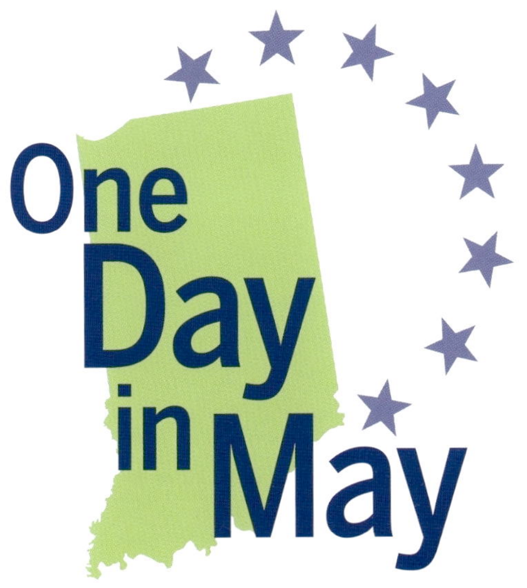

One
Day
in
May

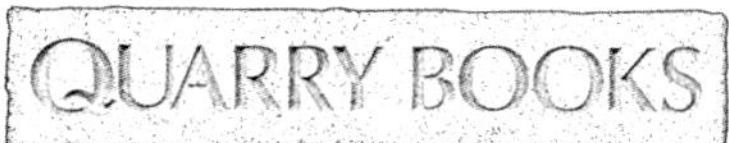

An Imprint of

INDIANA UNIVERSITY PRESS
Bloomington & Indianapolis

One Day in May

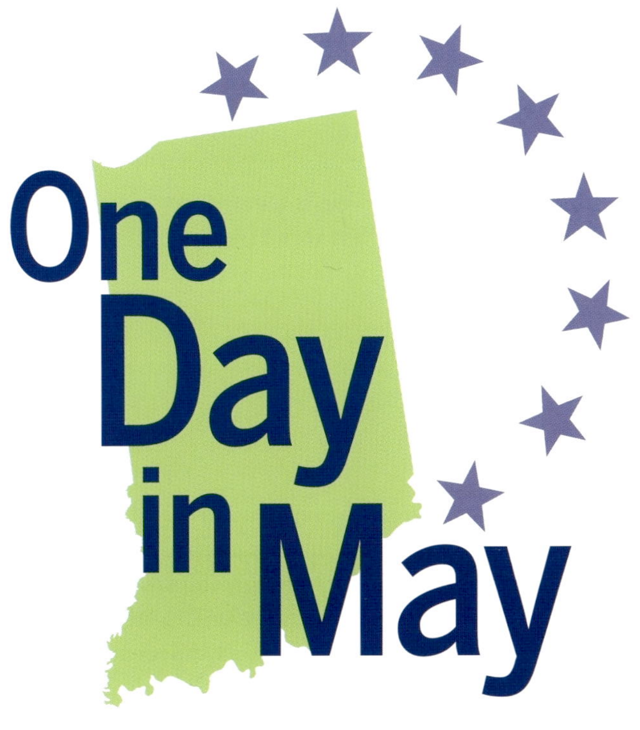

24 Hours in the Life of Indiana

Edited by

INDIANA UNIVERSITY PRESS

This book is a publication of

Quarry Books
an imprint of
Indiana University Press
Office of Scholarly Publishing
Herman B Wells Library 350
1320 East 10th Street
Bloomington, Indiana 47405 USA

iupress.indiana.edu

This book is printed on acid-free paper.

Manufactured in Korea

Cataloging information is available from the Library of Congress.

ISBN 978-0-253-02548-7 (paperback)
ISBN 978-0-253-02591-3 (ebook)

1 2 3 4 5 21 20 19 18 17 16

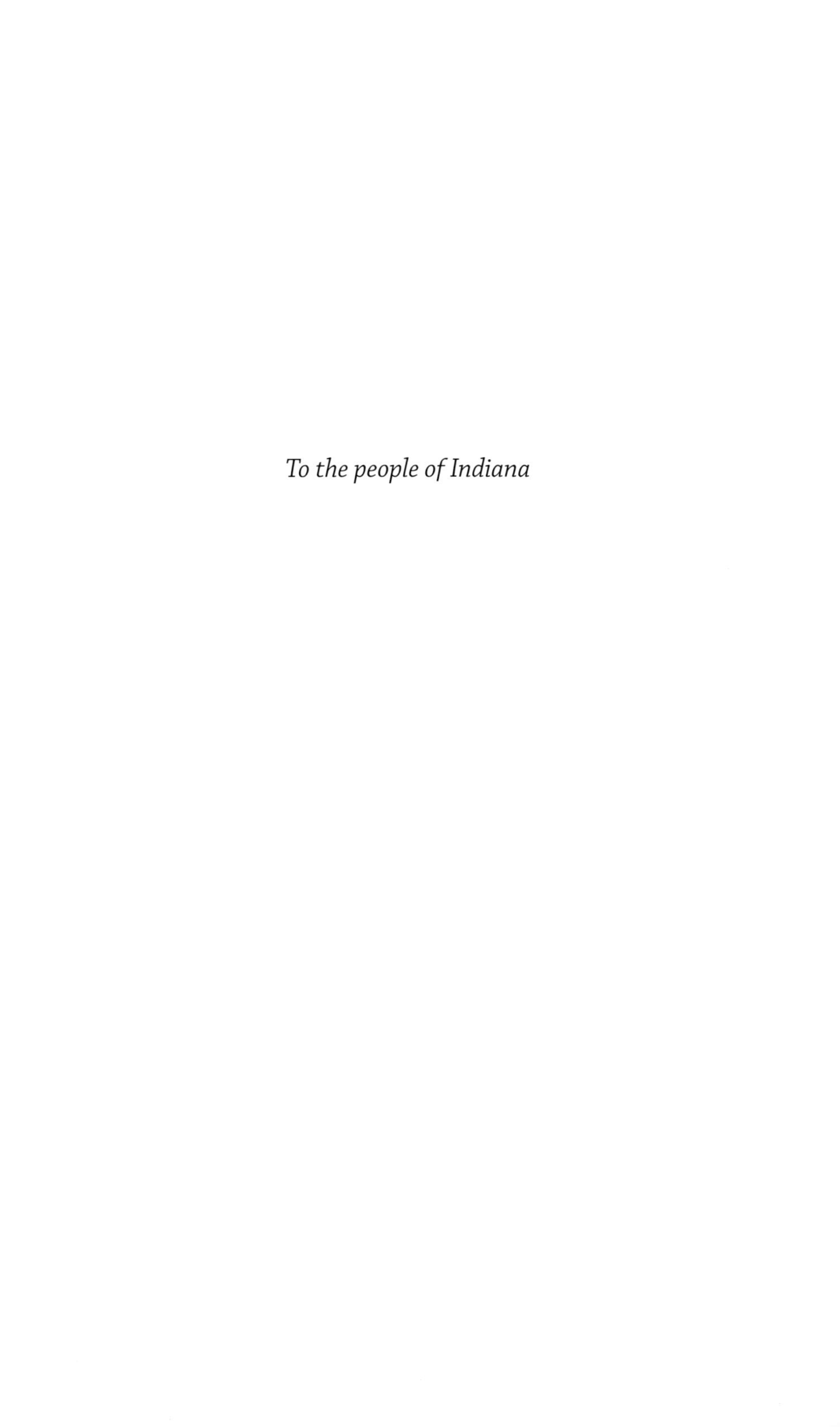
To the people of Indiana

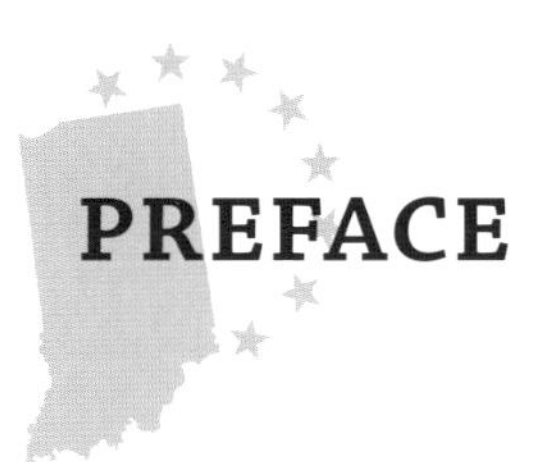

PREFACE

FRIDAY, MAY 20, 2016, was a typical spring day in the midwestern state of Indiana. The sun rose at 6:25 AM in Indianapolis and 7 minutes earlier in Fort Wayne, where it would reach 70 degrees before the day's end. It was a bright, sunny morning throughout most of the state; as the day progressed, clouds rolled in, rain fell, and nary a Hoosier spotted a sunset.

On the morning of May 20, 2016, the people of Indiana woke up—or came home from work—and got on with their day. The Greater Greenwood Lions Club began its spring garage sale at 9 AM. Items collected for months were sold by volunteers on the lawn in front of the Golden Corral restaurant. Two hours later and 43 miles south in Bloomington, food trucks pulled into the parking lots of the Chocolate Moose and Smith's Shoe Center, and lucky post–academic year residents of Btown stopped by to purchase and enjoy some tasty lunches. At 3:30 that Friday afternoon, to the west, in Terre Haute, members of the Central Christian Church sold tickets to their forthcoming Holy Cow Drop from the church's parking lot on Wabash Avenue. You simply had to drive up, pay $10 for a two-by-two-foot pasture square of your choice, and hope that the Holy Cow would do the rest and make you $10,000 richer. Looking south and moving into the early evening, the

Evansville Country Club hosted "Night of Adventure: aMaze & aMuse," an interactive fundraising event for adults featuring a zillion cool and undeniably eclectic things, including golf, a celebrity chef, a magician, an awesome dinner buffet and trivia competition, silent auctions, and—thank goodness—a cash bar. Way up north, and a couple of hours later, the 49'er Drive-In in Valparaiso opened its gates for its sixtieth year and offered a double-feature of *The Jungle Book* and *Captain America: Civil War*, beginning at 8:15 PM. For those more adventurous and soon-to-be hard of hearing, at about the same time, the heavy metal supergroup HELLYEAH rocked the stage at Pierce's Entertainment Center in Fort Wayne, the latest stop in their We're All in This Together tour.

Indeed, it was a normal spring day in the Hoosier State, paradoxically full of the mundane and mighty, surprise and same-old, all wrapped in routine. Cows were milked, eggs gathered, and some plowing got done before the rain. From Lake Michigan to the Ohio River folks biked, drove, or walked to work—or stayed home for their jobs. The last day of school for many children; the springboard into the weekend for most adults. The interminable construction and traffic delays on State Road 37 plodded on, while overhead, planes flew into and out of Indianapolis International Airport on time. Like every day, new Hoosiers were born on May 20, 2016, and for some, it was their last.

But it was not an *entirely* typical day. On May 20, 2016, in Indiana's two-hundredth year, Hoosiers chose to share their Friday together with the future. Hundreds across the state—and we mean everywhere—took photos that symbolized something meaningful about those twenty-four hours and sent them to us at Indiana University Press. After a considered (and sometimes agonizing) selection process, we settled on over 140 photographs from across Indiana that we felt best represented the slice of Hoosier life that was that Friday. To synchronize the entire state to the same time zone, we had to adjust the times of those handful of photographs taken from the extreme northwestern and southwestern corners by one hour. We also edited some descriptions a bit and added a few details here and there for clarification.

So, enjoy, reflect, and appreciate our state once again. Hey, not all the pictures are professionally impeccable . . . but they are real and stand collectively as the essence of Indiana, the blood and bones of what unfolded across the hours in that One Day in May.

Indiana University Press

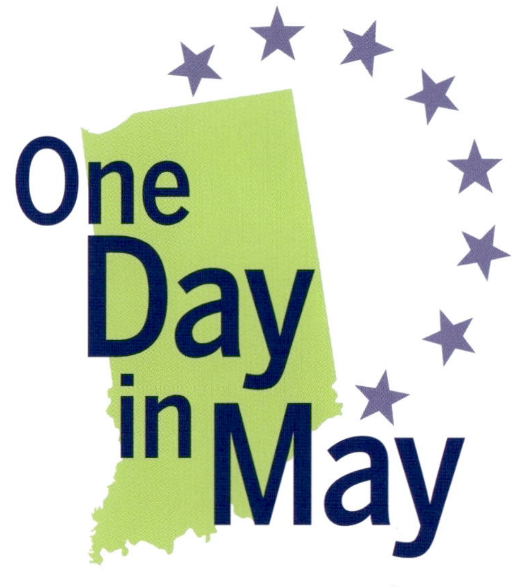

One
Day
in
May

24

HOURS

IN THE LIFE OF INDIANA

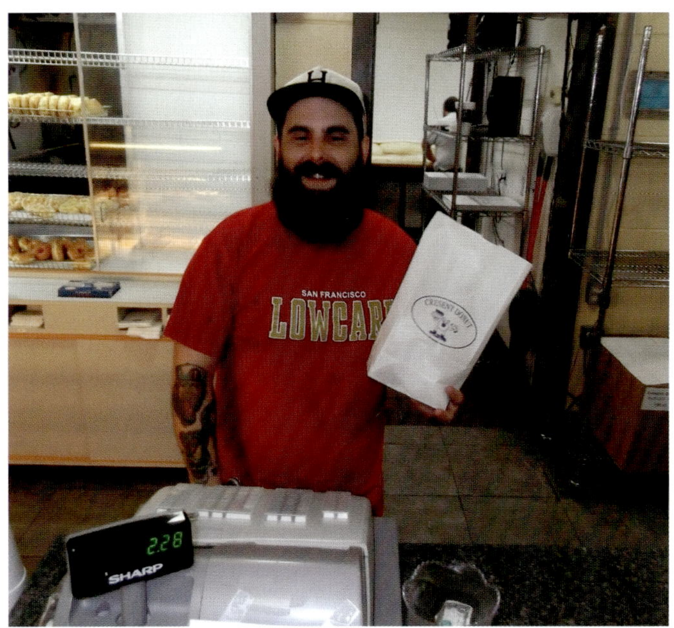

2:44 AM

Bloomington

Picking up my "after work snack" of fresh cake donuts from Jason at Cresent Donut Shop.

Photo by Mark Richardson

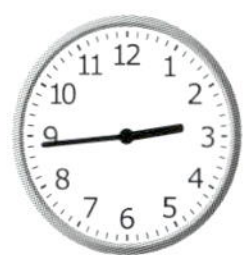

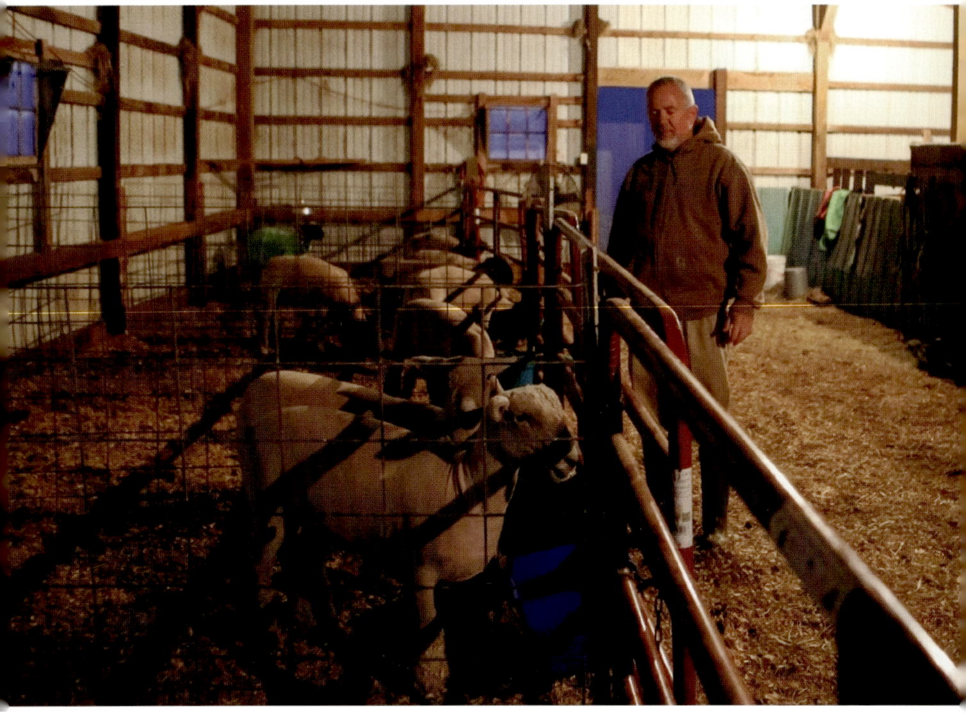

6:04 AM

Columbus

Purdue-trained veterinarian Steve Newton tends to the sheep on his farm an hour earlier than normal before heading off to a 6:30 AM staff meeting at Hope Veterinary Clinic.

Photo by Greg Jones

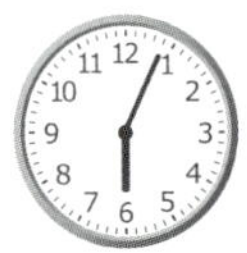

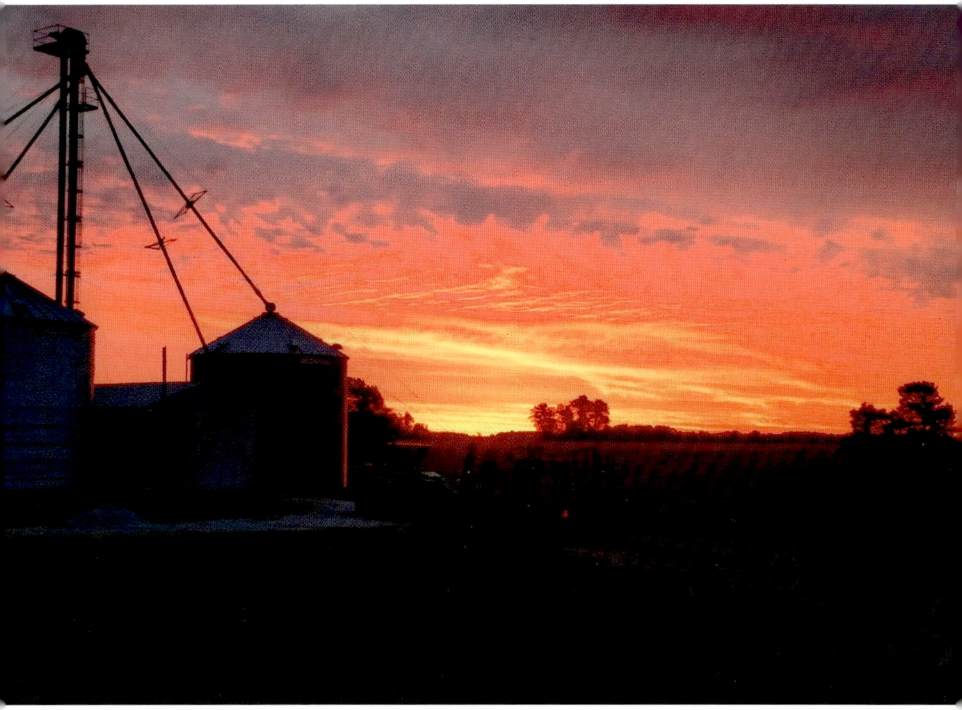

6:12 AM

Zenas

Another wonderful Hoosier sunrise.

Photo by Rebecca Sargent

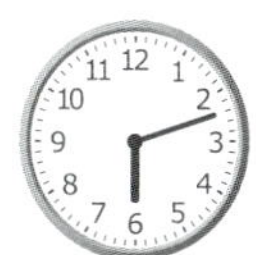

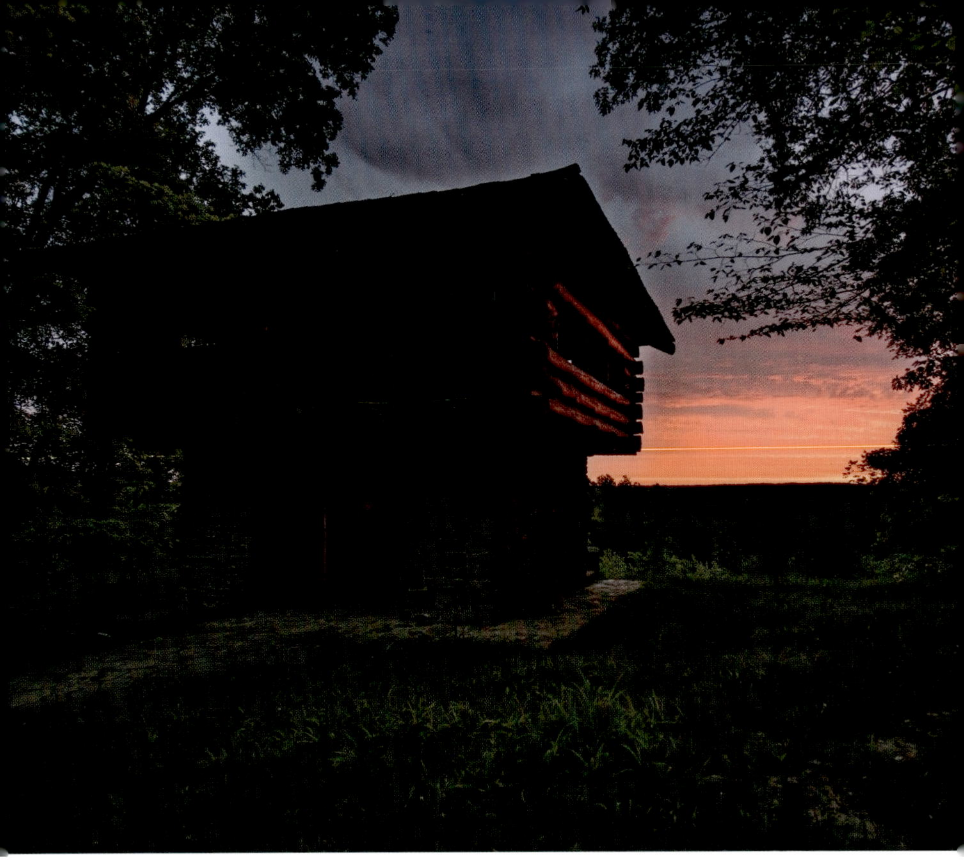

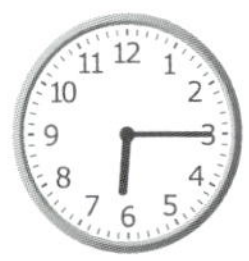

6:15 AM

Nashville

Sunrise at the North Lookout Tower in Brown County State Park.

Photo by Norberto Nunes

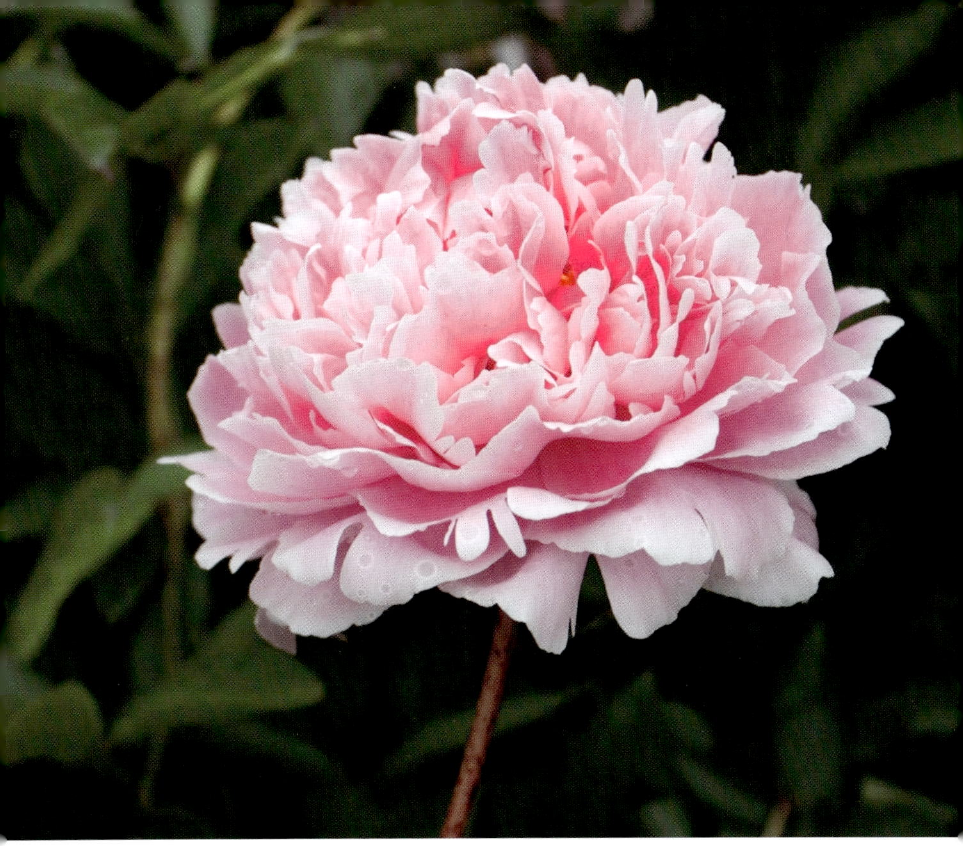

6:30 AM

New Harmony

Pink peony from Fragrant Farms at first light.

Photo by Janet Lorence

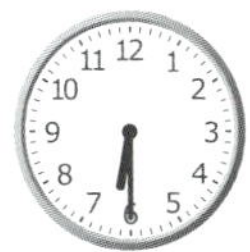

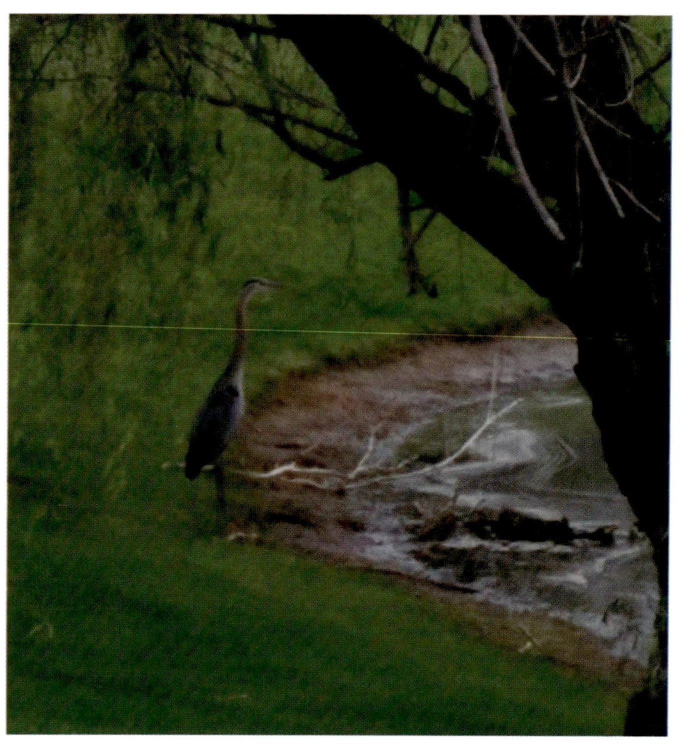

6:30 AM

Indianapolis

Krishna, our resident blue heron at Wildcat Run,
awake with the rest of us.

Photo by Bob Brault

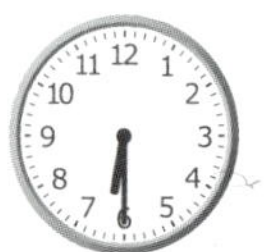

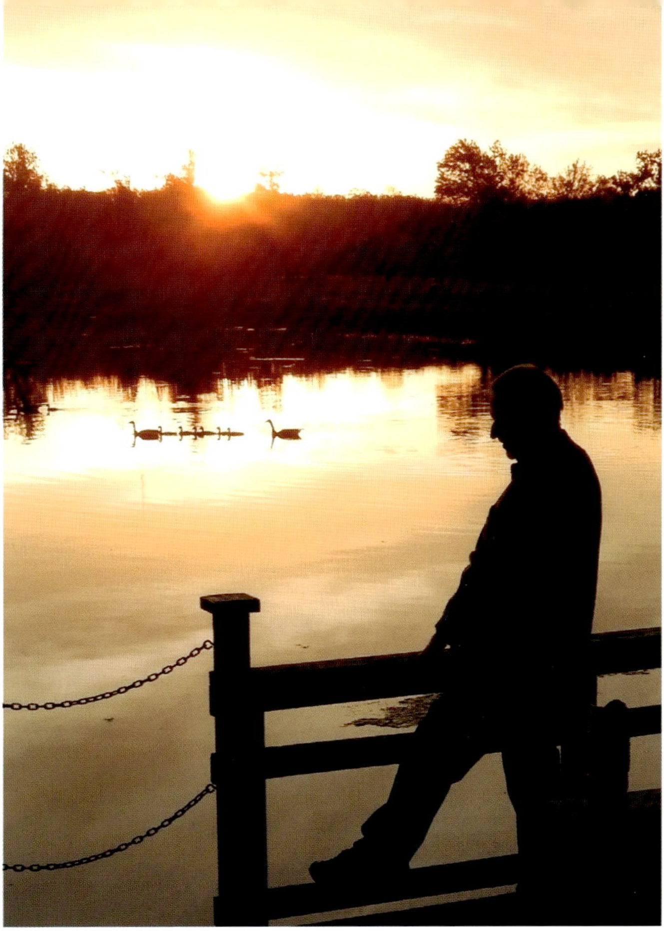

6:32 AM

Bluffton

Sunrise meditation at Kunkel Lake,
Ouabache State Park.

Photo by Gwen Daugherty

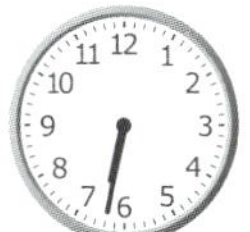

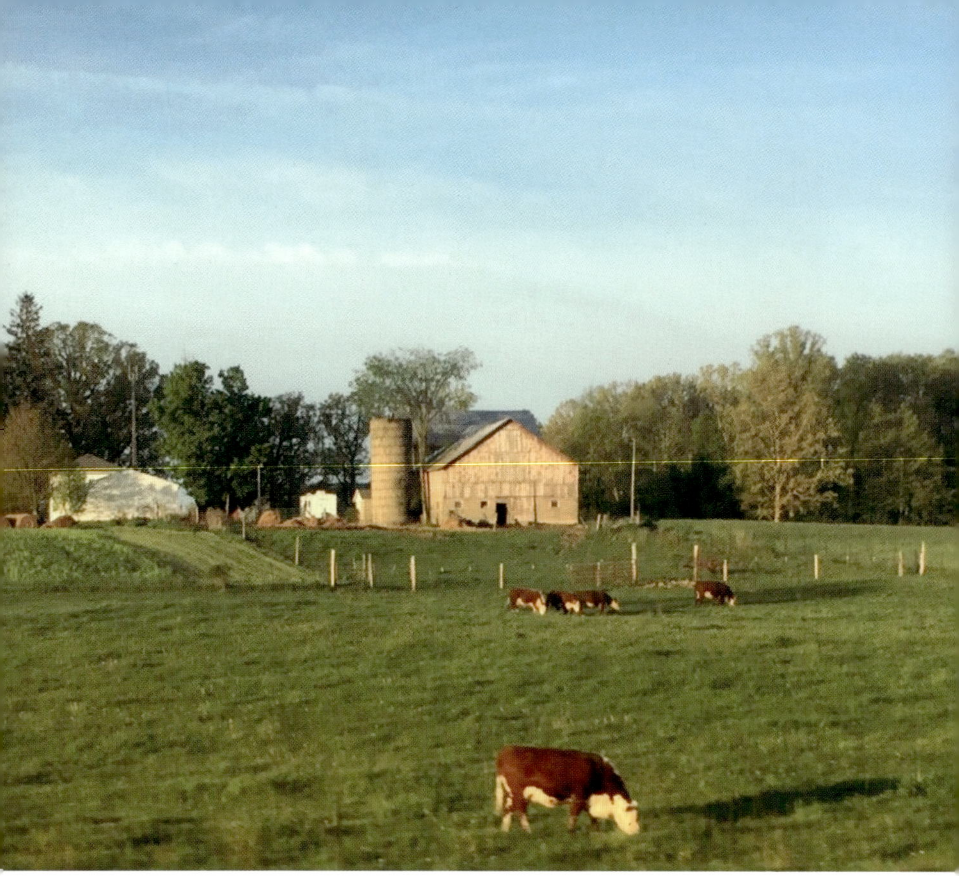

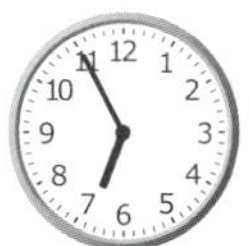

6:55 AM

Angola

Cows doing what they do.

Photo by Victoria McCourt

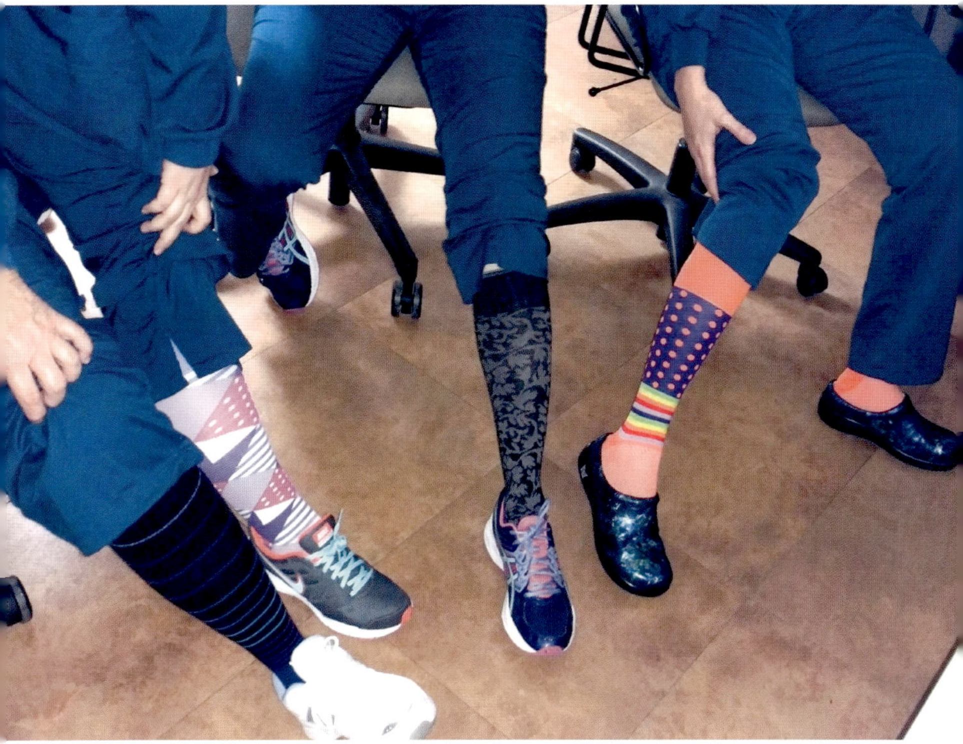

6:59 AM

Fort Wayne

Nurses compare snazzy support stockings as they
get ready to start their day in the Cardiovascular
ICU at Parkview Regional Medical Center.

Photo by Susan Chemey

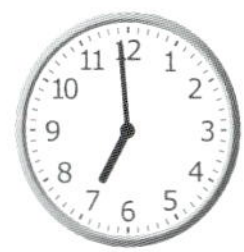

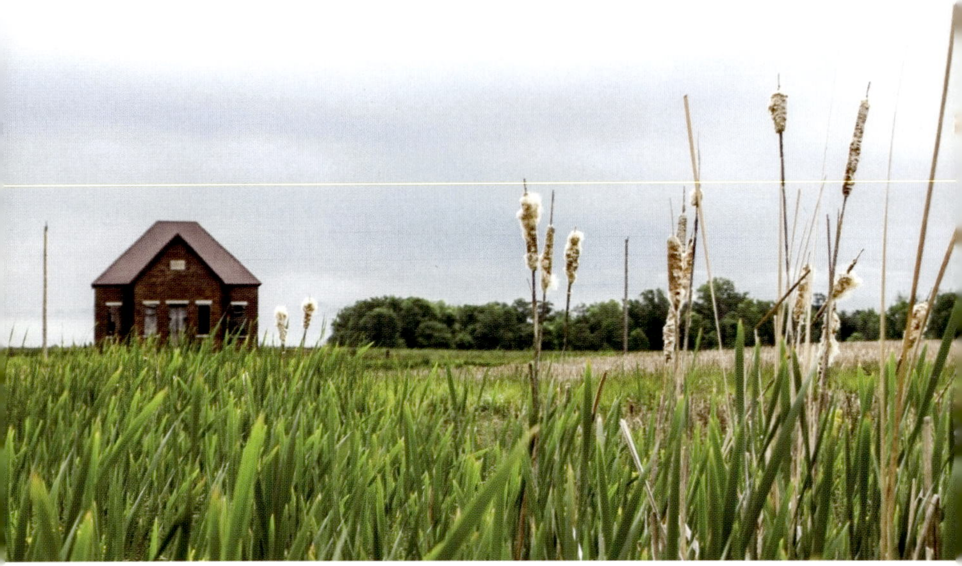

7:00 AM

Columbus

Cattails in the tall grass watching over an old
Petersville schoolhouse in the distance.

Photo by Shannon Malanoski

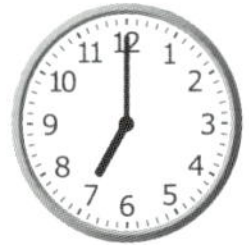

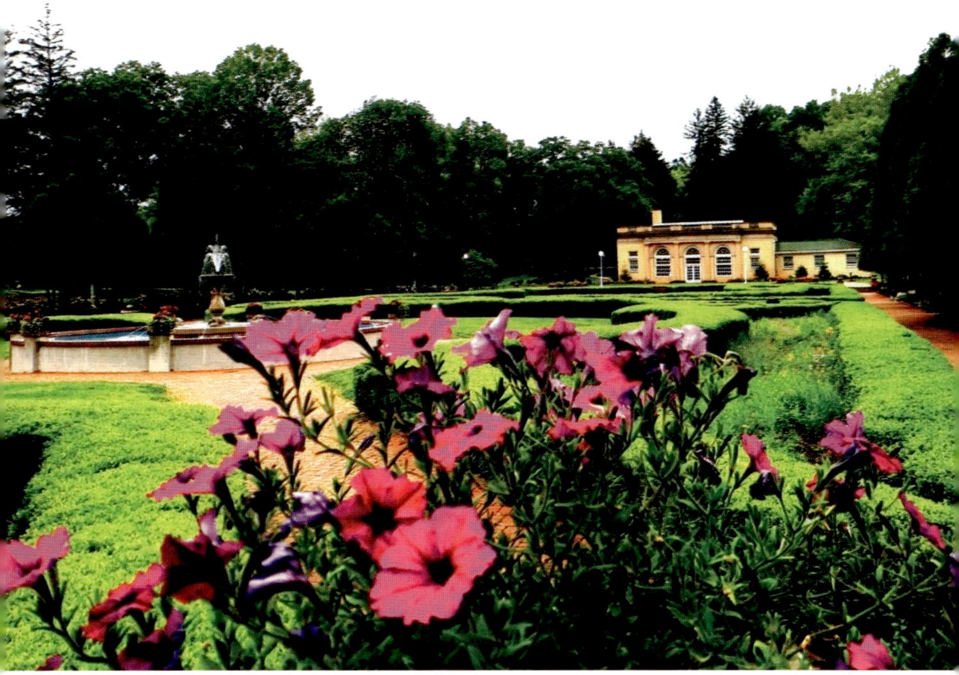

7:00 AM

West Baden Springs

Early morning stroll around the gardens of the historic West Baden Springs Hotel.

Photo by Kristal Painter

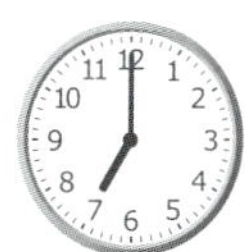

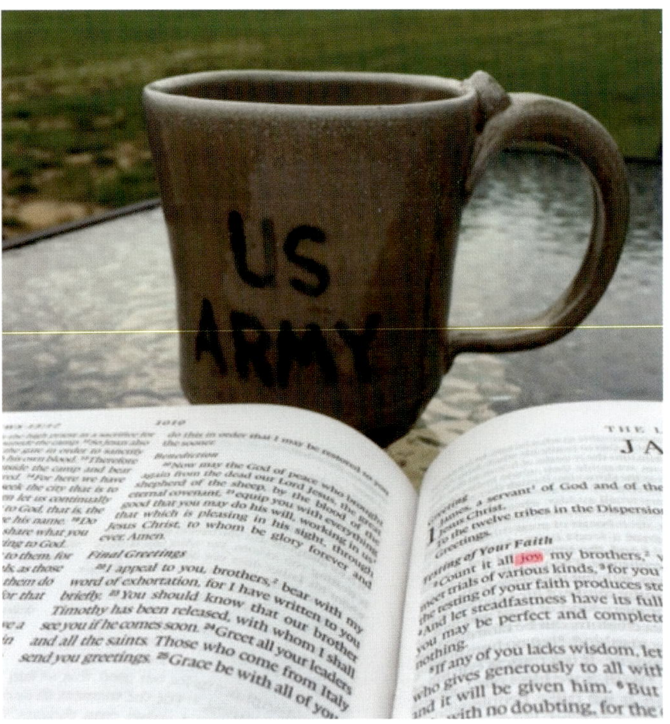

7:06 AM

Newport

Praying for the safety of my son who is deployed in Afghanistan and for my daughter who landed in Haiti yesterday for a two-month internship with Northwest Haiti Christian Mission.

Photo by Amy Tolbert

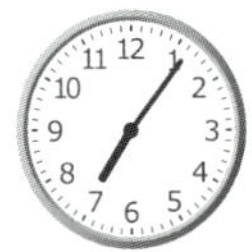

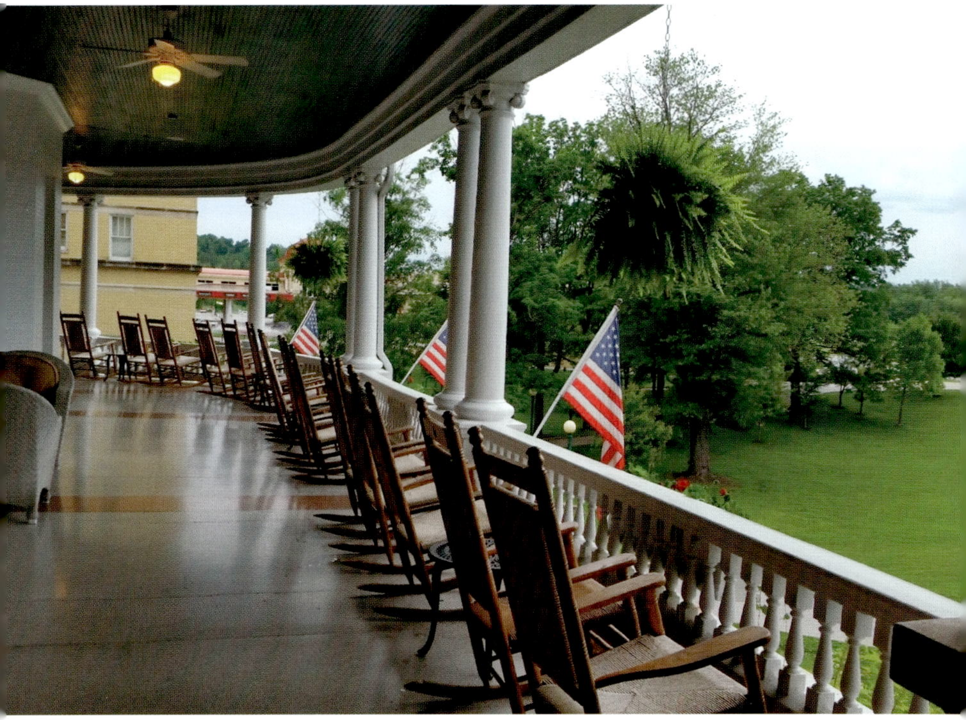

7:30 AM

French Lick

Coffee on the beautiful front porch of the
French Lick Springs Hotel. I could sit here all day.

Photo by Julia Federle

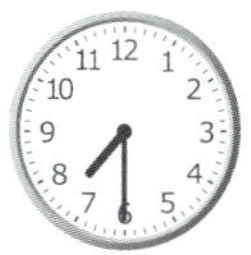

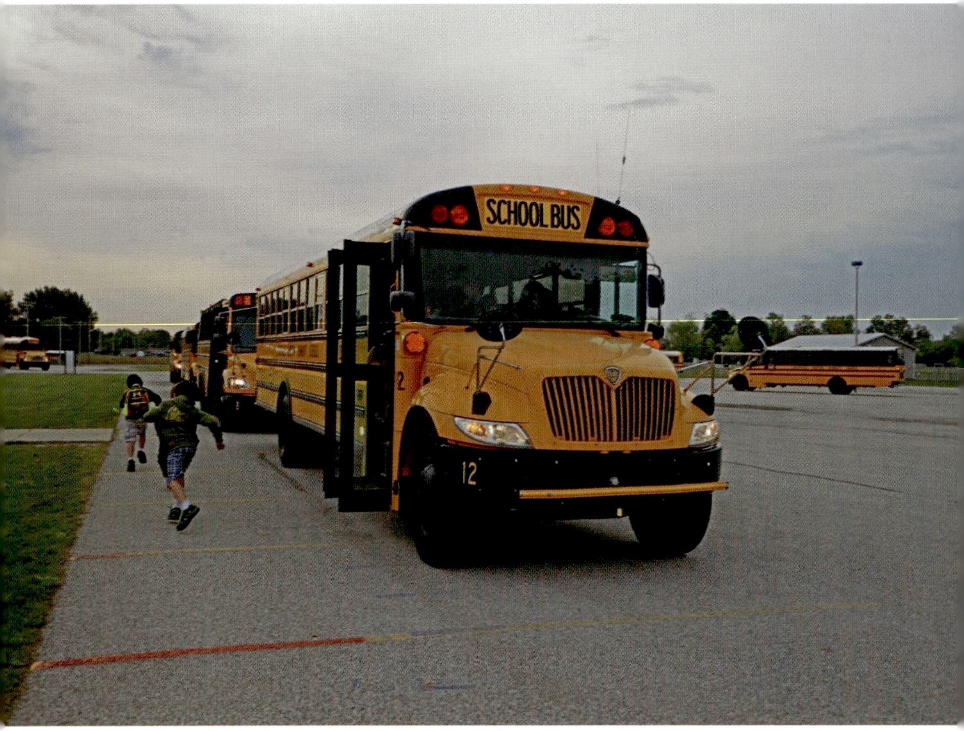

7:40 AM

Centerville

The start of the last day of school at Centerville-Abington Elementary!

Photo by Mark Campbell

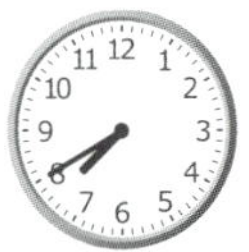

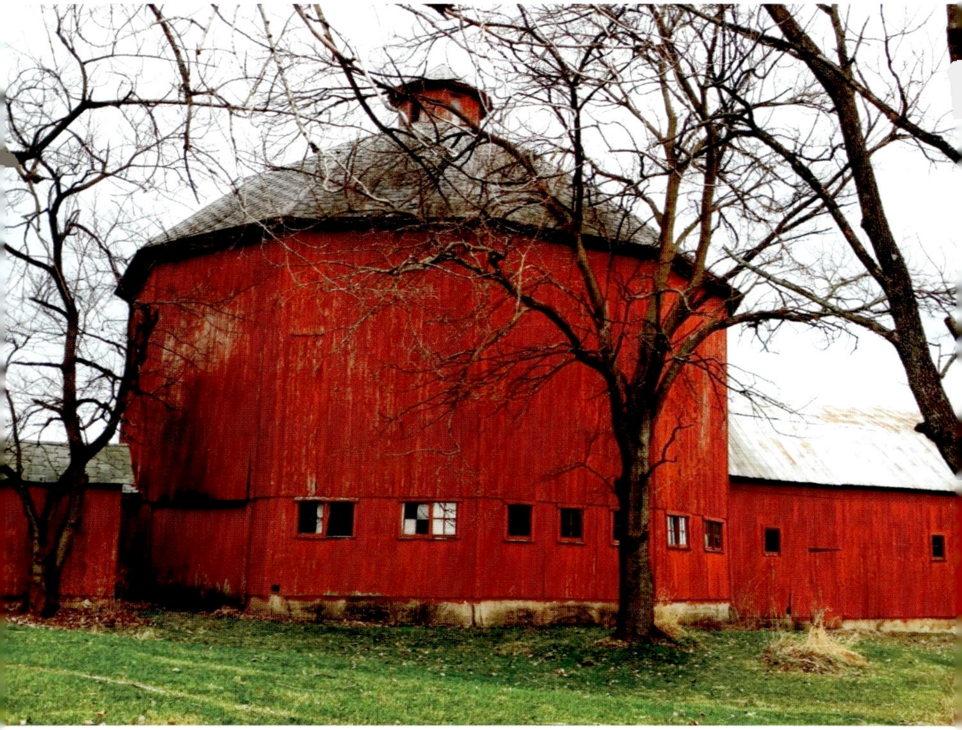

8:15 AM

Culver

That's one red, round, and ready barn.

Photo by Daniel Holderman

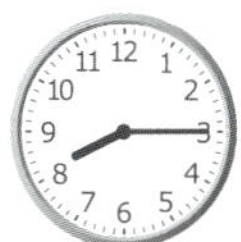

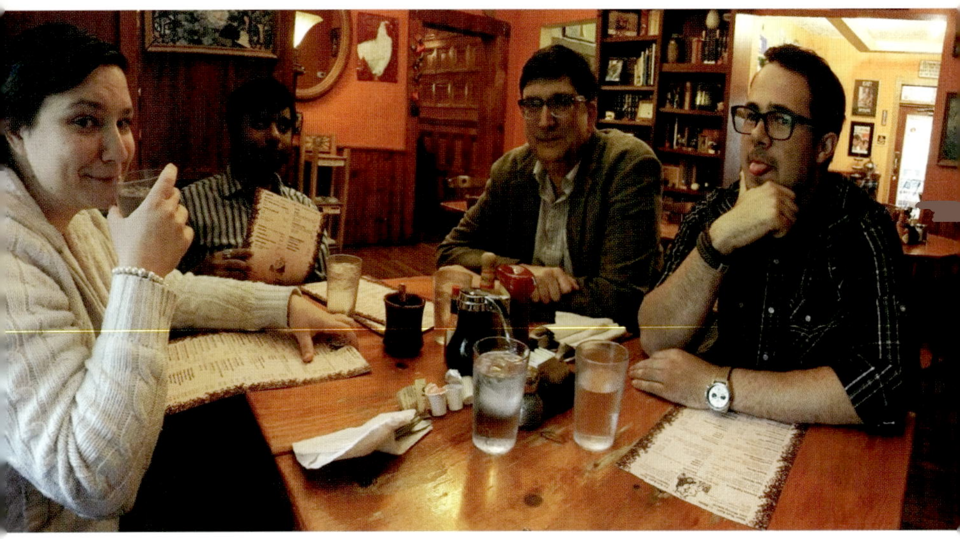

8:15 AM

Bloomington

Graduate students enjoying breakfast at the
Runcible Spoon before summer research,
conferences, and job interviews.

Photo by Dan Johnston

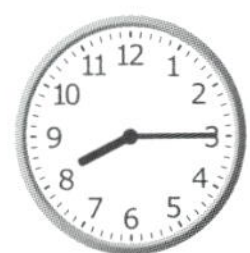

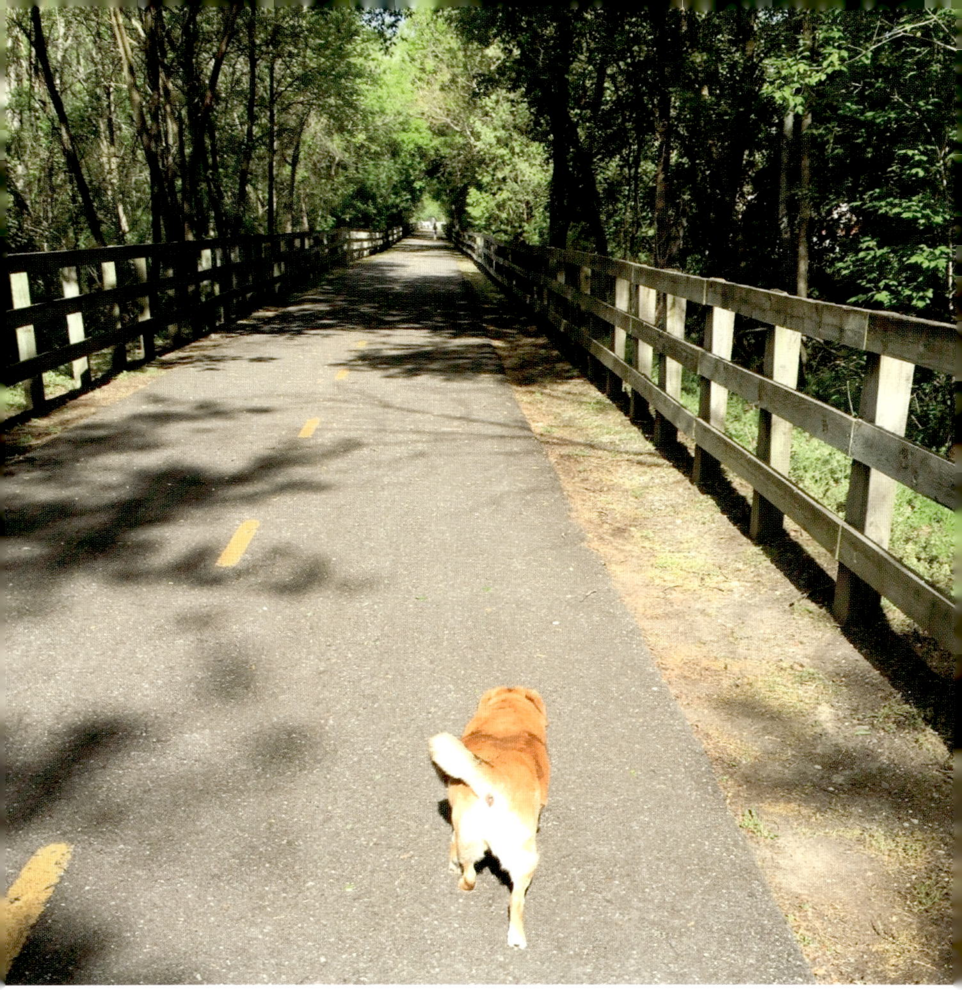

8:30 AM

Hobart

Walking Della Pugsley on the Oak Savannah Trail.

Photo by Jane Dudley

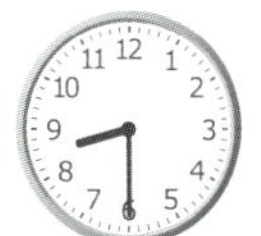

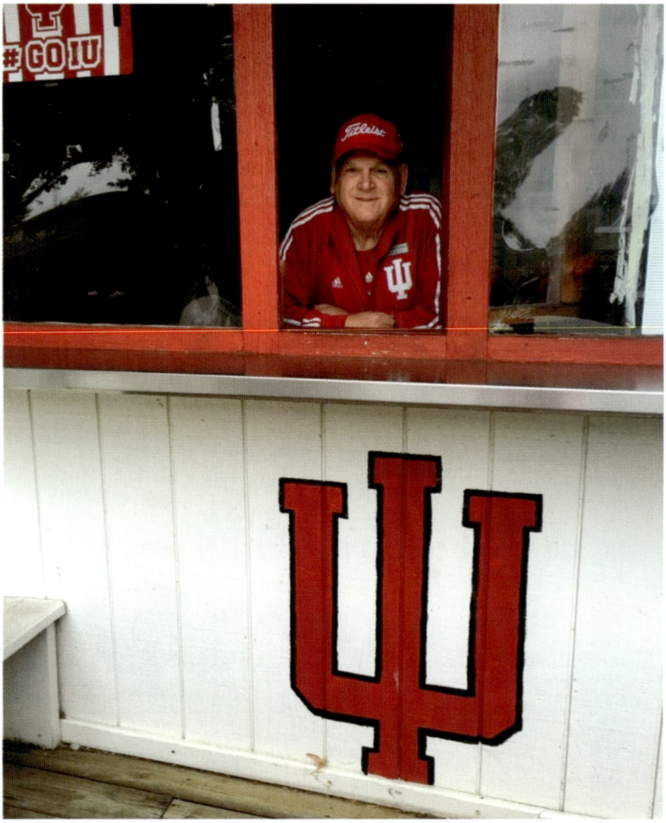

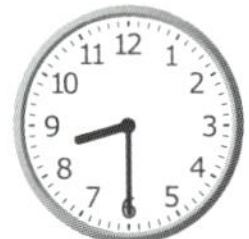

8:30 AM

Bloomington

Dog Shack Dave in his IU shack selling hot dogs
at Eagle Pointe Golf Course at Lake Monroe.

Photo by Jeannie Pratt

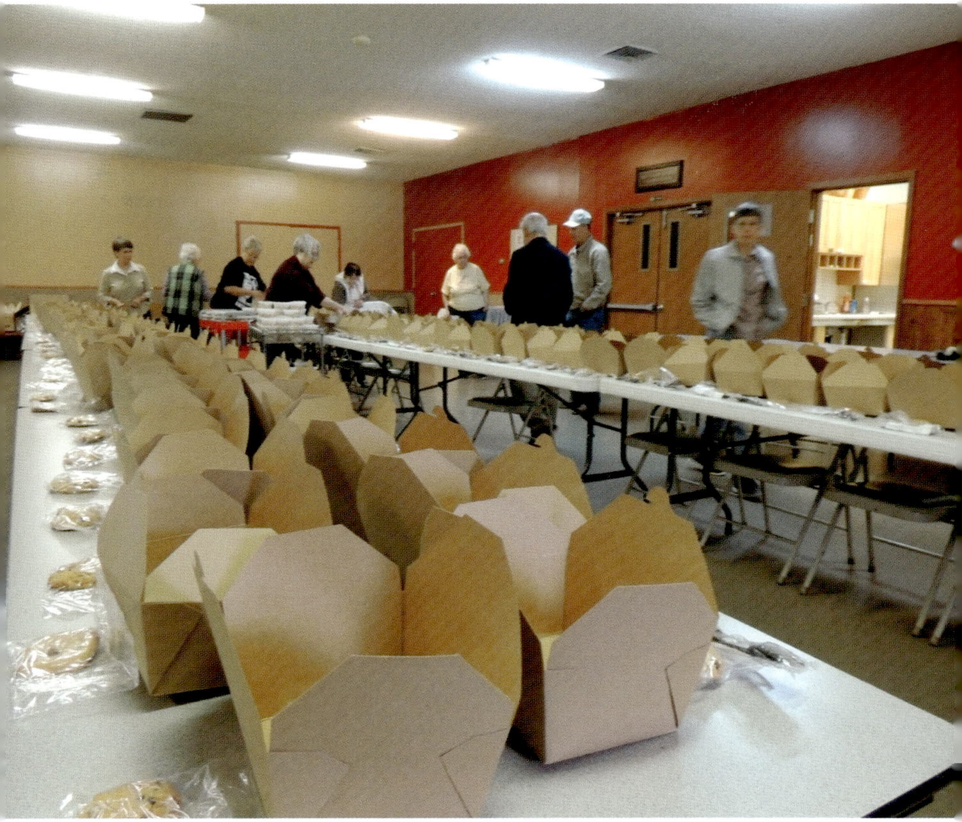

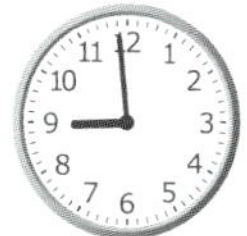

8:59 AM

Walkerton

Members of the Walkerton United Methodist
Church prepare box lunches for factory workers and
others in the community.

Photo by John Turner

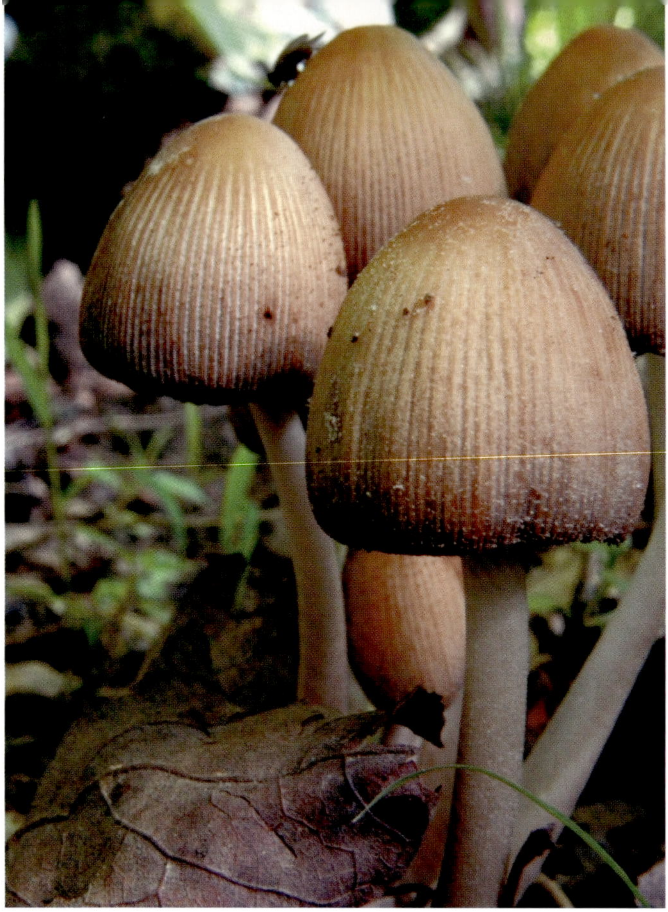

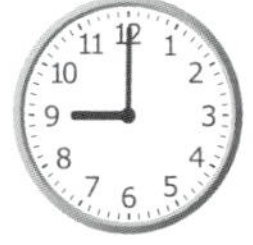

9:00 AM

Cuzco

Beautiful beings are often unseen.
The mushrooms in the woods near my house
are here and gone so quickly.

Photo by Stacy Graan-Wilson

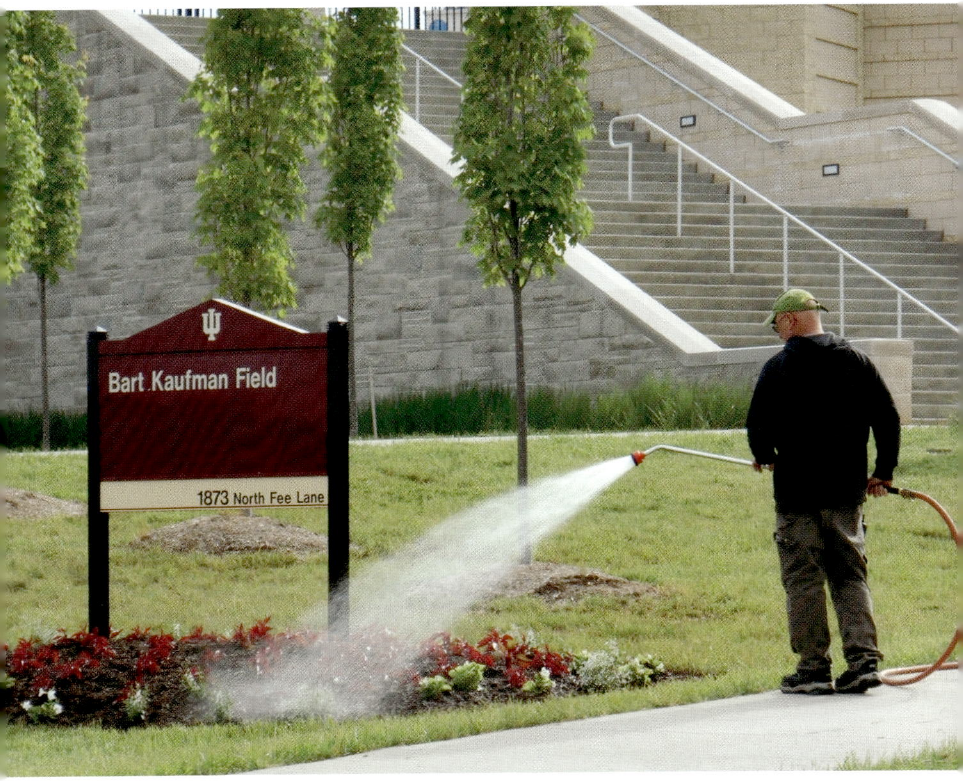

9:00 AM

Bloomington

Groundskeeper maintains the natural beauty
of the Indiana University Bloomington campus.

Photo by Gary Loos

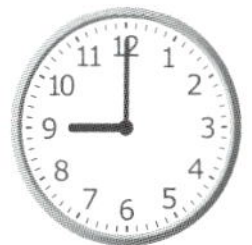

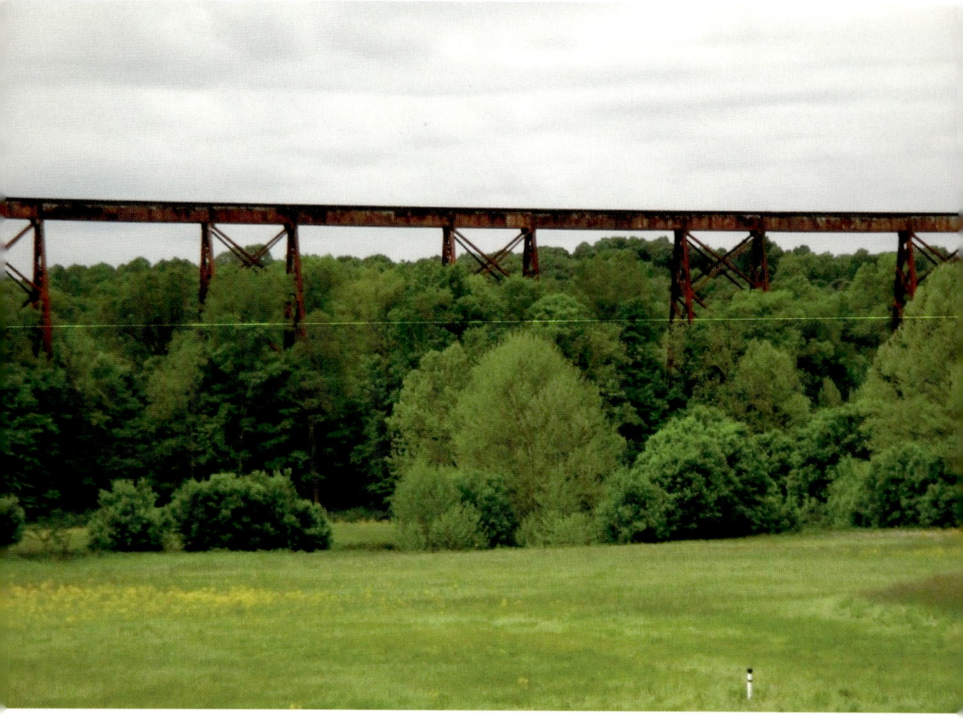

9:21 AM

Greene County

Tulip Trestle, east end of the viaduct toward Solsberry. This was as close to the viaduct as I could get today as the road was closed for paving for the first time ever.

Photo by Linda Long

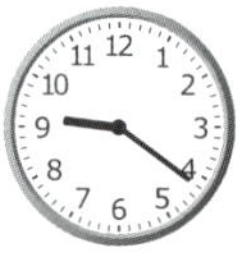

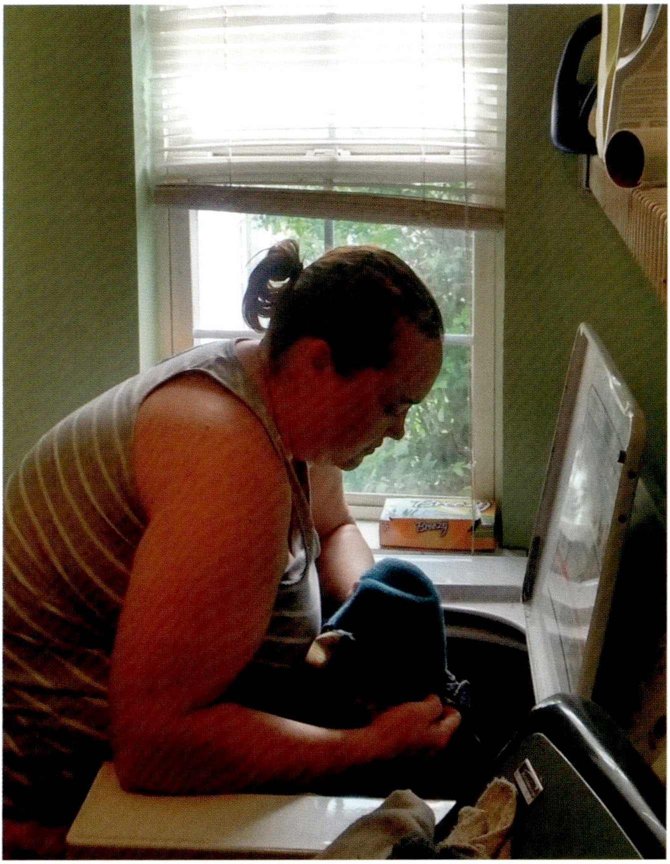

9:30 AM

Indianapolis

Laundry and sunshine on a perfect day in May.

Photo by Nikki Wiles

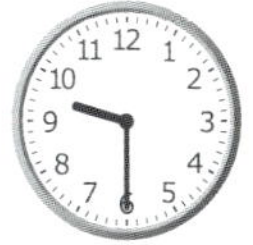

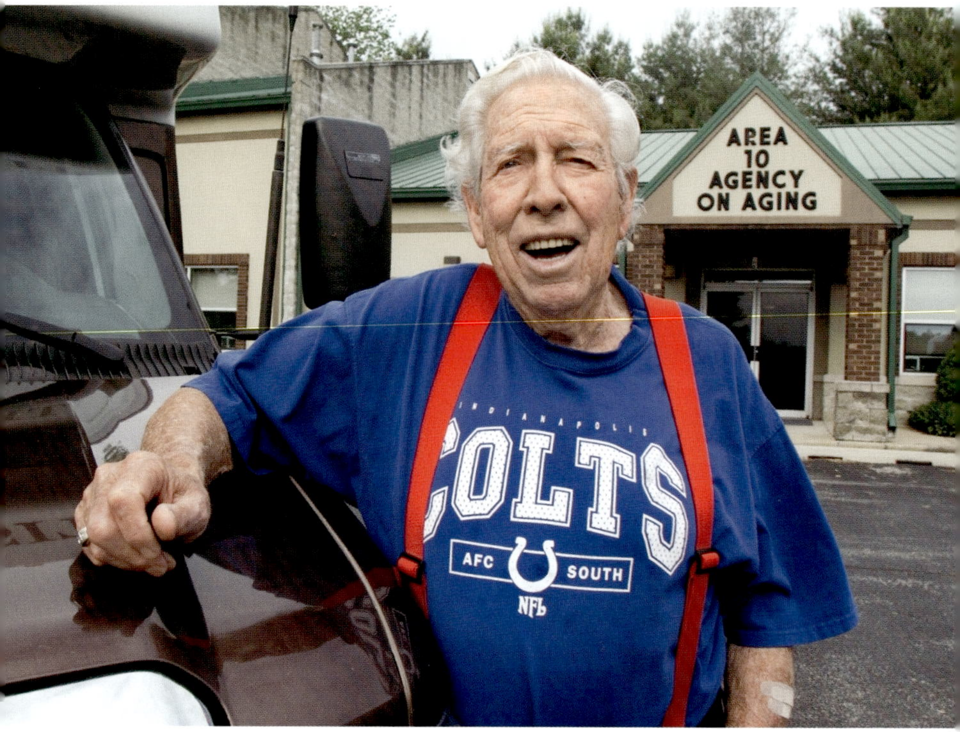

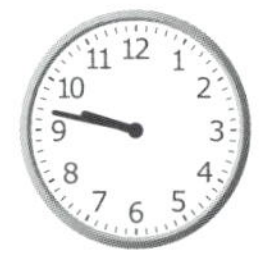

9:47 AM

Ellettsville

Eighty-four-year-old retired plumber Ike Grimes
rides a Rural Transit bus three times a week
to work out on exercise equipment at the
Area 10 Agency on Aging headquarters.

Photo by Richard Fields

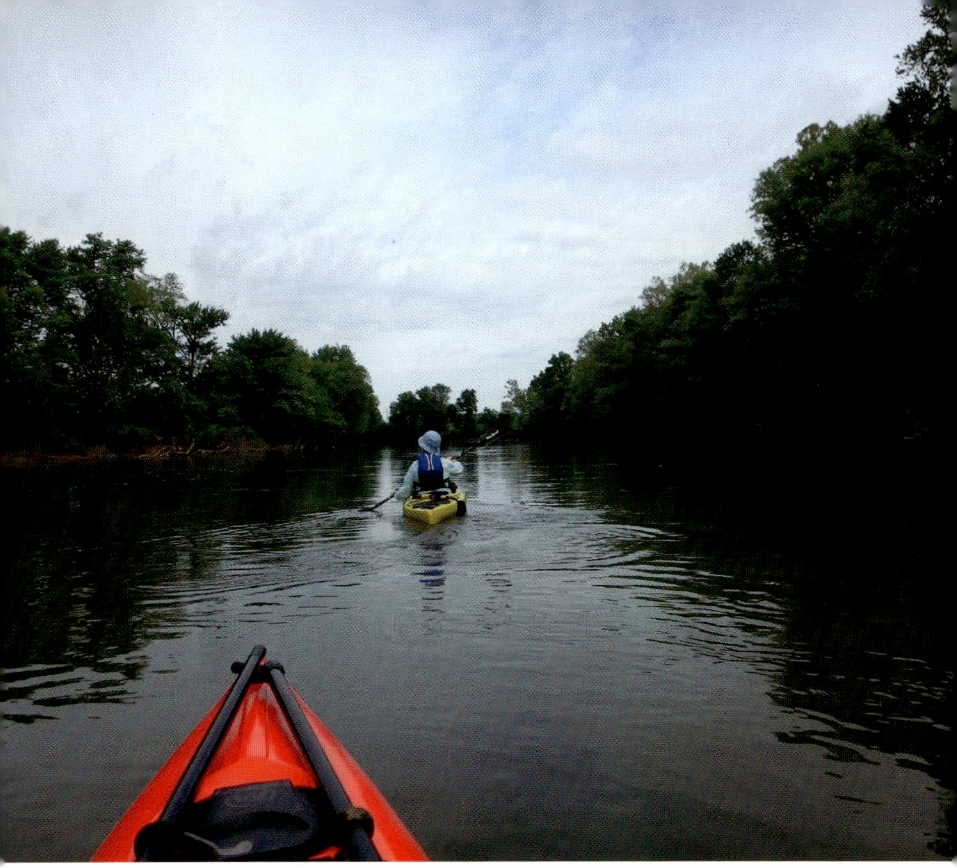

10:00 AM

Owen County between Spencer and Gosport

Kayaking the White River!

Photo by Kelly Bogan

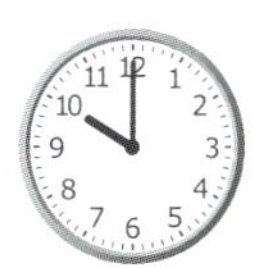

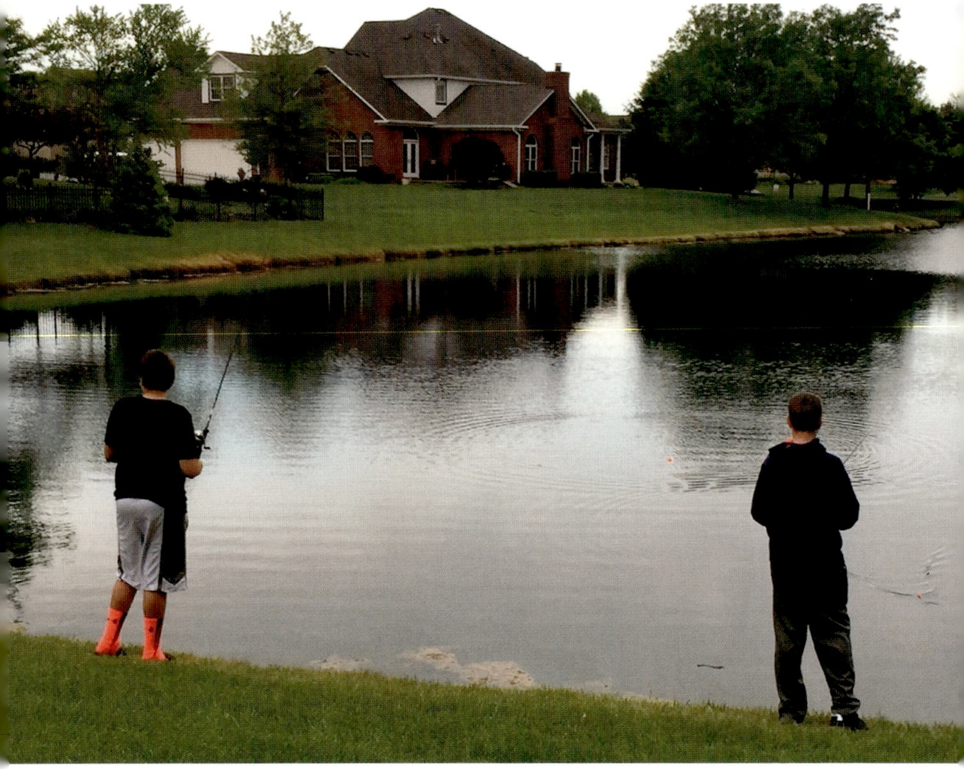

10:00 AM

Lebanon

My twelve-year-old son and his friend fishing. Some joys in life are timeless.

Photo by Courtney Bowyer-McCollum

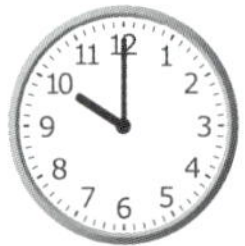

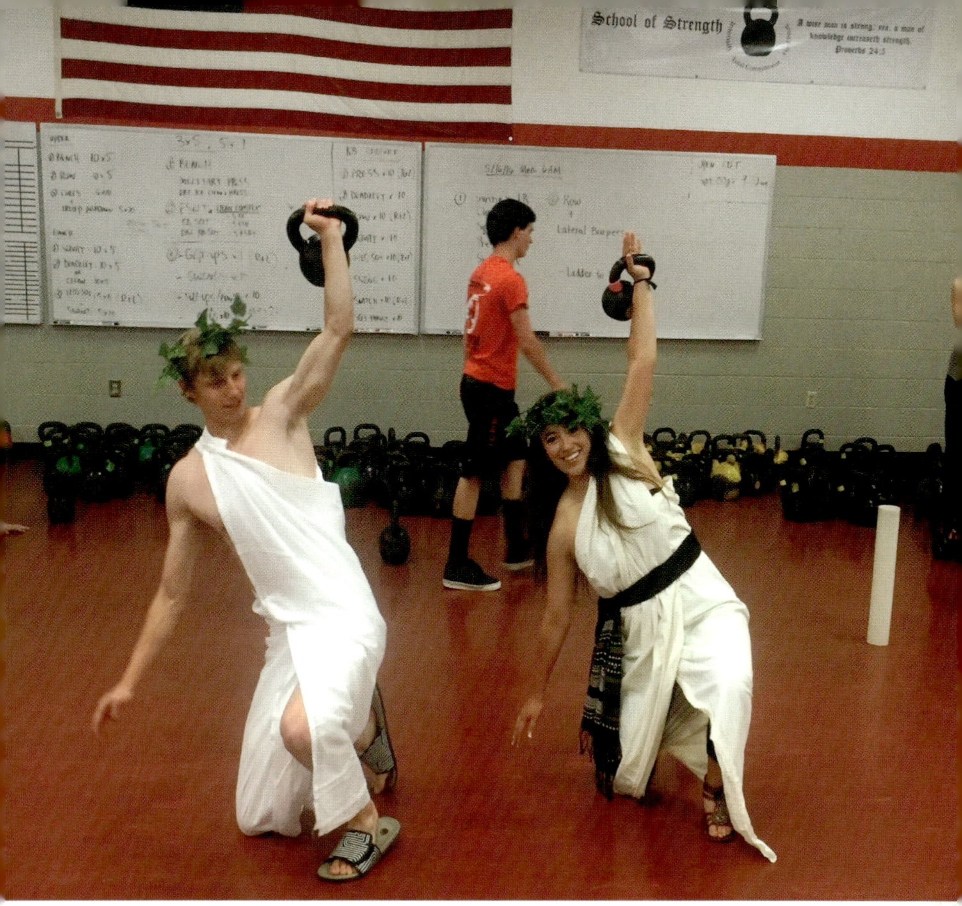

10:07 AM

Greenwood

Senior Week, Toga Day, at Center Grove High School. Perfect for Olympic weightlifting at the School of Strength!

Photo by Christina Randall

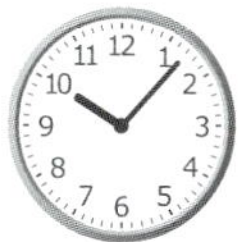

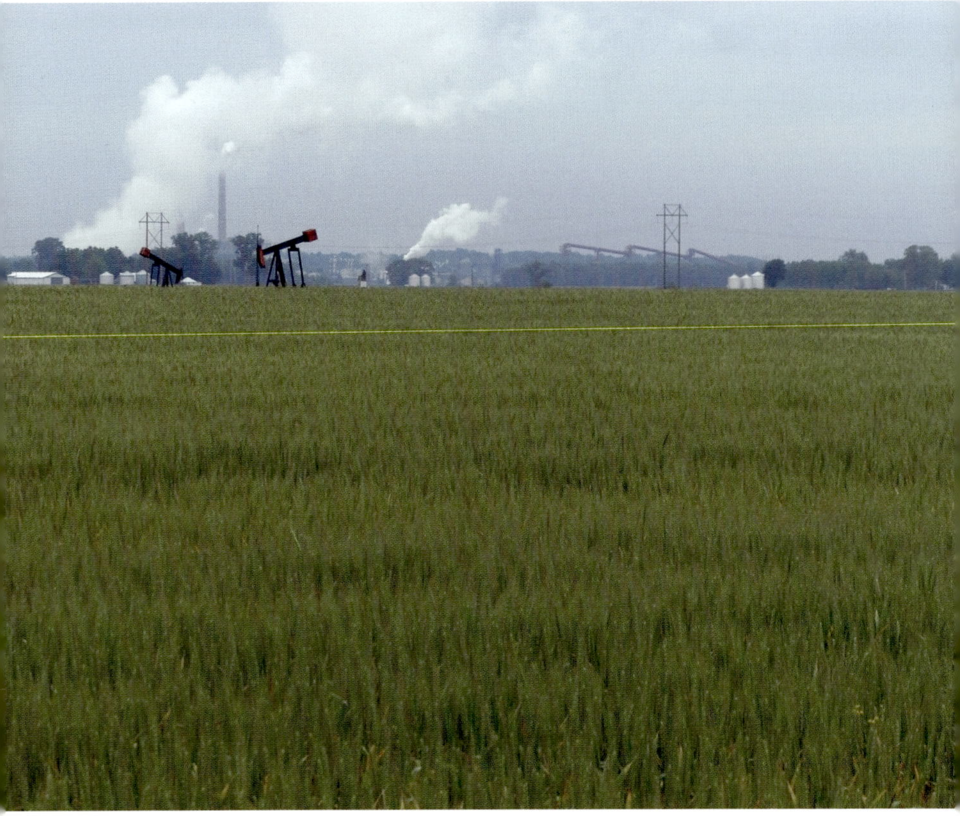

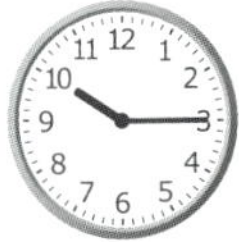

10:15 AM

Posey County

Horsehead oil pumps at work off of State Road 62.

Photo by Mary Ann Michna

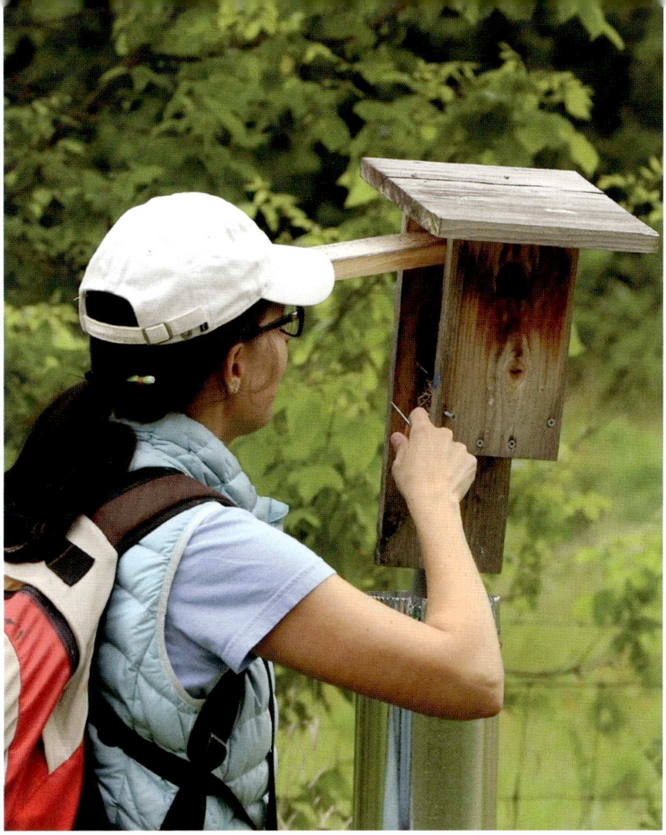

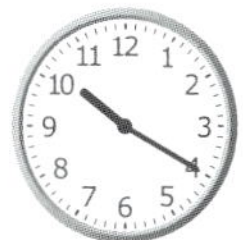

10:20 AM

Bloomington

Indiana University Bloomington biologist Kim Rosvall eagerly peeks into a nest box to see if a tree swallow's eggs have hatched. Her research team has set up nearly 200 nest boxes around Bloomington in order to study female competition and reproduction in this remarkable species.

Photo by Elizabeth George

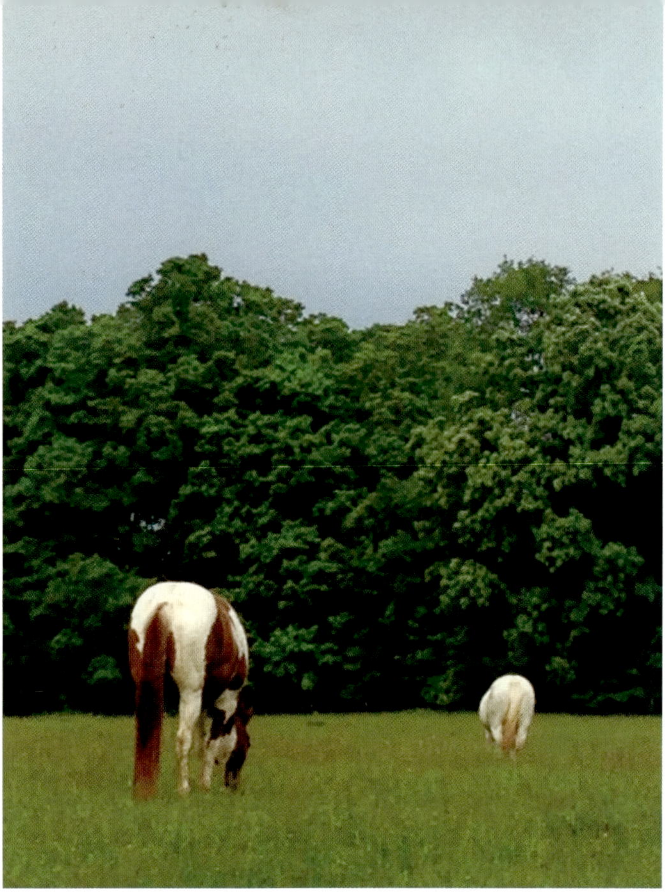

10:30 AM

Bloomington

Mares enjoying their morning turnout.

Kari Gillesse

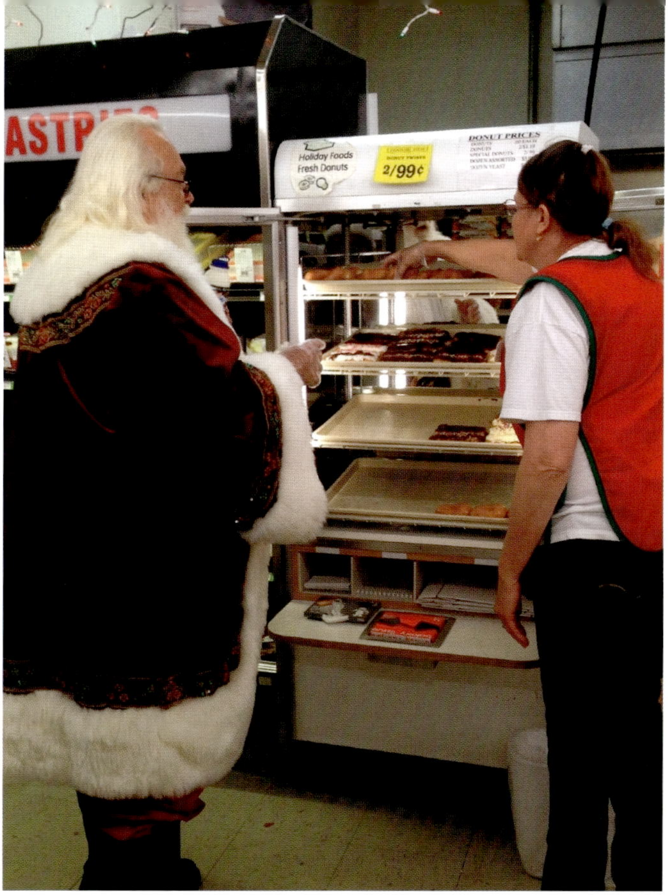

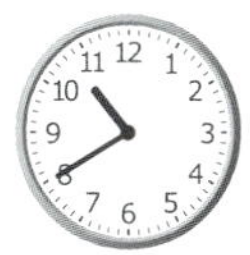

10:40 AM

Santa Claus

Santa grabbing a donut from the local bakery.

Melissa Brockman

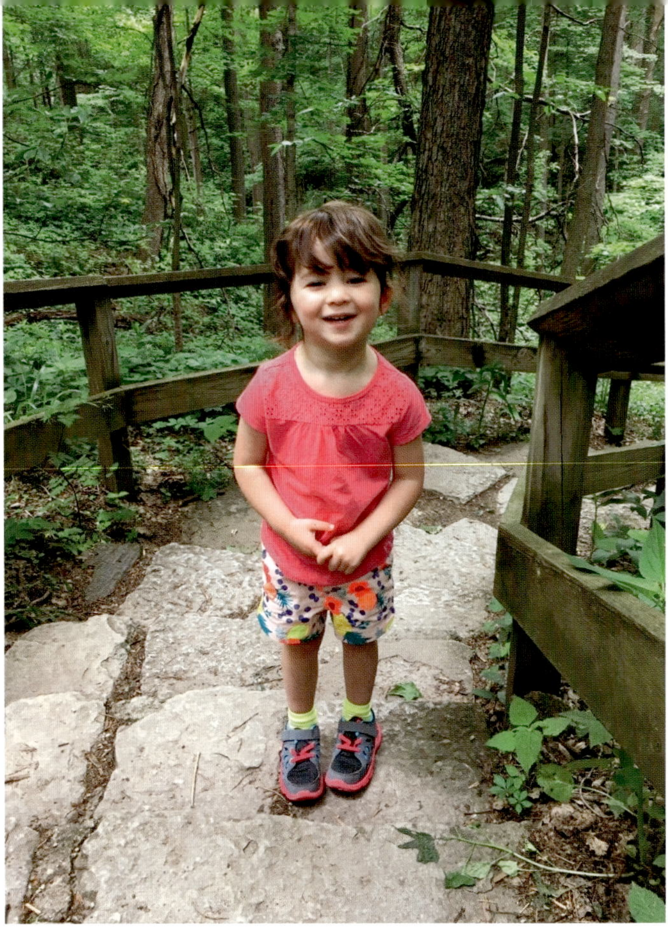

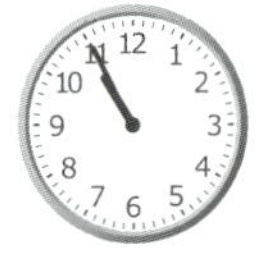

10:55 AM

Indianapolis

Hiking at Holliday Park with my three-year-old daughter.

Photo by Erin Gobel

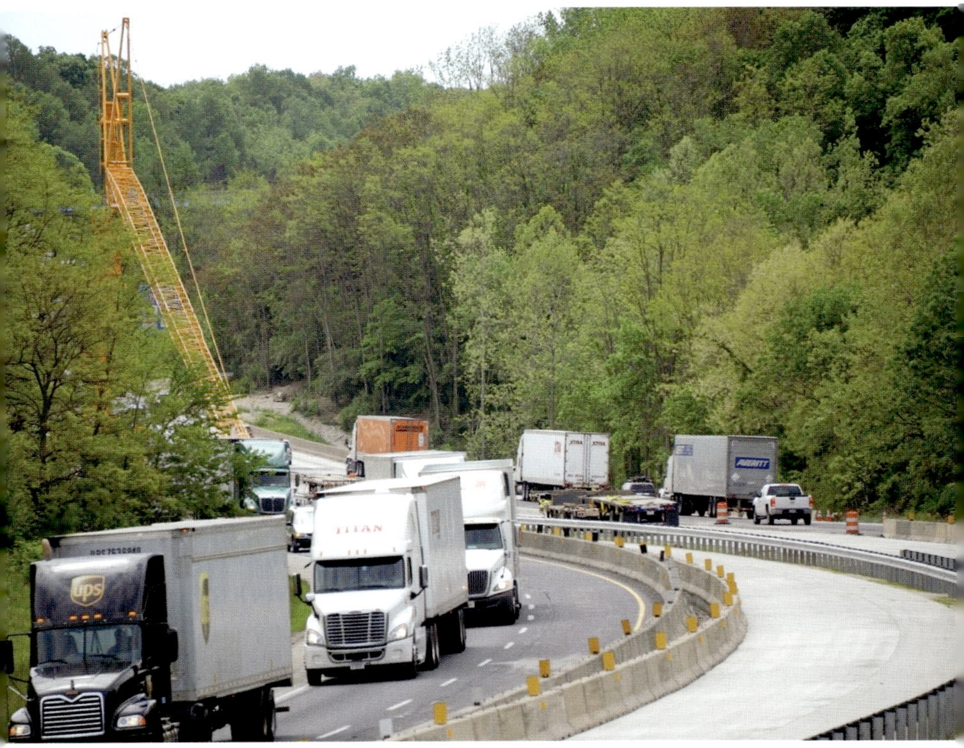

11:07 AM

Lafayette

The construction, widening of I-65, and repair of the
Wildcat Creek Bridge continue.

Photo by Marsha Williamson Mohr

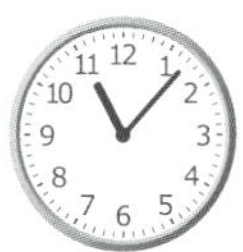

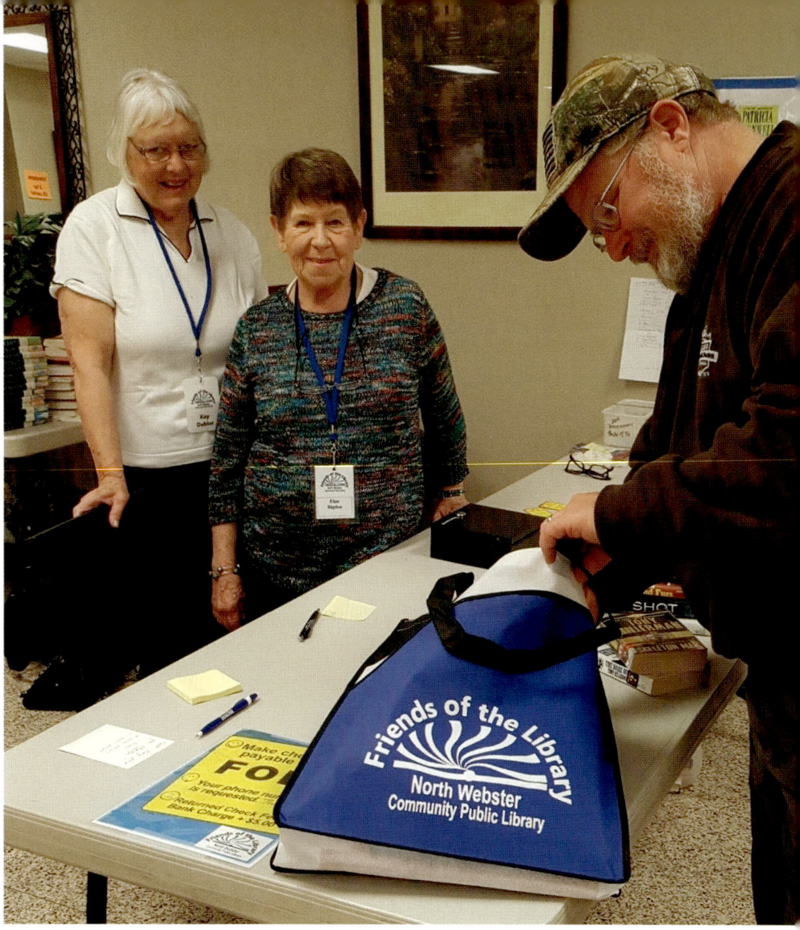

11:15 AM

North Webster

Great buys at the library's book sale!

Photo by Helen Leinbach

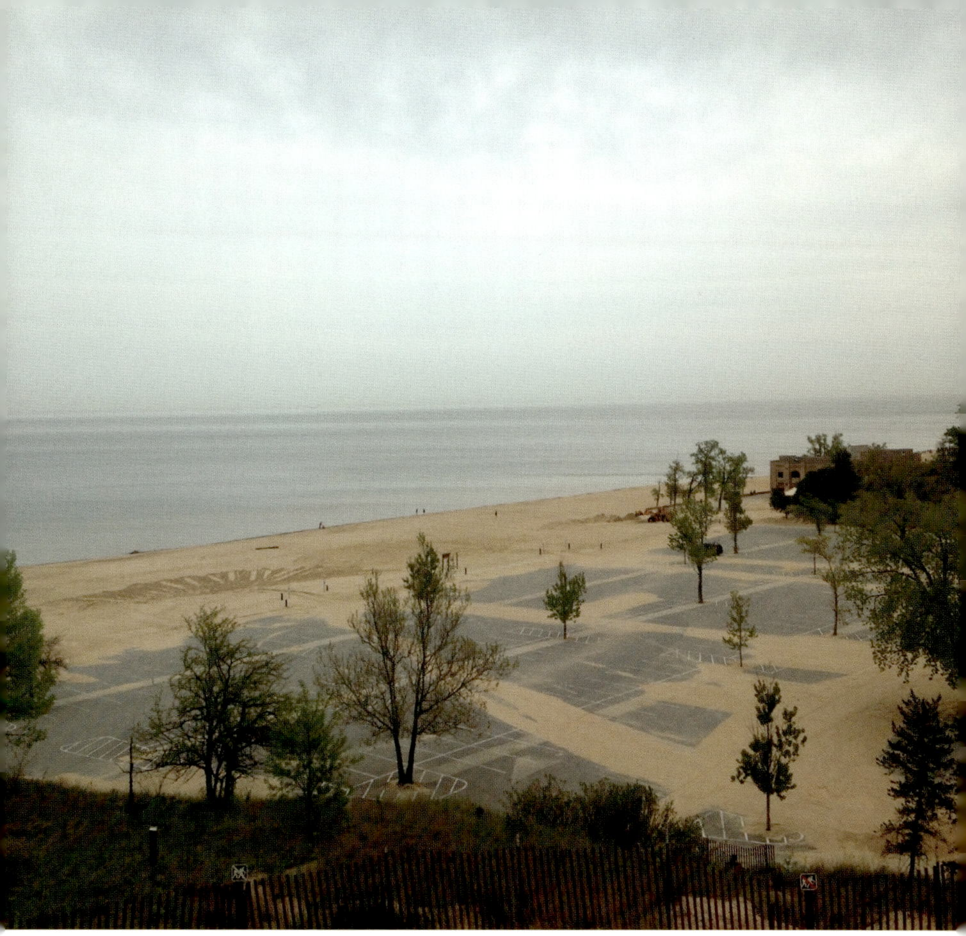

11:21 AM

Chesterton

Indiana Dunes State Park beach from the
observation deck.

Photo by Mikayla Larson

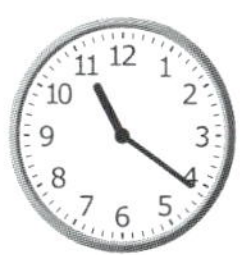

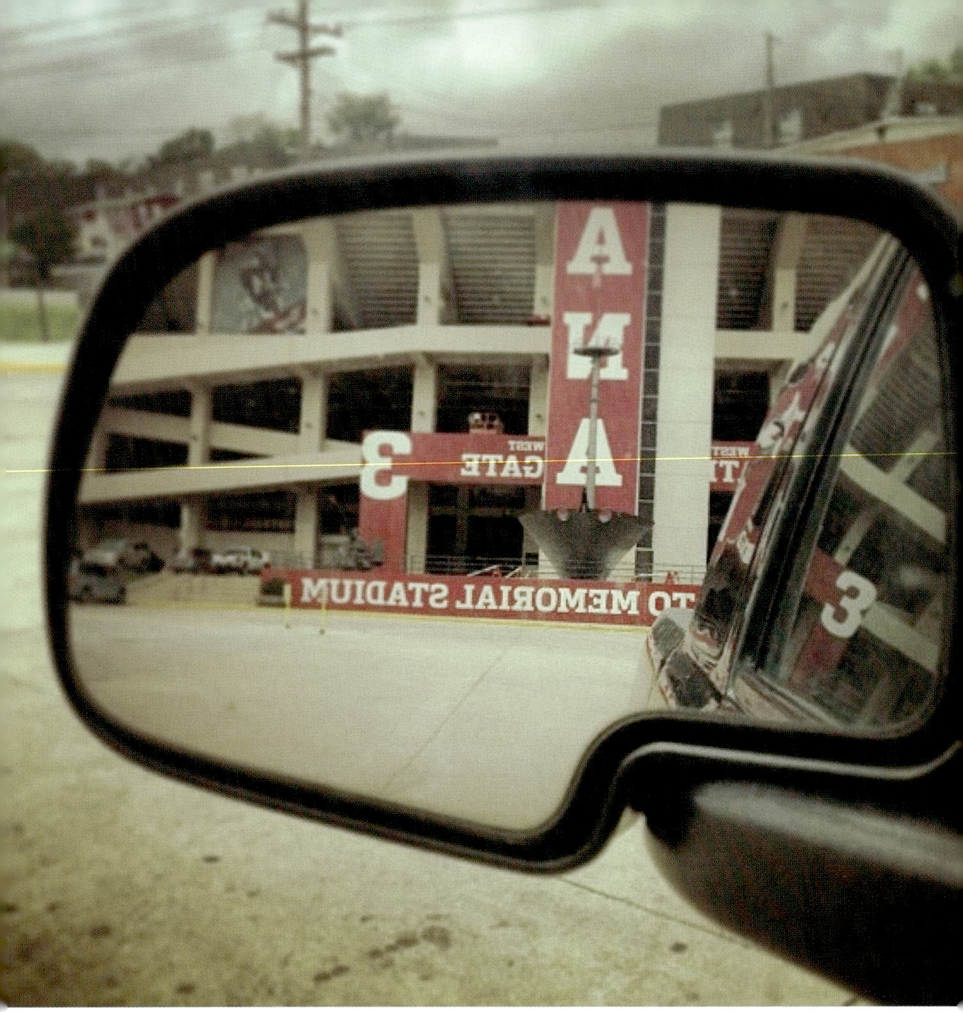

11:25 AM

Bloomington

Leaving Memorial Stadium after
laying down the new turf.

Photo by Richard Howenstein

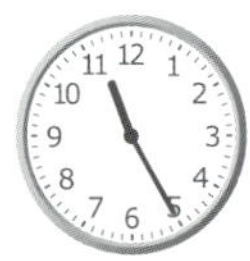

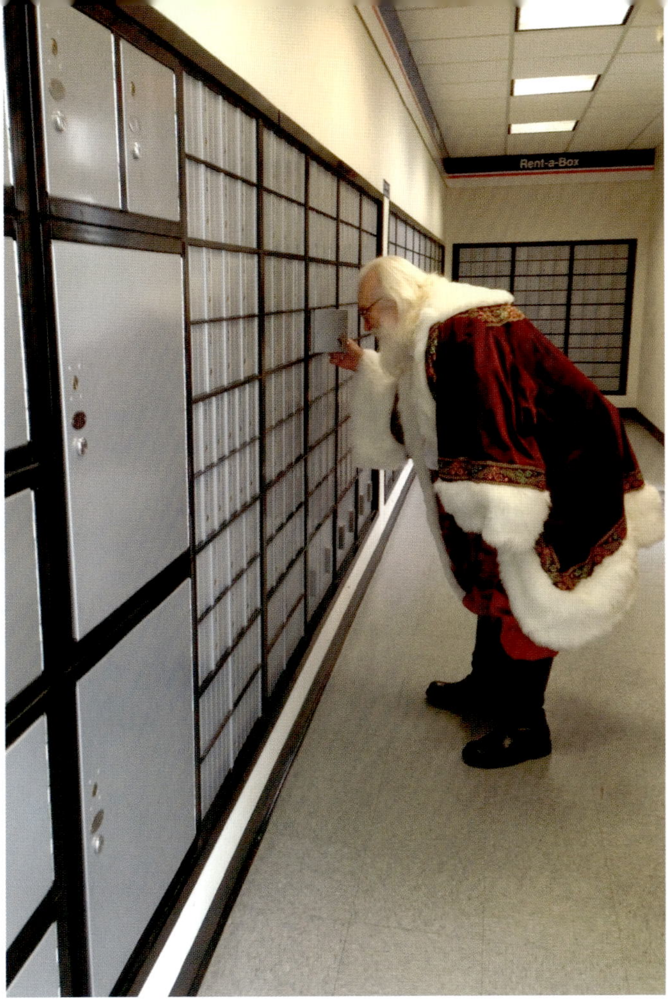

11:30 AM

Santa Claus

Santa checking his mailbox.

Photo by Julie Schnell

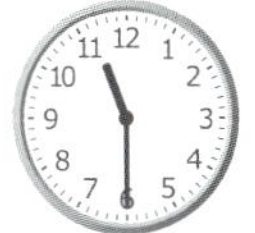

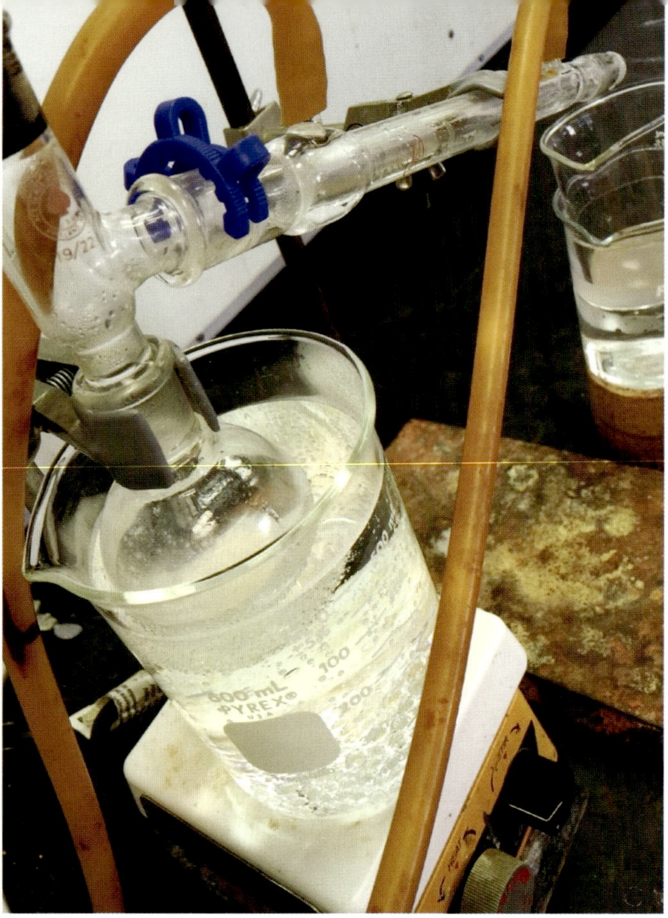

11:30 AM

Indianapolis

Aspiring premedical student performing a distillation during an Organic Chemistry lab at IUPUI (Indiana University–Purdue University Indianapolis).

Photo by Emma Ng

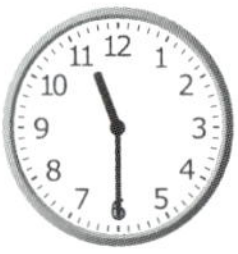

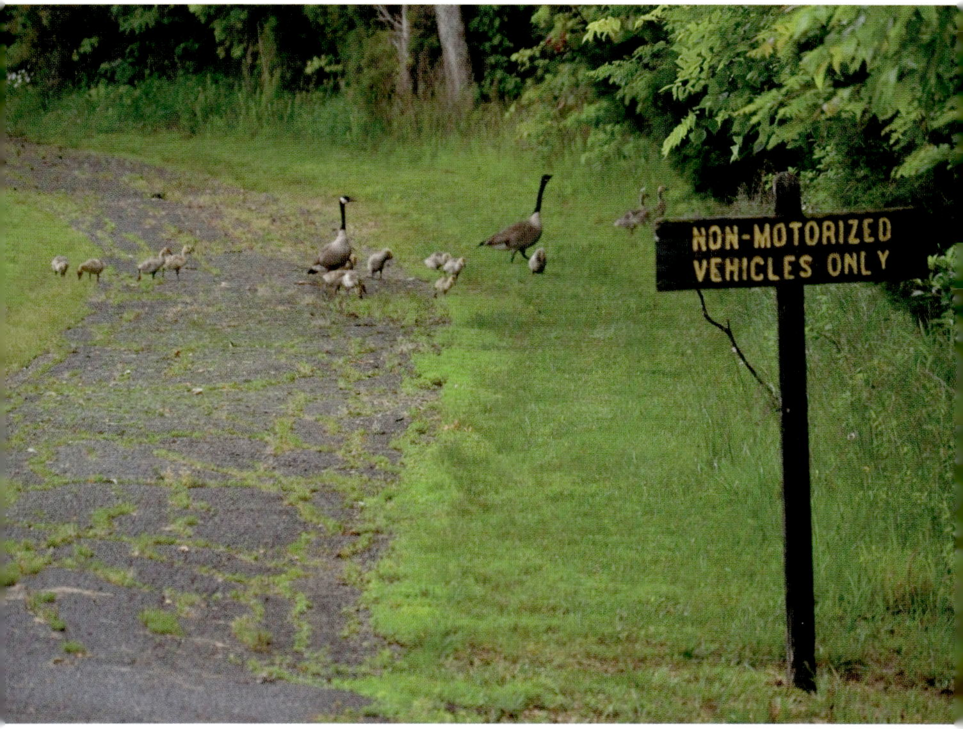

11:30 AM

Dubois County

These Canada Geese don't mind the wet weather as they lead their goslings toward Patoka Lake reservoir.

Photo by Carol Preflatish

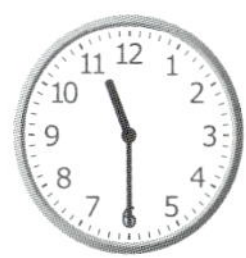

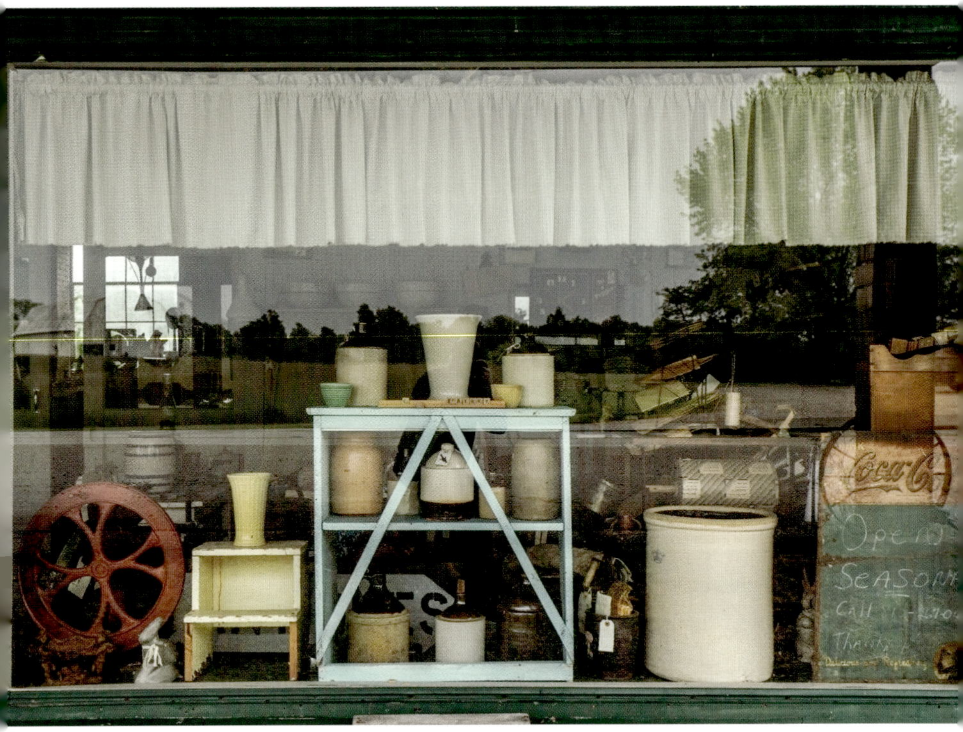

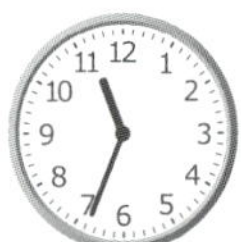

11:34 AM

Sulphur

Yesterday on display. Store window of a closed antique store at the intersection of Indiana Route 62 and Main Street.

Photo by Bob Gwaltney

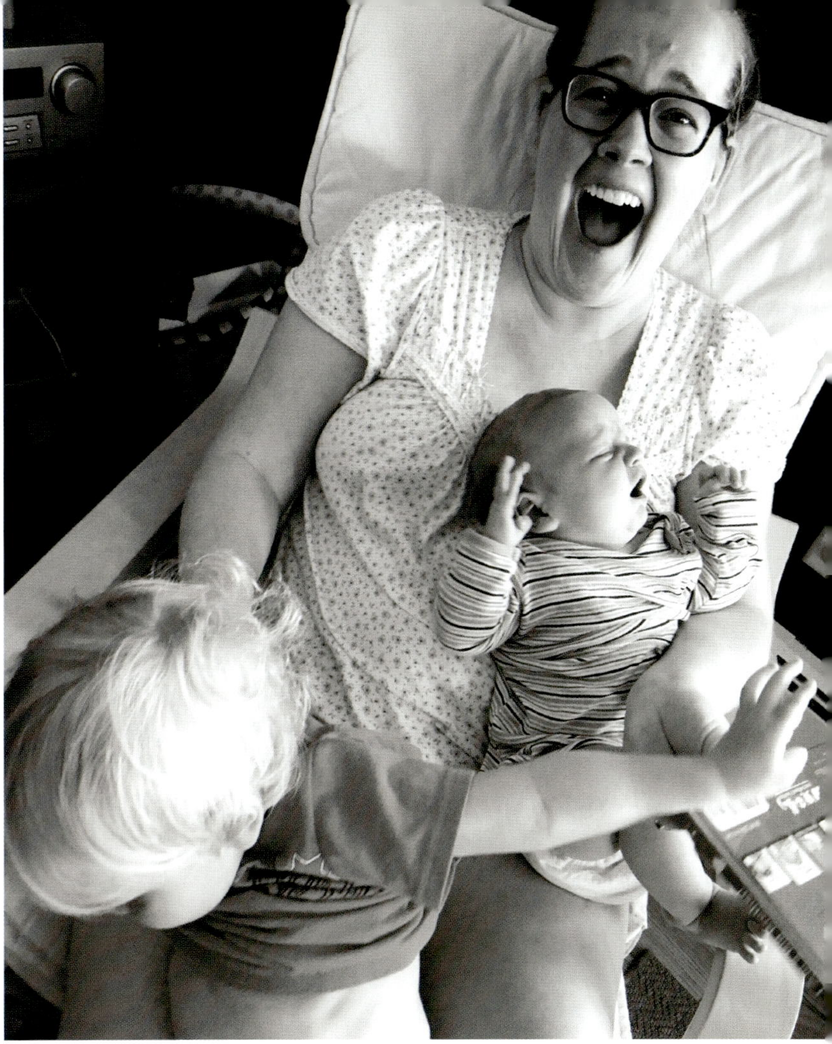

11:44 AM

Jonesboro

One book, one mom, two boys—who wins?

Photo by Herb Peterson

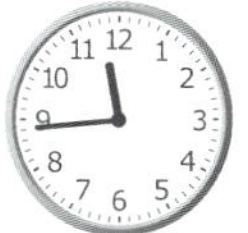

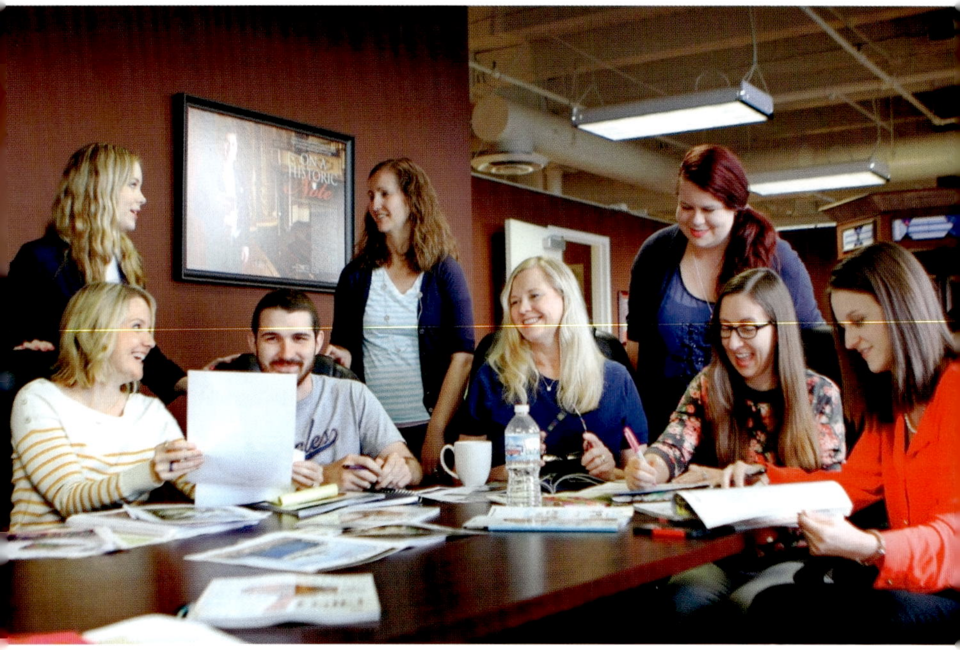

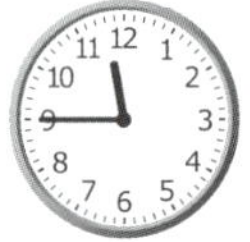

11:45 AM

Evansville

With page layouts and production schedules in front of them, the staff of Tucker Publishing Group in Evansville, Indiana, gather to discuss their latest publication of *Evansville Living*.

Photo by Evansville Living

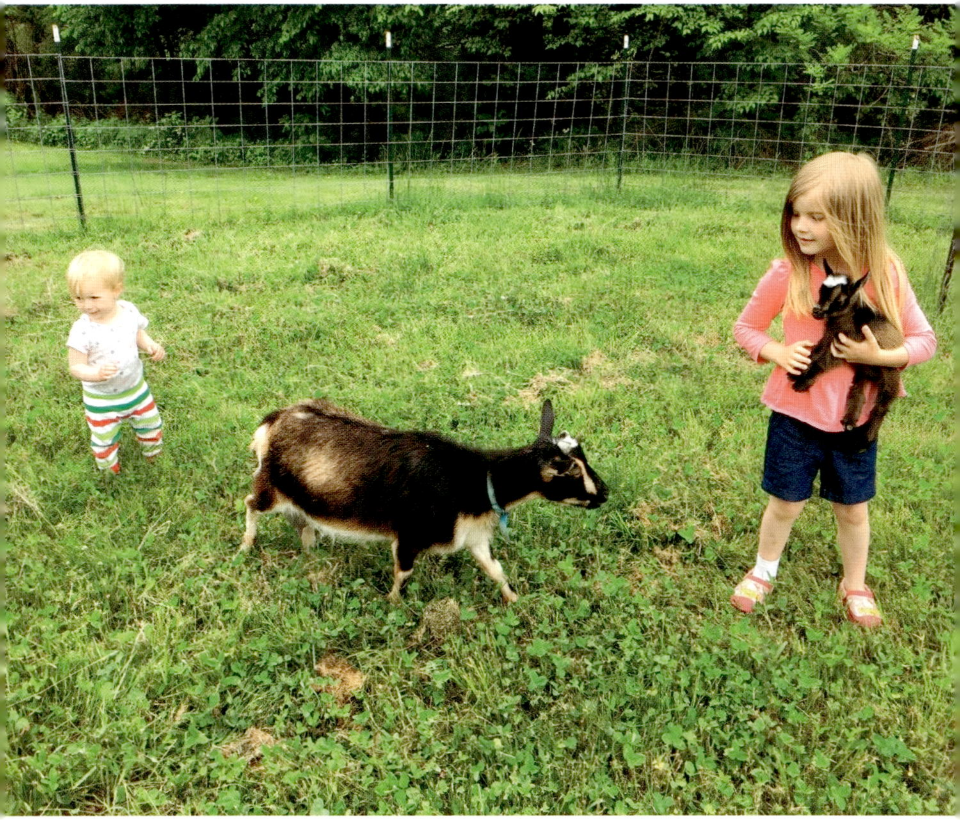

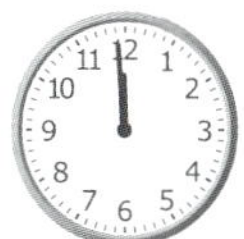

11:59 AM

Deputy

My girls spending time with their goats
before the rain settles in!

Photo by Erin Malcomb

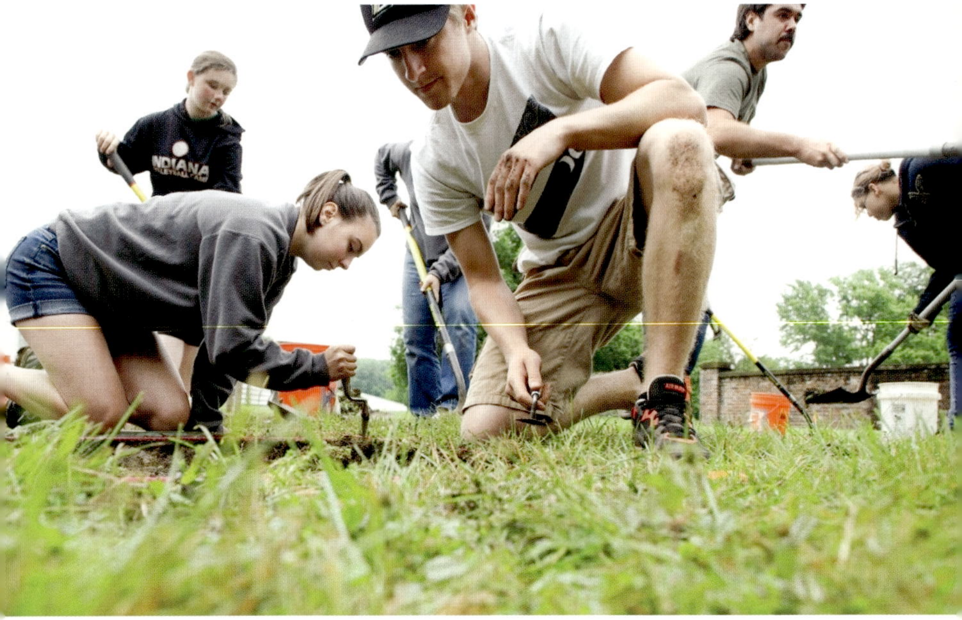

12:07 PM

New Harmony

New University of Southern Indiana students start
an archaeological dig during the second week
of the USI Archaeology Field School.

Photo by Erin McCracken

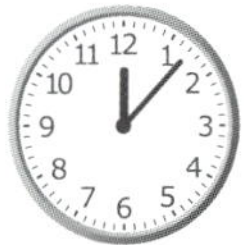

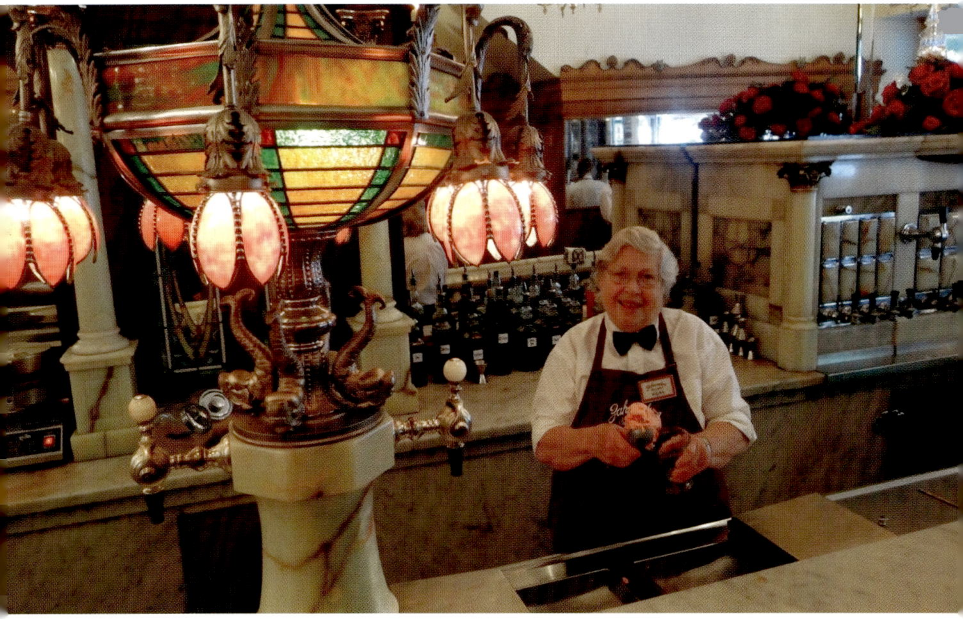

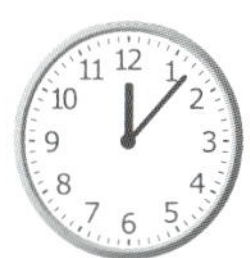

12:07 PM

Columbus

Chief soda jerk Wilma Essex Hair serving up raspberry and chocolate ice cream at Zaharakos Ice Cream Parlor.

Photo by Marilyn Brackney

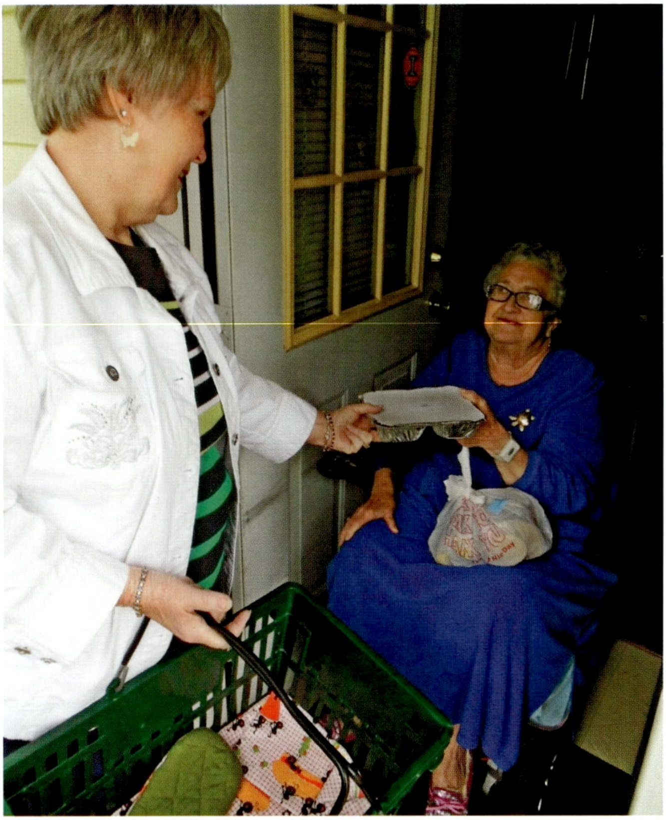

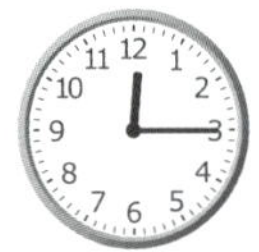

12:15 PM

Bloomington

Meals on Wheels volunteer Carolyn Anderson
delivers a hot noon meal to client
Alice Vaughn in her home.

Photo by Kathy Romy

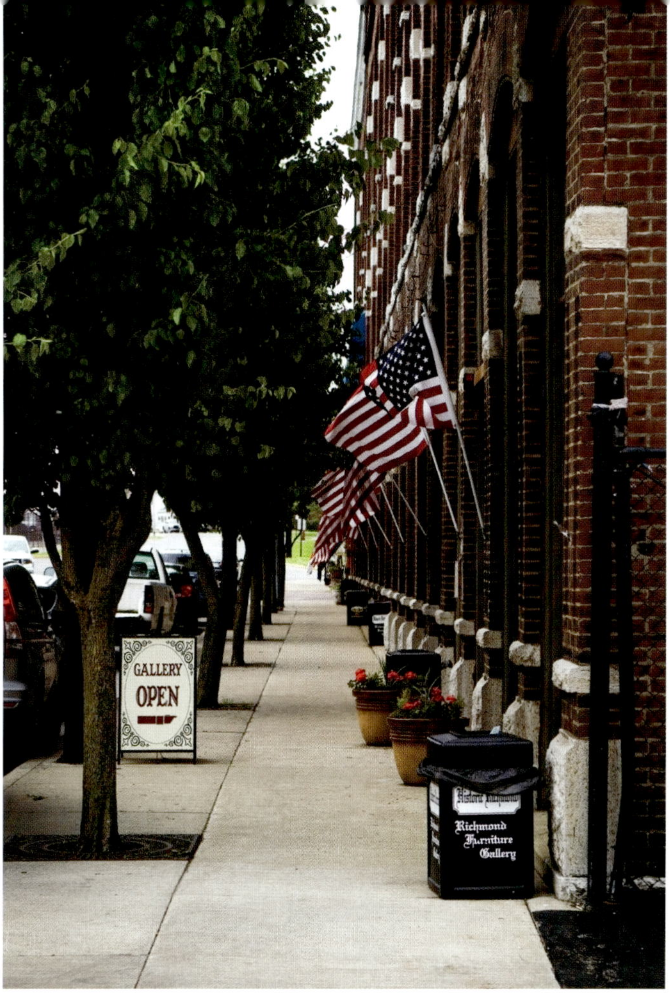

12:27 PM

Richmond

Lunchtime view down the sidewalk in the historic Richmond Depot District.

Photo by Taylor Gregory

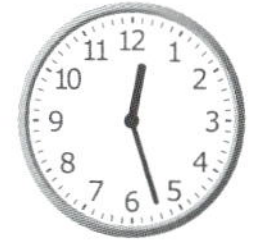

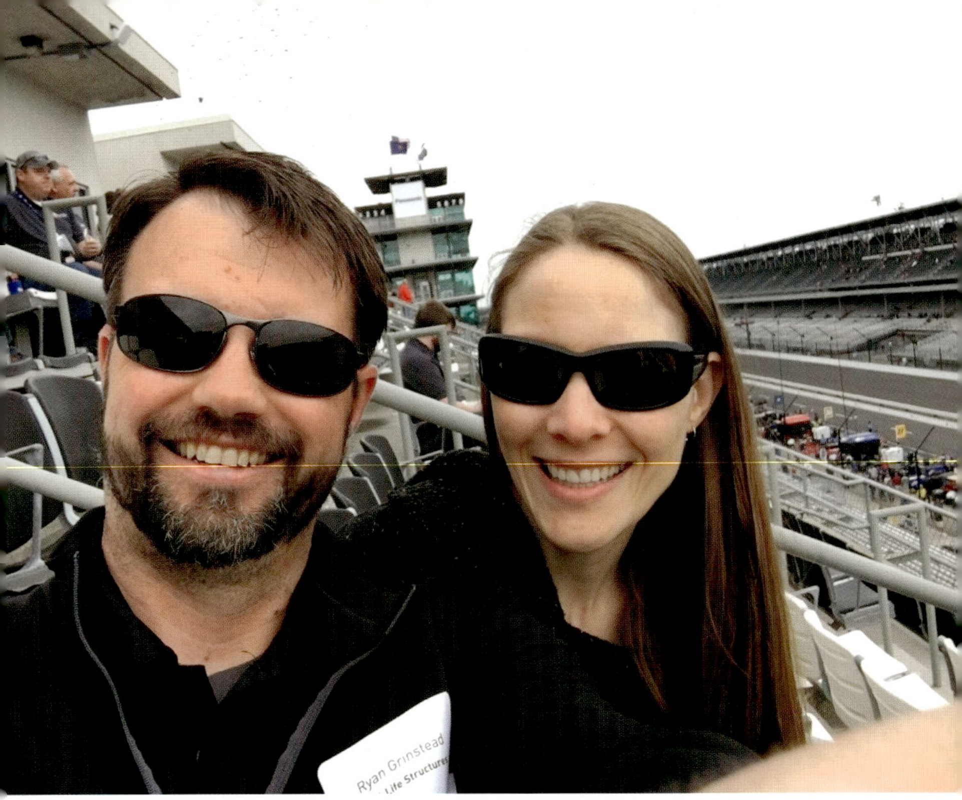

12:29 PM

Indianapolis

Fast Friday at the Indianapolis Motor Speedway!

Photo by Katherine Matthen Grinstead

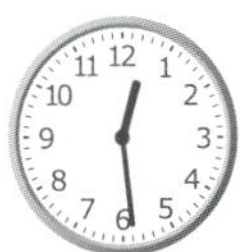

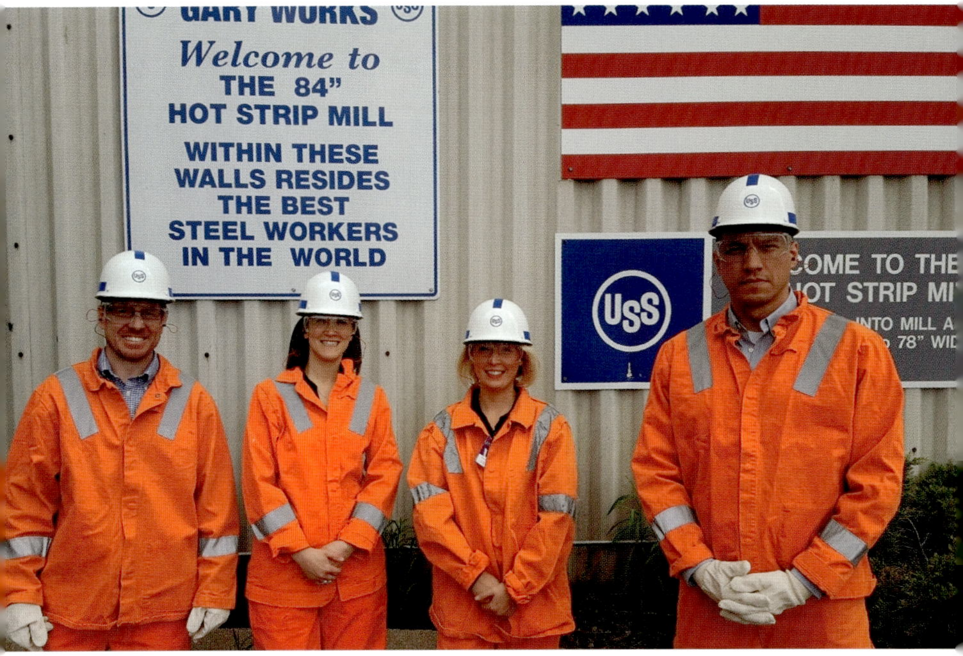

12:30 PM

Gary

Staff members of Congressman Pete Visclosky tour
U.S. Steel's Gary Works.

Photo by Amy Blaker

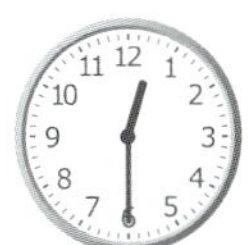

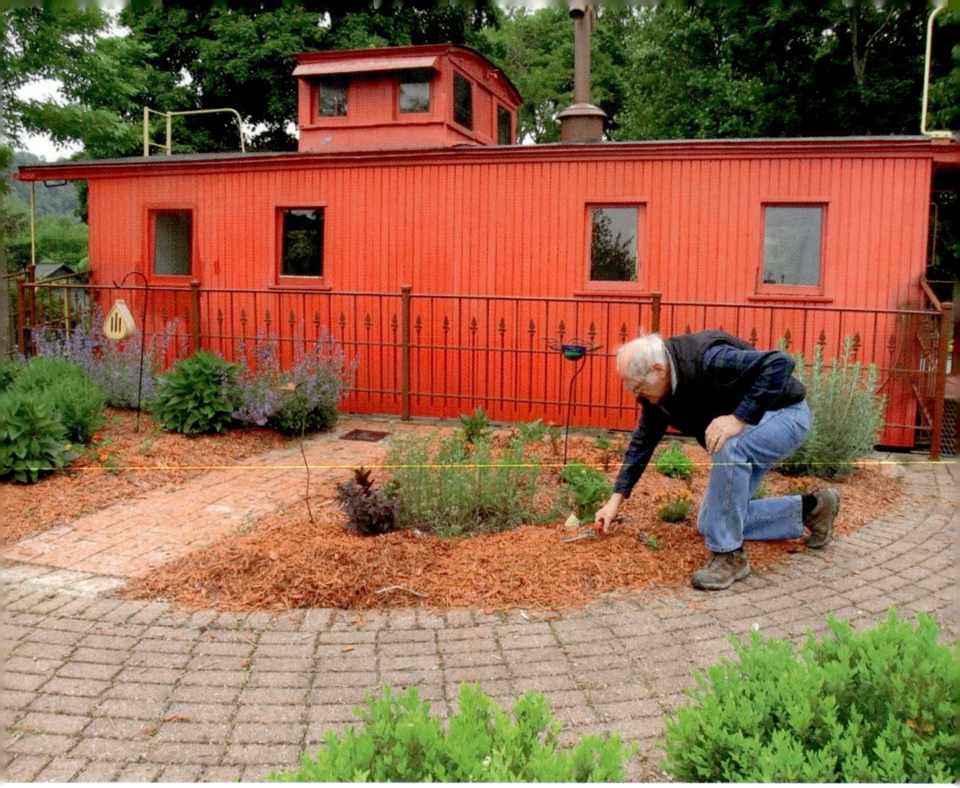

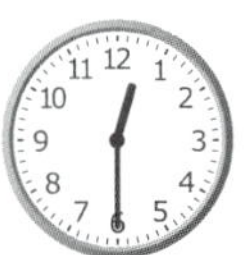

12:30 PM

Madison

Jefferson County Historical Society volunteer Michael Moore creates a Monarch Waystation for butterflies in Harriet's Garden at the Heritage Center.

Photo by Michael Moore

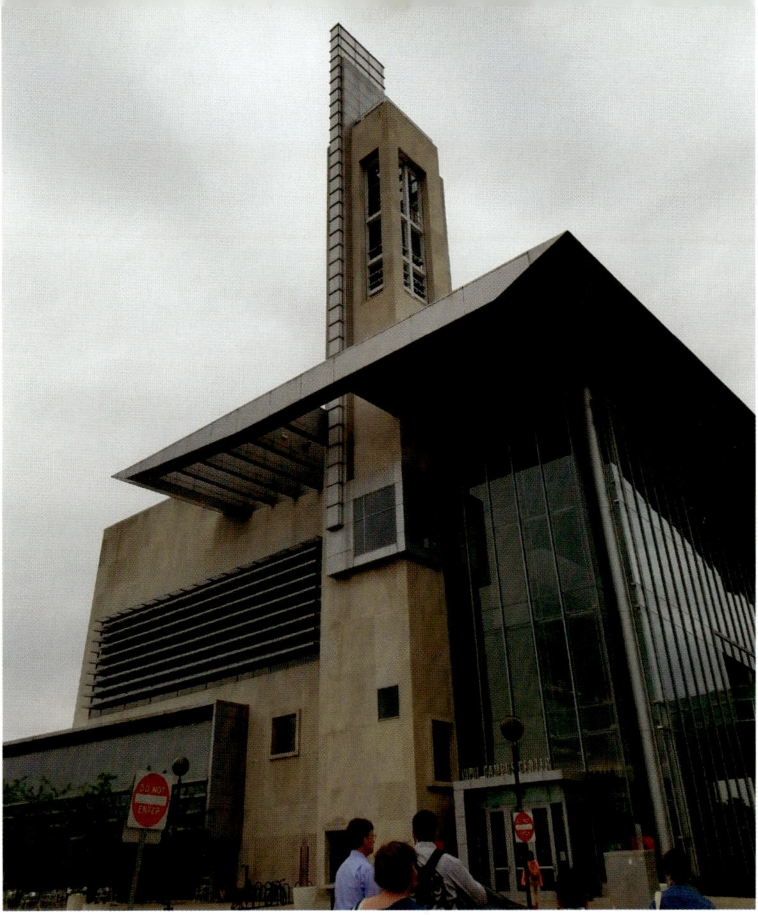

12:45 PM

Indianapolis

Clouds rolling in over Statewide Libraries Day at the IUPUI Campus Center. Indiana University Libraries faculty and staff from all campuses are meeting here to share ideas and discuss the topics of the day.

Photo by Michelle Hahn

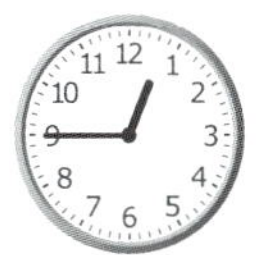

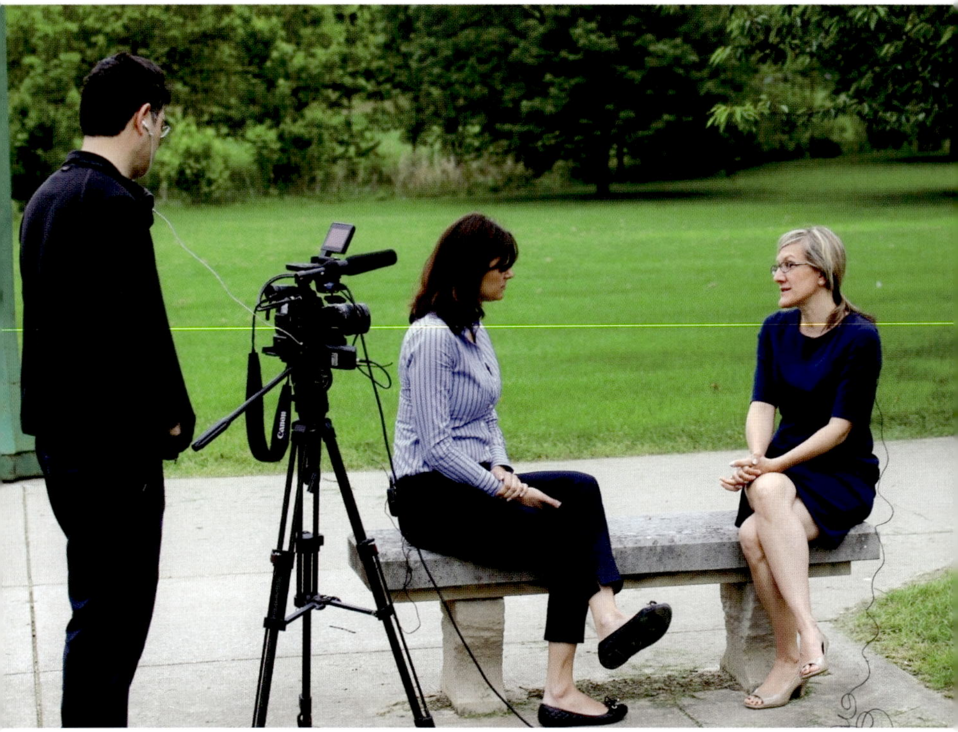

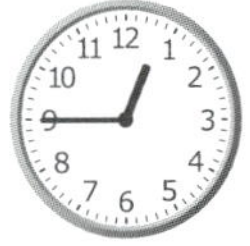

12:45 PM

Bloomington

PBS NewsHour reporter Yasmeen Qureshi, with her cameraman Daniel, interview IU Bloomington School of Education professor Suzanne Eckes about recent legal issues regarding transgender student rights.

Photo by Scott Witzke

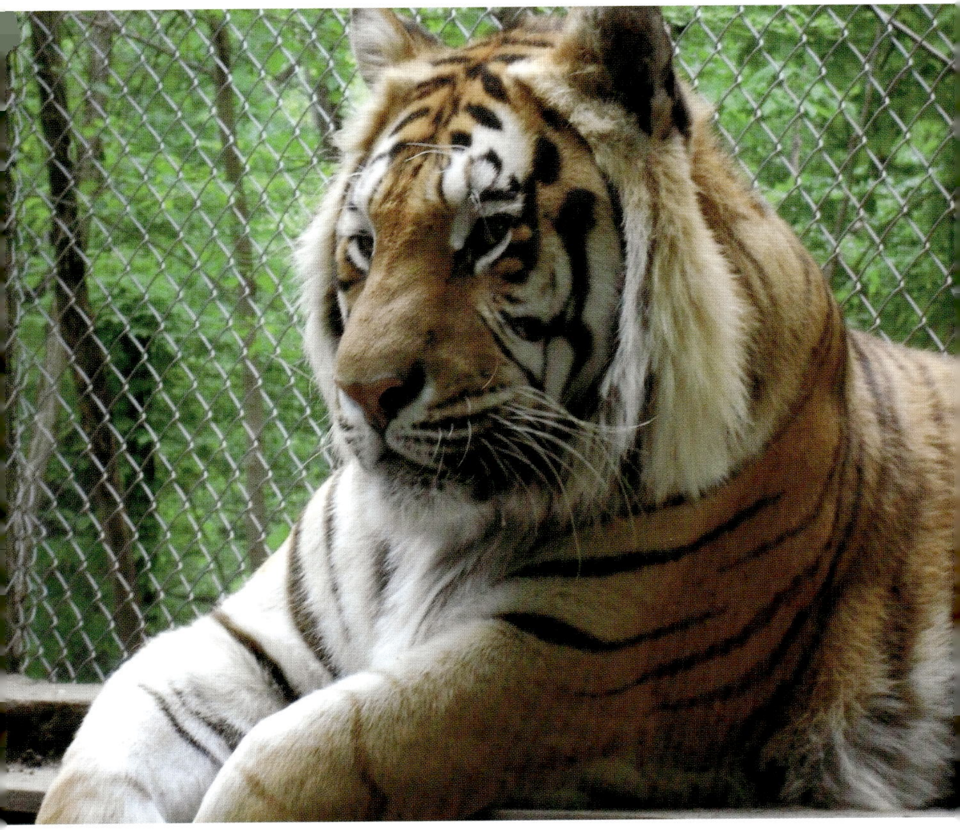

1:00 PM

Center Point

A lazy Friday for the tigers at the Exotic Feline
Rescue Center.

Photo by Kelly Staten

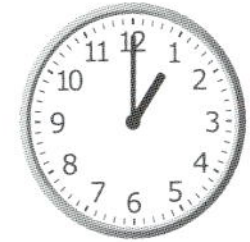

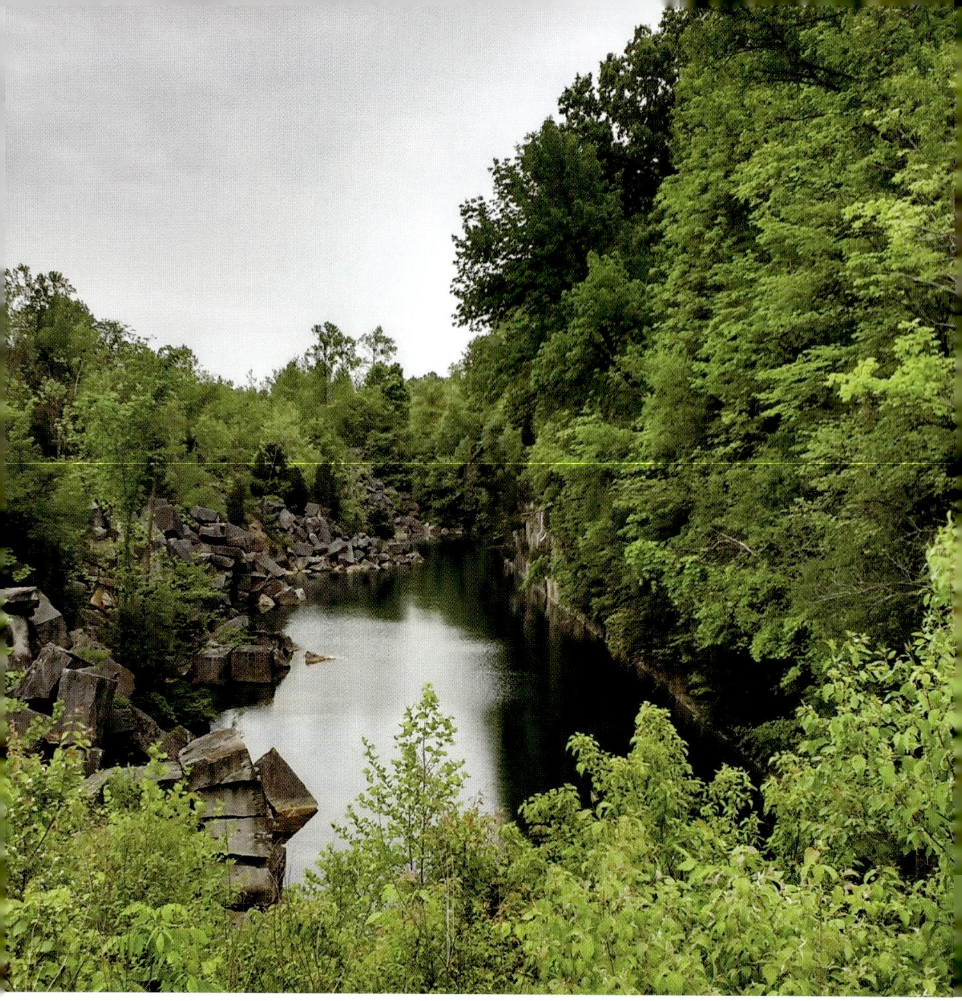

1:00 PM

Bloomington

One of southern Indiana's iconic abandoned quarries.
Beauty in abandonment, as nature takes it back.

Photo by Rebecca Winkle

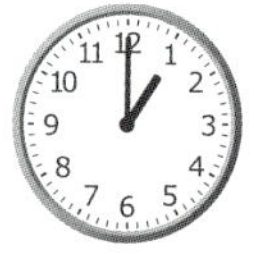

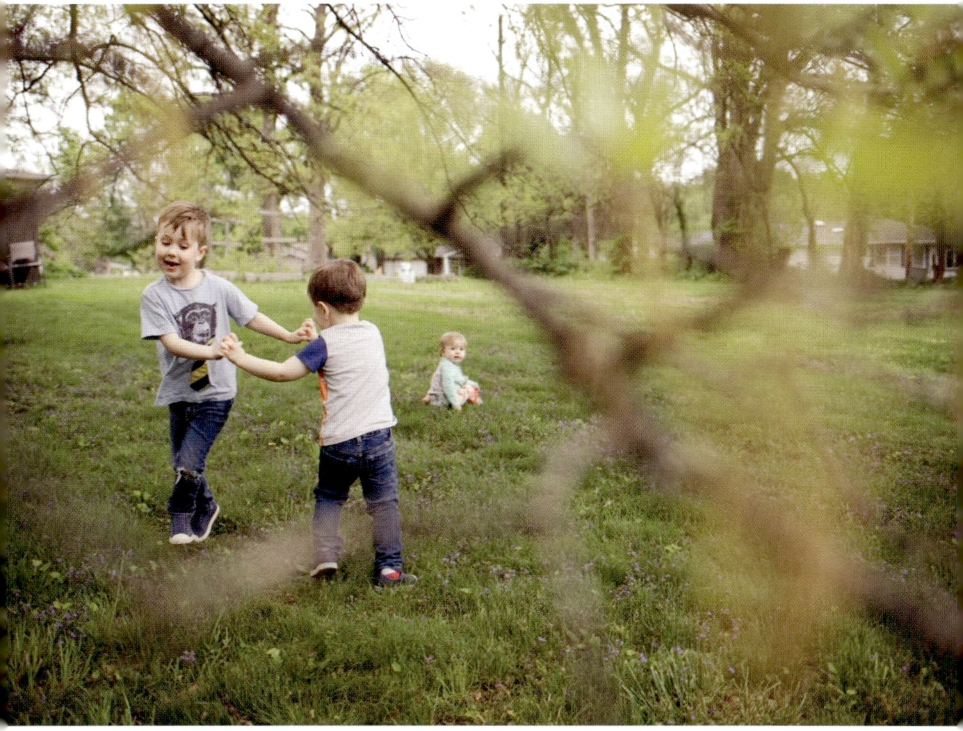

1:07 PM

Valparaiso

My sons playing Ring around the Rosie in our backyard while their baby sister watches.

Photo by Rebecca Hoyle

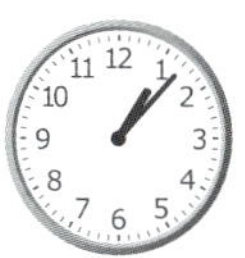

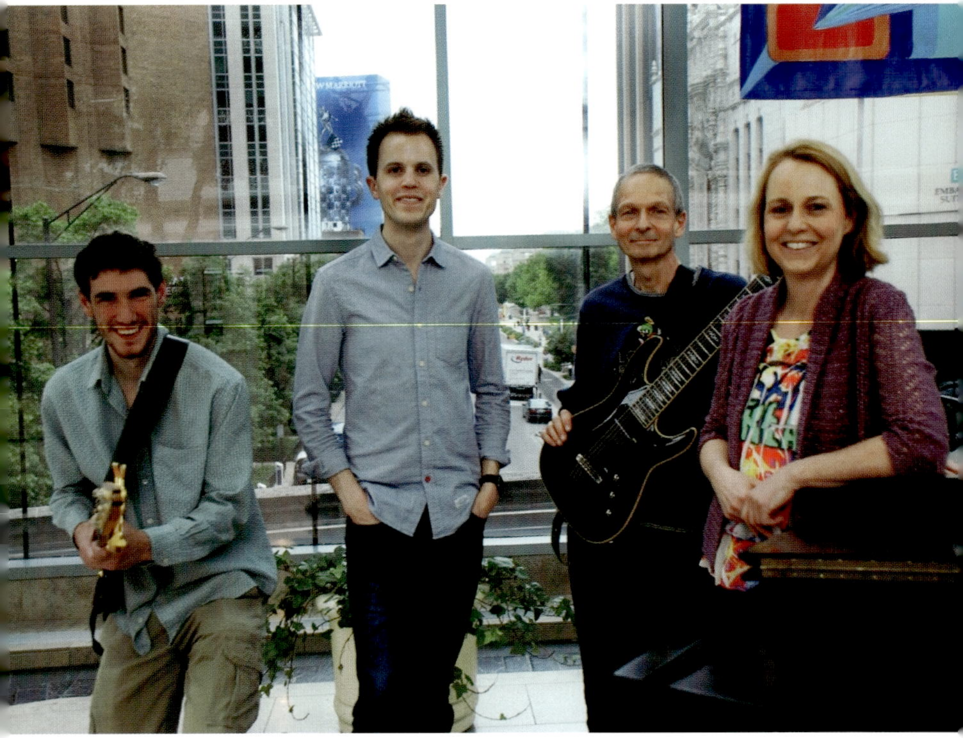

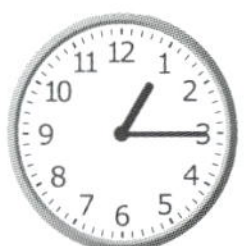

1:15 PM

Indianapolis

The Time Flies performs a lunch concert at the
Artsgarden, Circle Centre Mall.

Photo by Monika Herzig

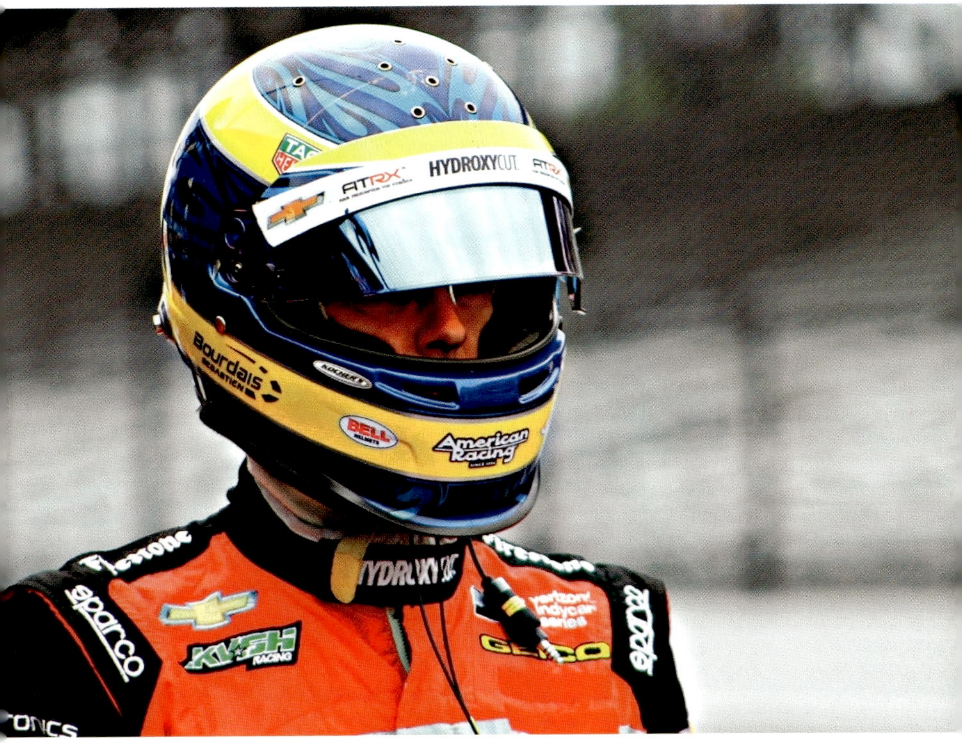

1:16 PM

Indianapolis

IndyCar driver Sébastien Bourdais surveys the track in preparation for practice for the hundredth running of the Indianapolis 500 at the Indianapolis Motor Speedway.

Photo by Kate Shoup

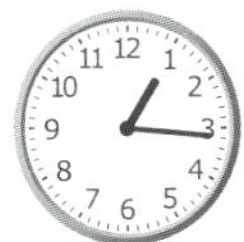

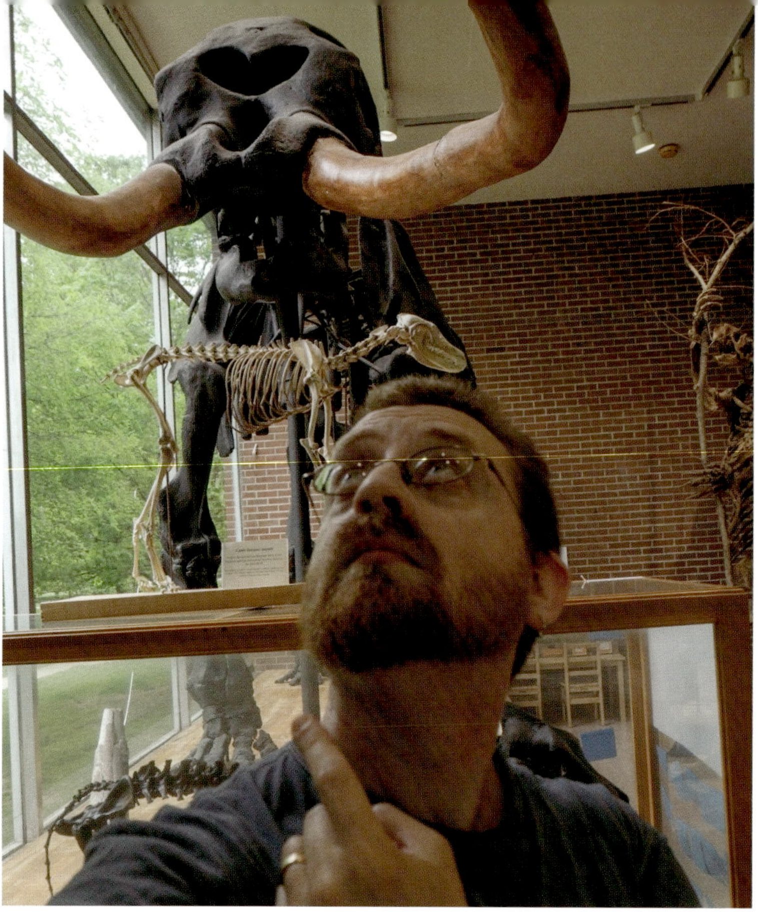

1:29 PM

Richmond

At the Joseph Moore Museum at Earlham College,
checking out the skeleton of an American mastodon
and other mammals that once roamed Indiana
during the Pleistocene Epoch.

Photo by Travis Poling

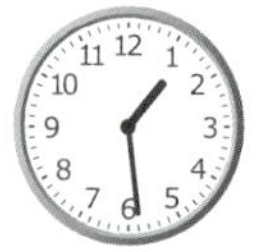

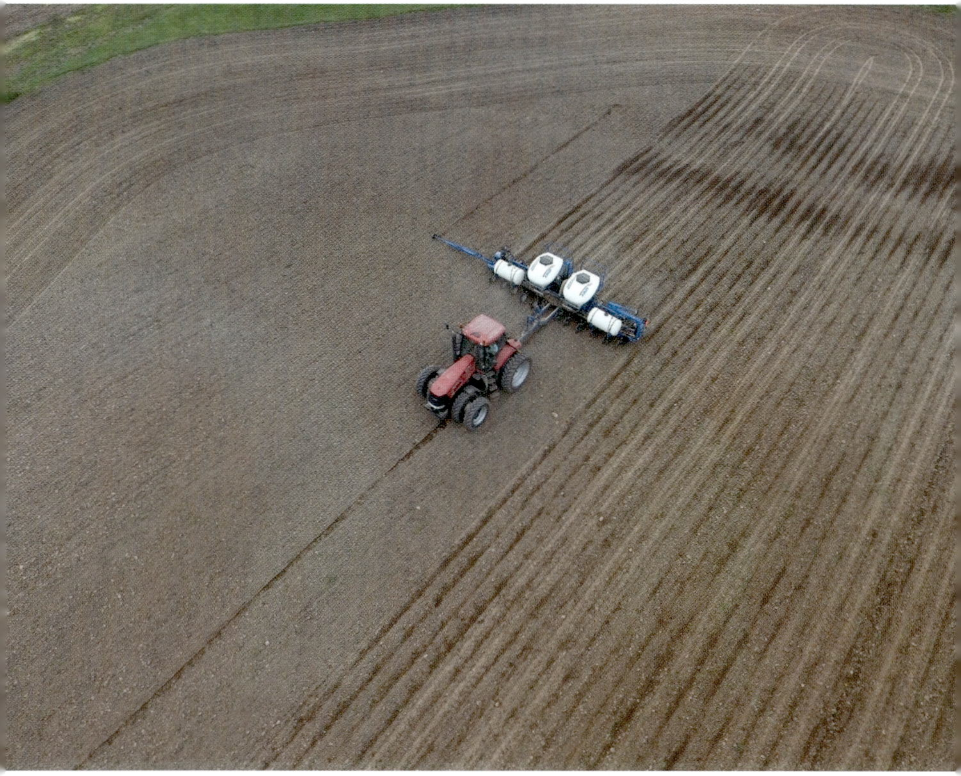

1:30 PM

Centerville

Drone captures me planting corn on a farm that has been in our family for over eighty years.

Photo by Steve Bode

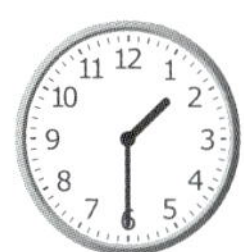

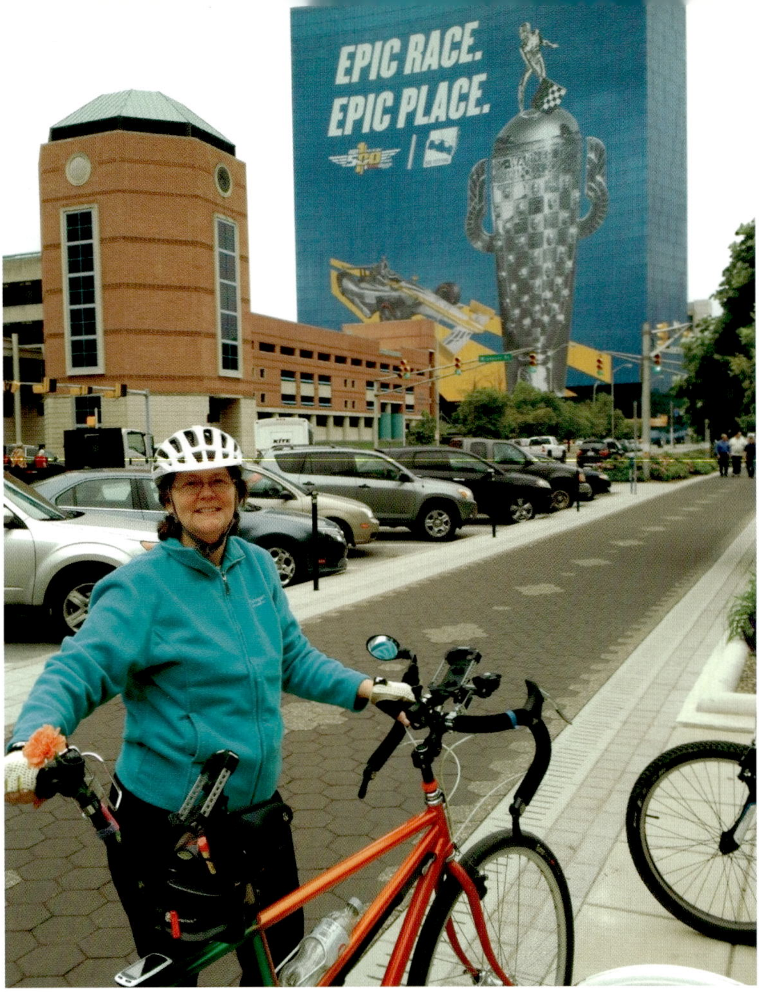

1:33 PM

Indianapolis

Biking the world's biggest small town!

Photo by Vance Hodges

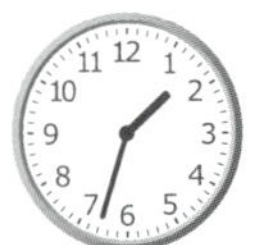

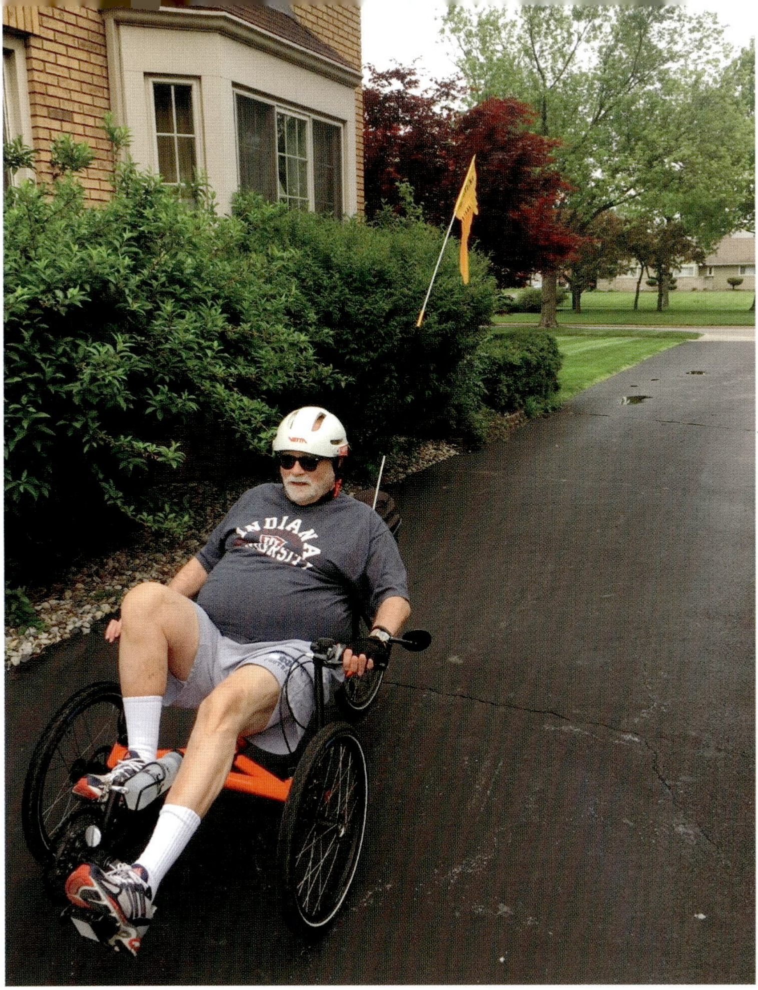

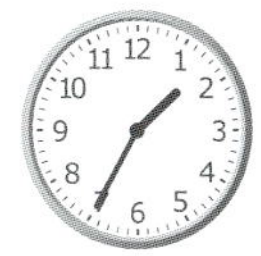

1:35 PM

Fort Wayne

A retired editor, I'm finishing an hour-long tricycle ride. My problems with balance keep me off bikes.

Photo by Craig Klugman

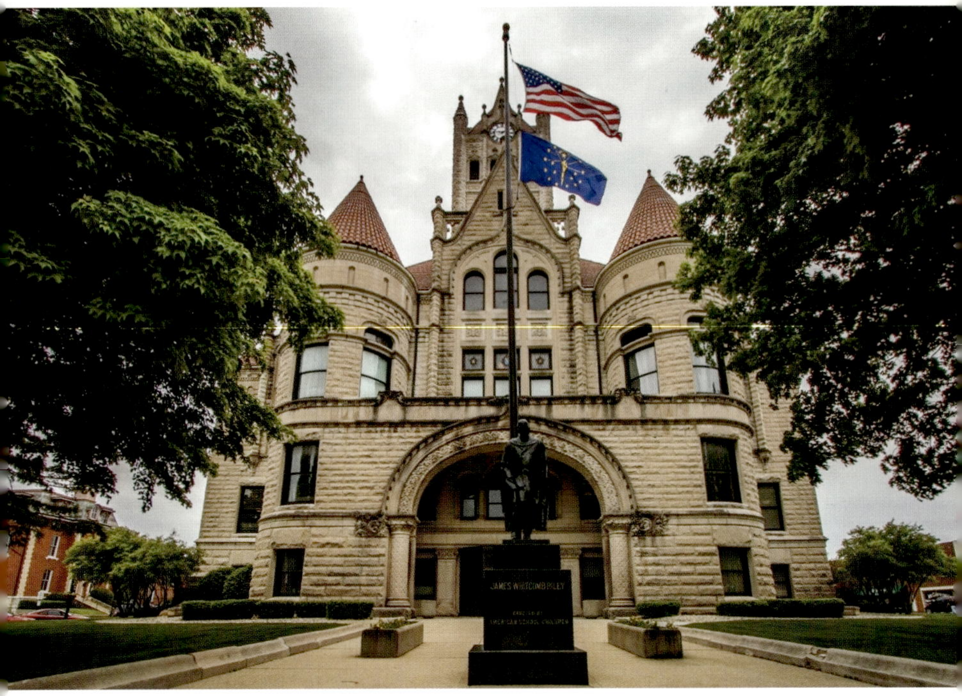

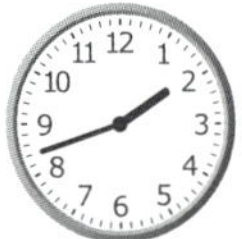

1:42 PM

Greenfield

Standing in front of the Hancock County
Courthouse and the statue of
James Whitcomb Riley.

Photo by Brad Brown

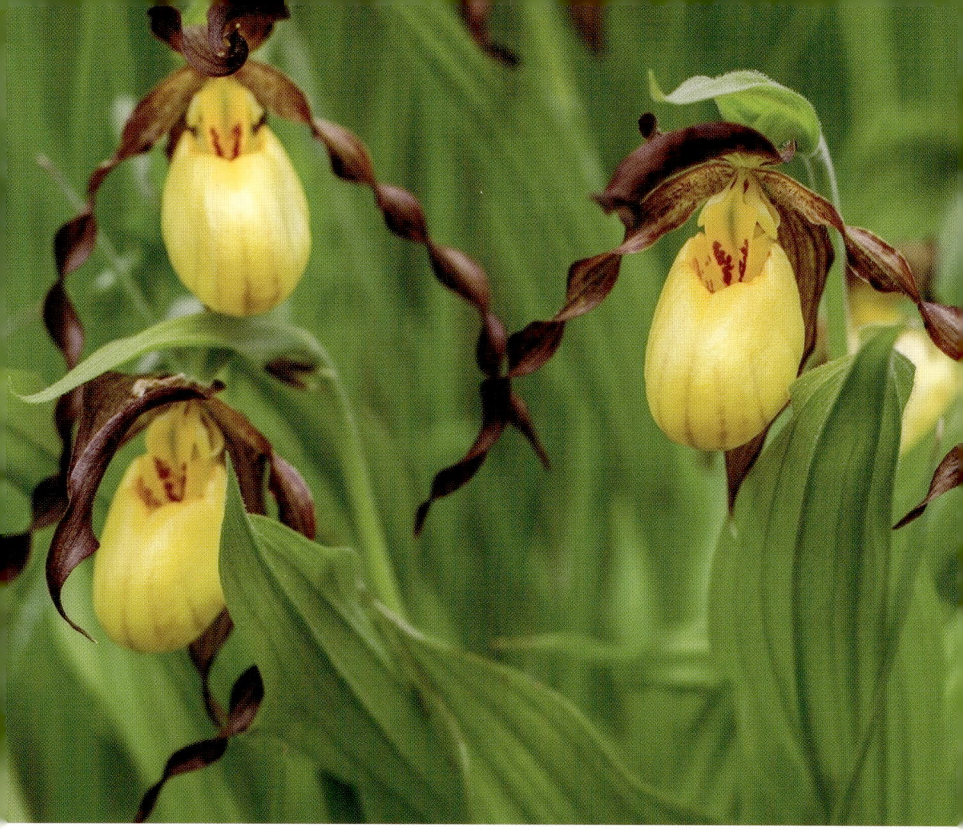

2:00 PM

Steuben County

Discovering a yellow lady's slipper orchid
while hiking on this beautiful day along Trail 3
in Pokagon State Park.

Photo by Kemuel Badger

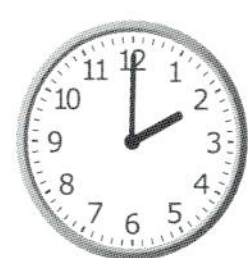

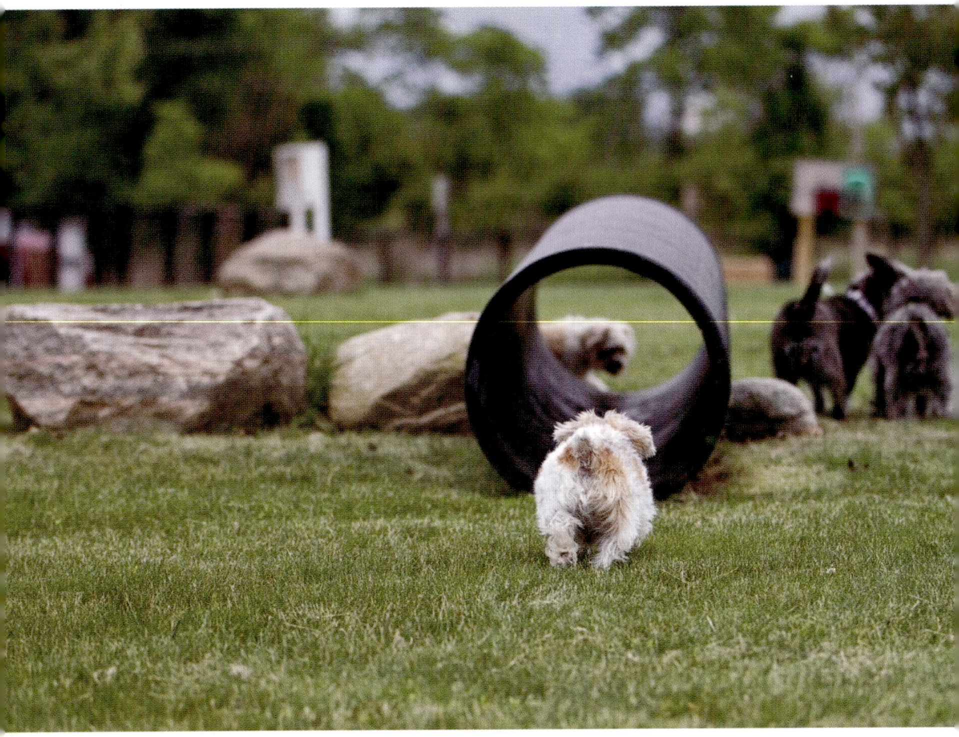

2:00 PM

Greenfield

Our first trip to Rover's Run Bark Park
after a long winter!

Photo by Susan Cook

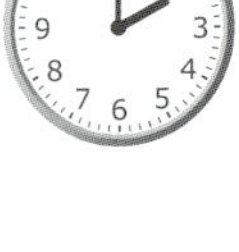

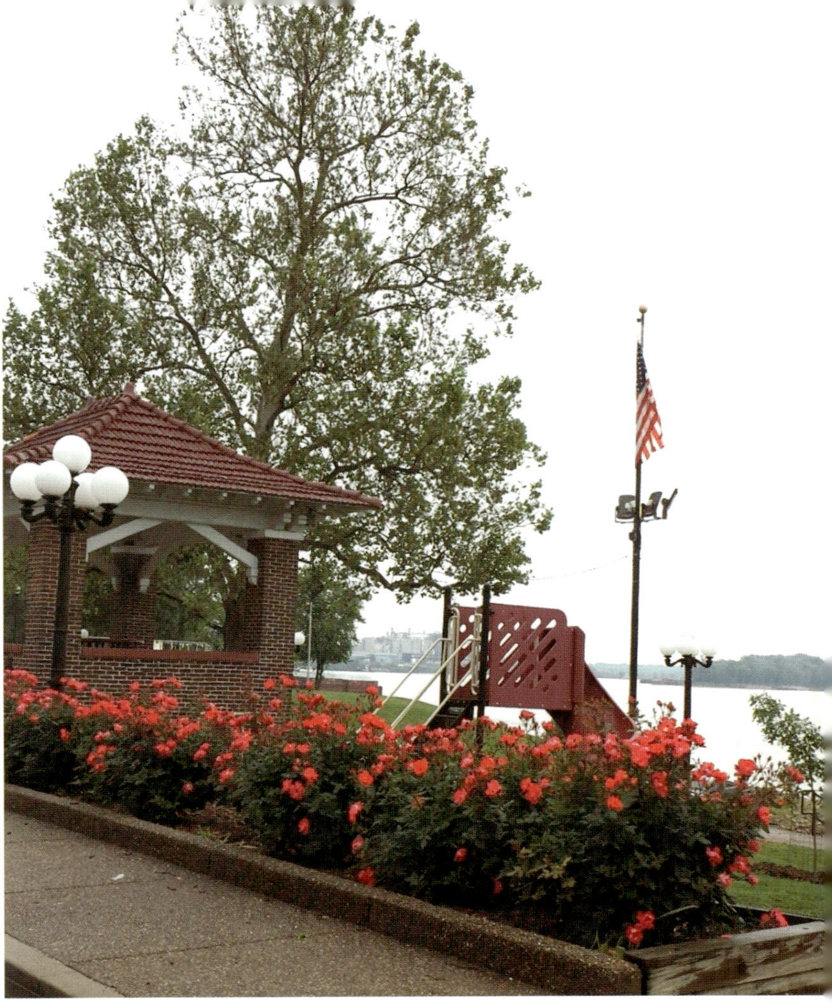

2:15 PM

Mount Vernon

Enjoying Sherburne Park on the Ohio River,
even if it is a rainy day.

Photo by Rebecca Higgins

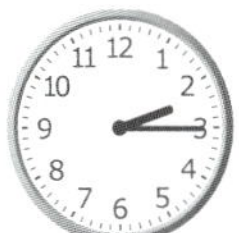

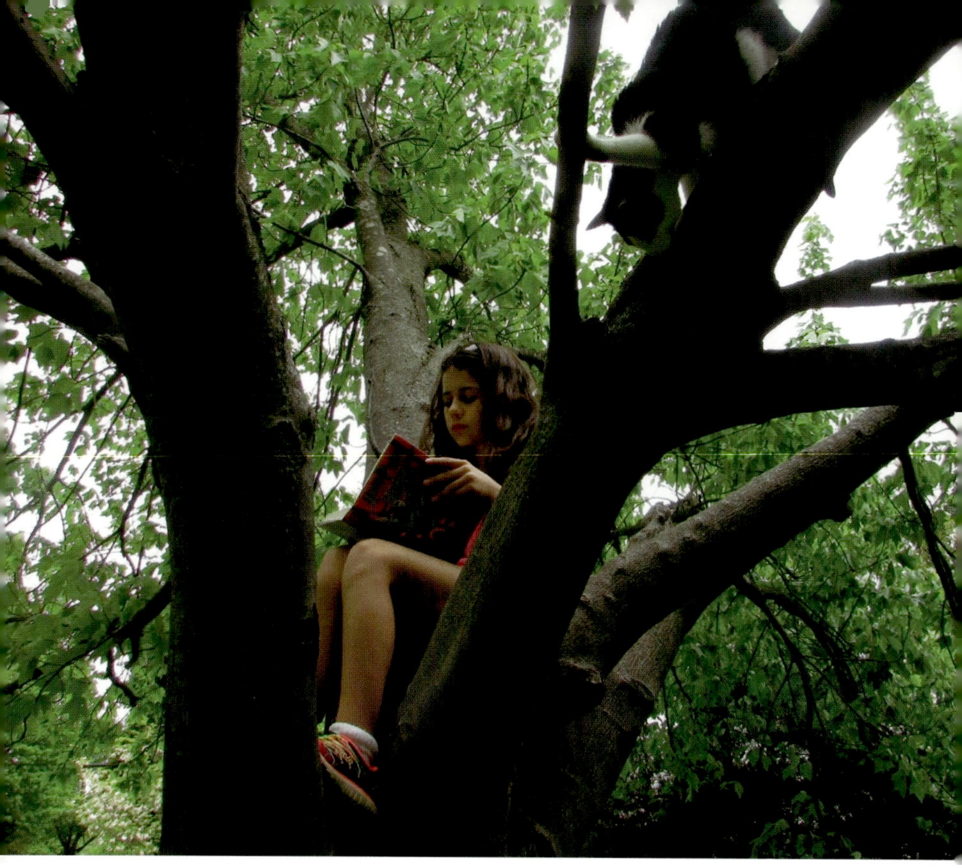

2:21 PM

South Bend

Spending a quiet afternoon in Hogwarts
with cat Chester.

Photo by Melanie Garcia

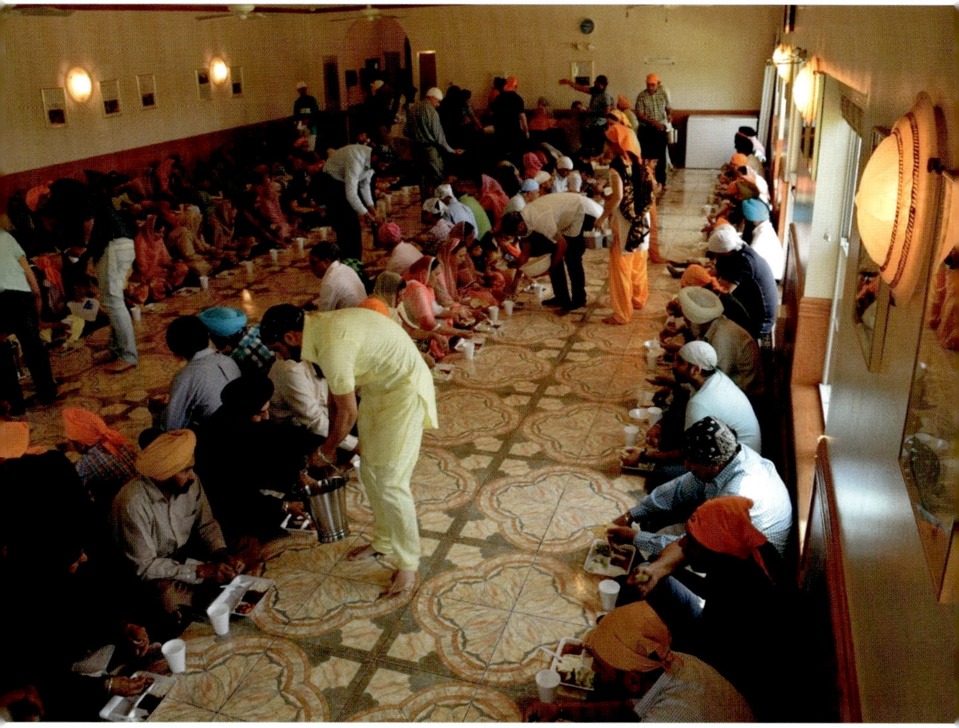

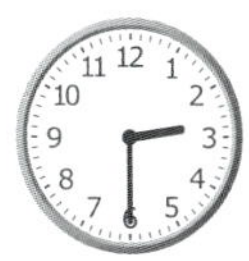

2:30 PM

Crown Point

Volunteers from the Sikh Religious Society serving
food in the Langar Hall free community kitchen.
Everyone sits down on the floor and eats
the same food to ensure equality.

Photo by Jaspal Gothra

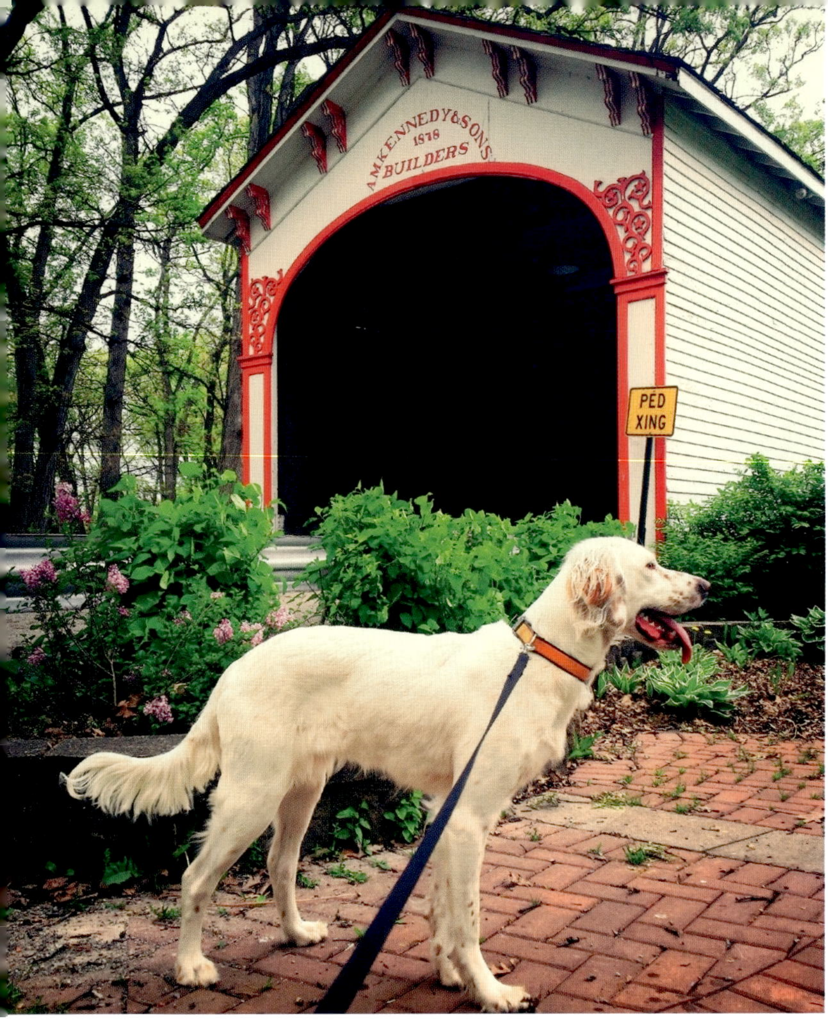

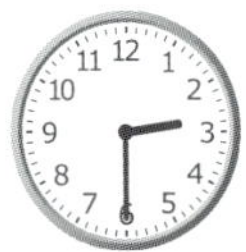

2:30 PM

Crown Point

My daily walk past the Milroy or Shelhorn Covered
Bridge at the Lake County Fairgrounds.

Photo by Christine Starrick

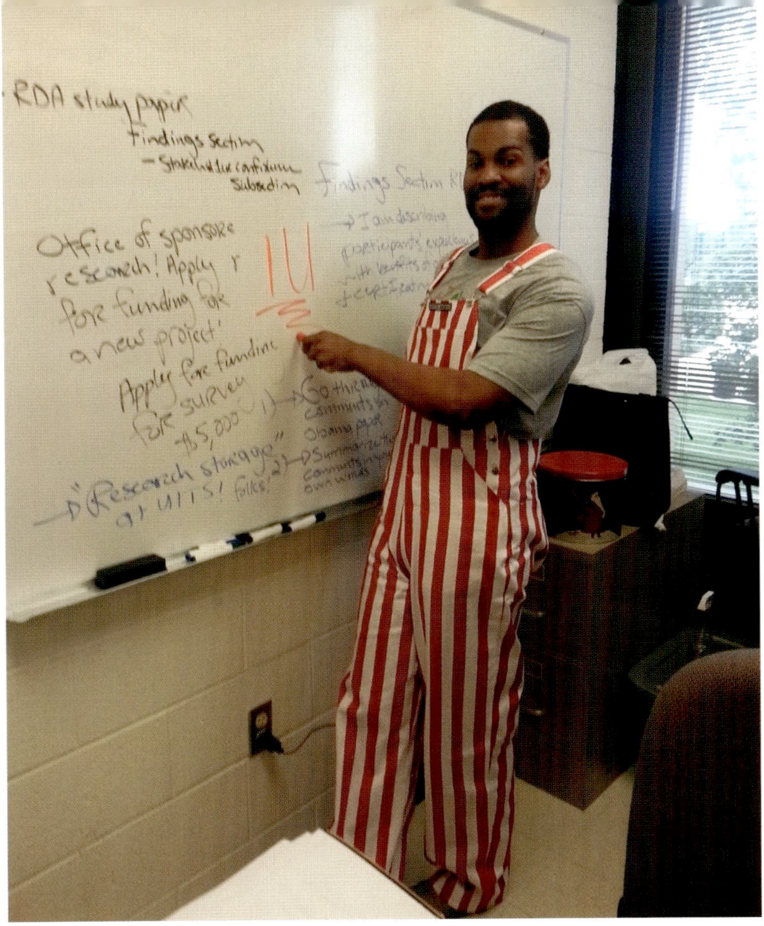

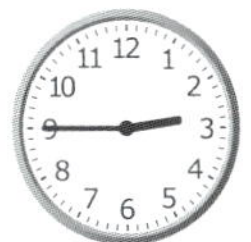

2:45 PM

Bloomington

Devan Donaldson, IU Bloomington associate professor of information and library science, shows Hoosier pride by wearing candy stripes while working in his faculty office.

Photo by Jane Lewis

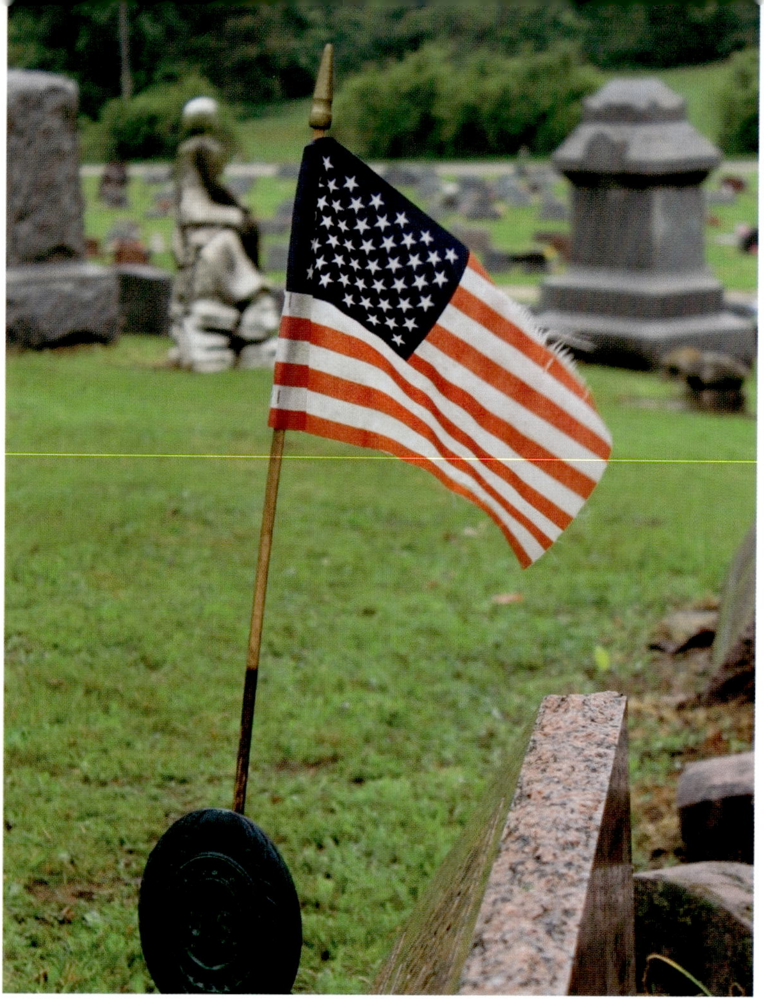

2:59 PM

Washington

Memorial Day will not be just another day in May
at the Oak Grove Cemetery.

Photo by Brenda Osmon

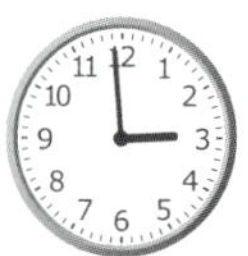

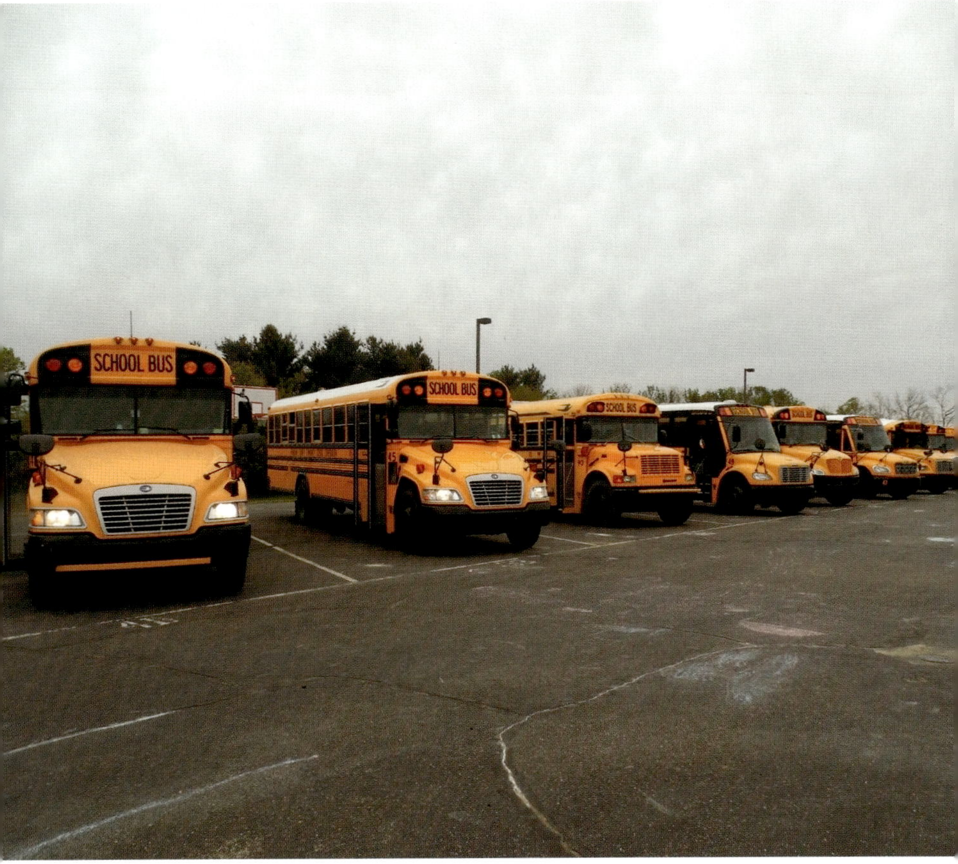

3:00 PM

Mt. Carmel

School's out for the summer!

Photo by Laura Frondorf

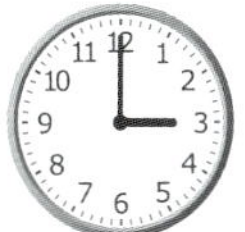

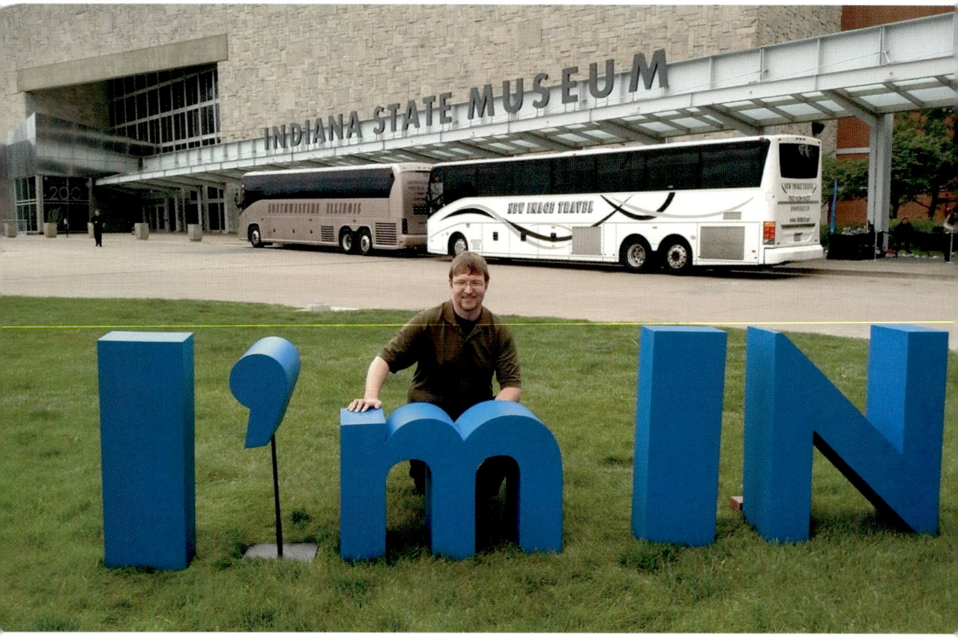

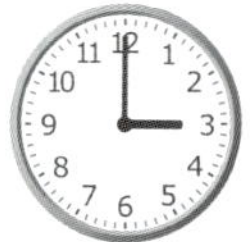

3:00 PM

Indianapolis

Celebrating the Bicentennial Legacy Project
at the Indiana State Museum.

Photo by Matthew Pope

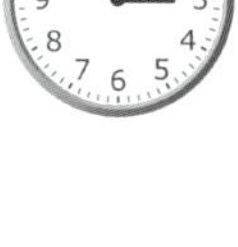

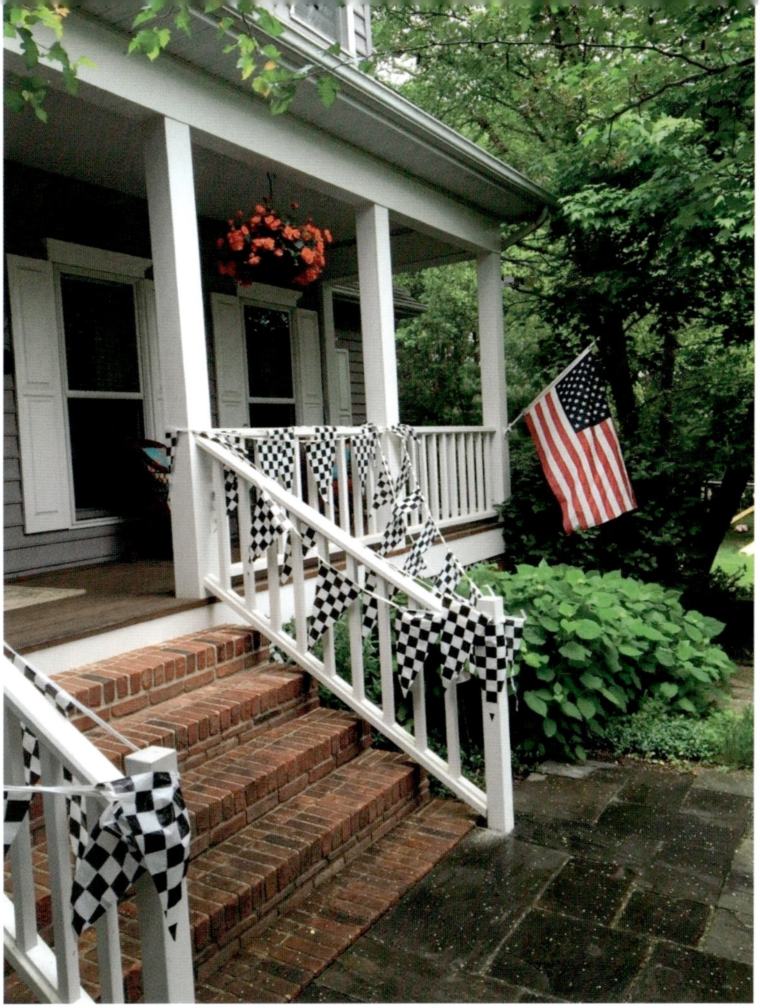

3:23 PM

Terre Haute

Getting ready for the race. God bless America
and God bless Indiana!

Photo by Suzi Unger

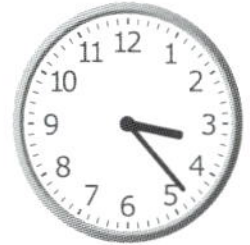

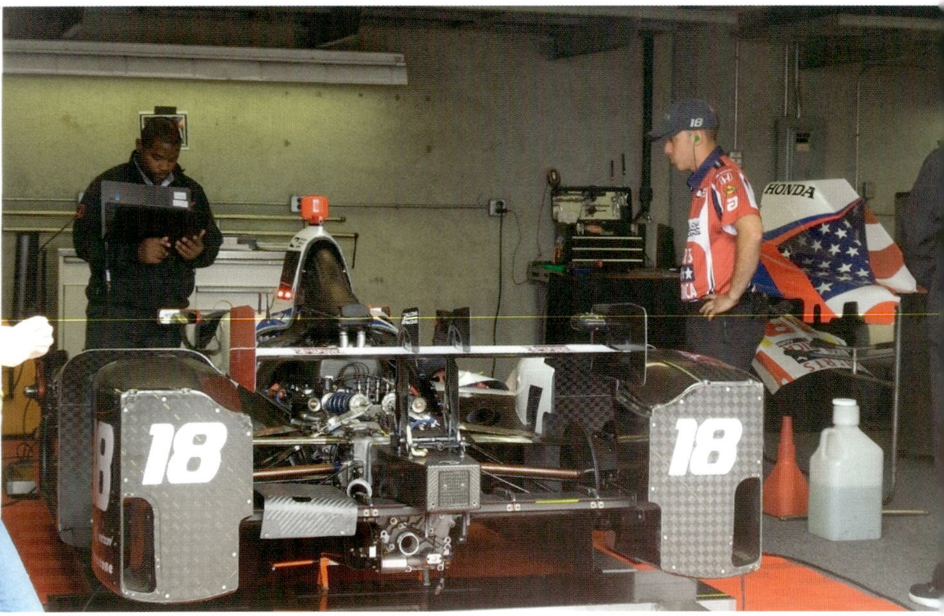

3:30 PM

Indianapolis

Figuring out what went wrong with the car
in qualifications. A very frustrating day
at the Indianapolis Motor Speedway
for the driver and team.

Photo by Susan Woods

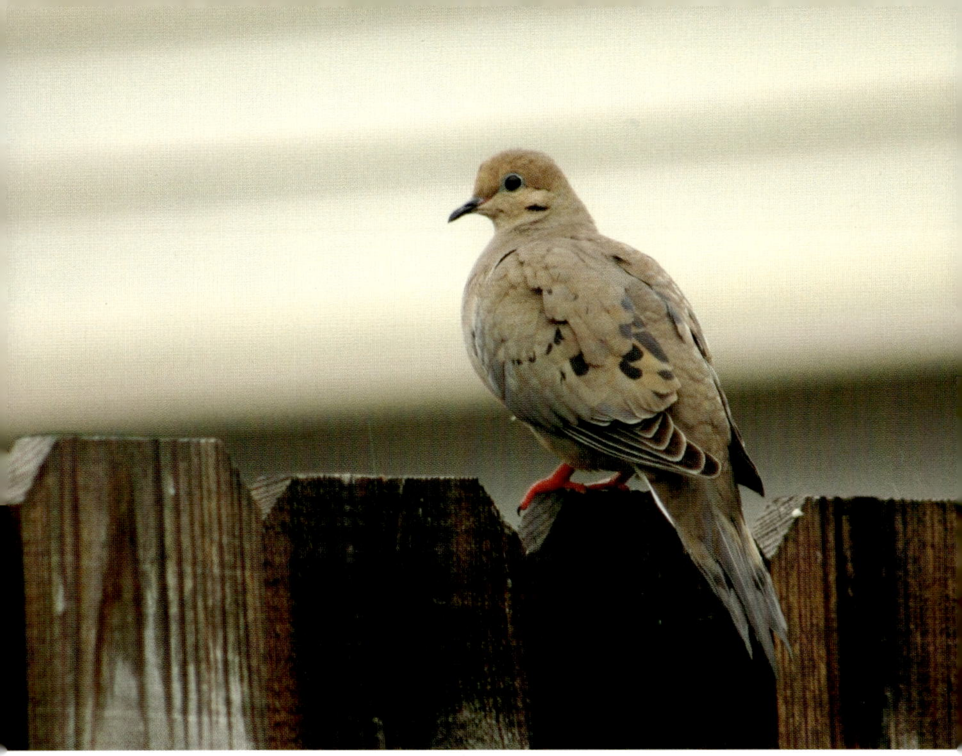

3:30 PM

Franklin

A mourning dove sitting on our backyard fence
shortly after the rain begins to fall.

Photo by JoAnne Davis

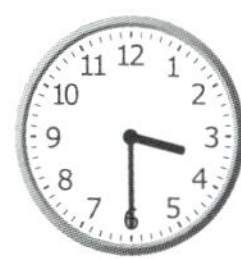

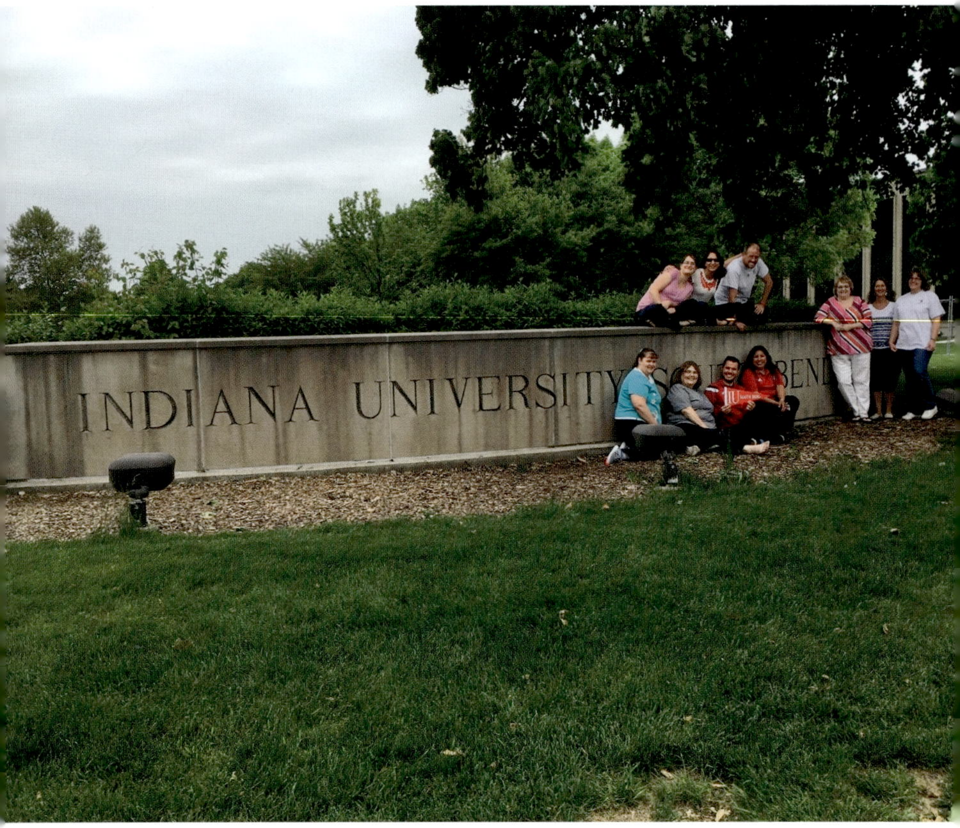

3:40 PM

South Bend

Admissions and financial aid staff
taking a break at IU South Bend.

Photo by Koren Scott

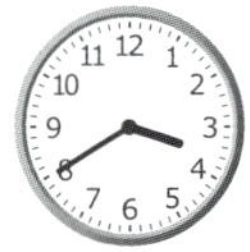

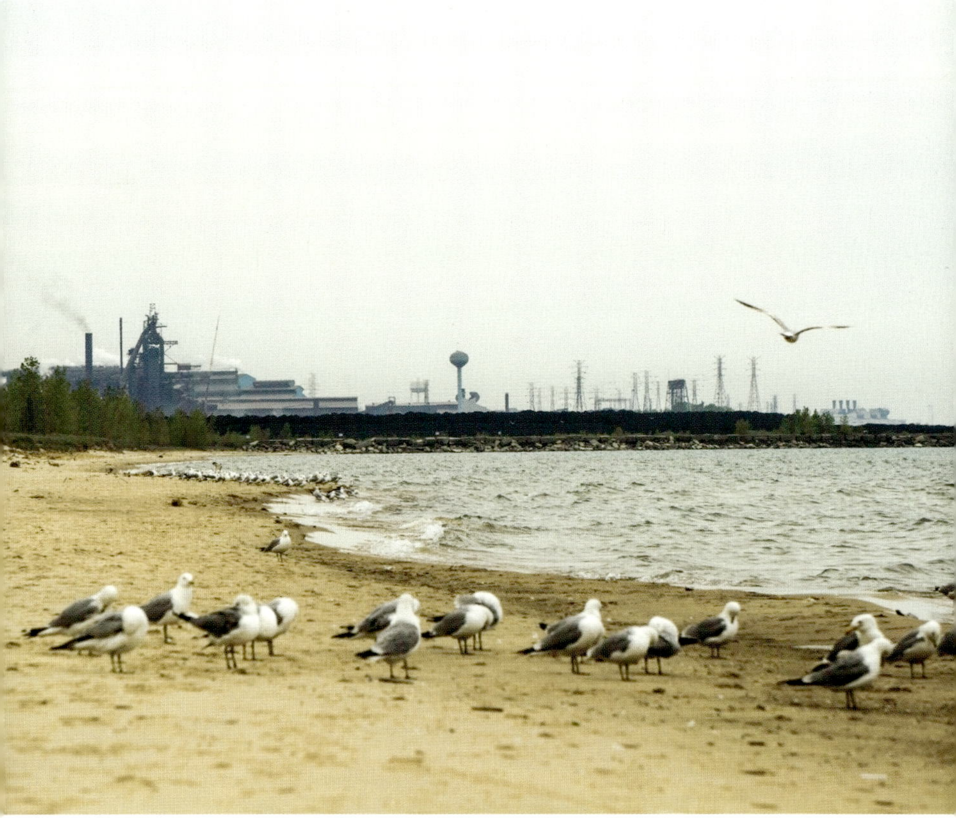

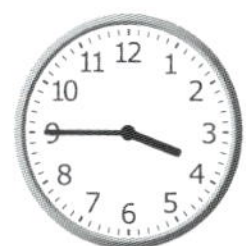

3:45 PM

Gary

The U.S. Steel Mill as seen from Miller Beach
on a hazy afternoon.

Photo by Scott Pederson

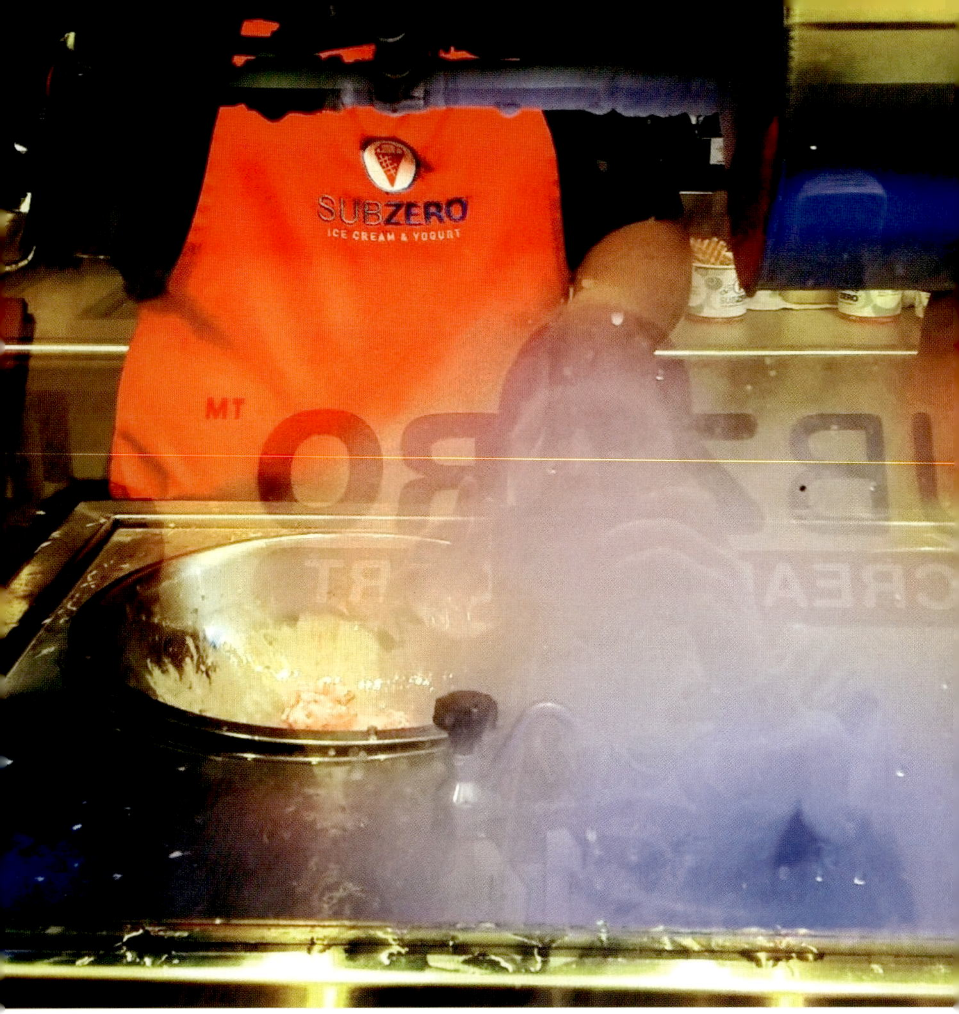

3:47 PM

Indianapolis

Chilling out with fro-yo at
Sub Zero Ice Cream & Yogurt.

Photo by Sarah Bahr

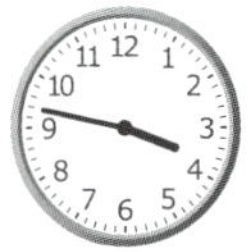

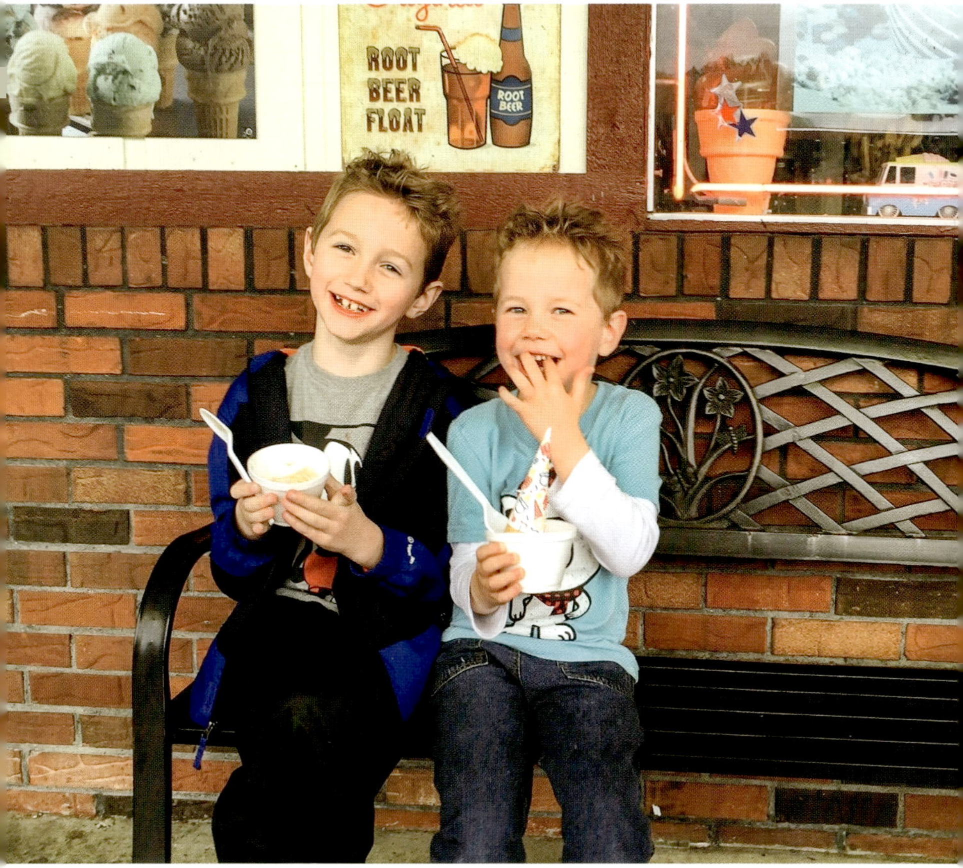

4:00 PM

Bloomington

After-school ice cream at Jiffy Treet,
a Btown institution since 1948.

Photo by Nichole Lynnette

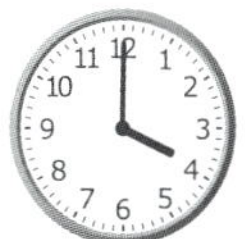

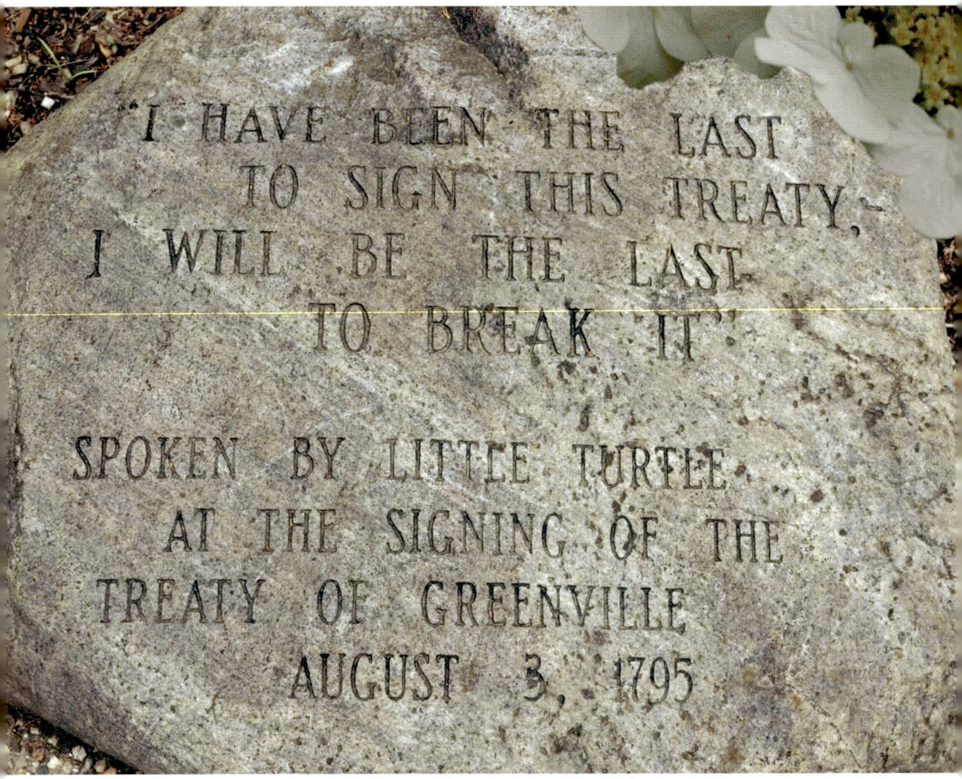

4:12 PM

Fort Wayne

Visiting Chief Little Turtle's grave site.

Photo by Sue Sells

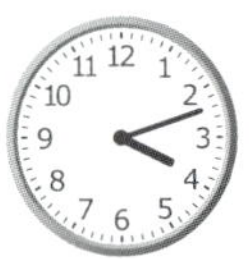

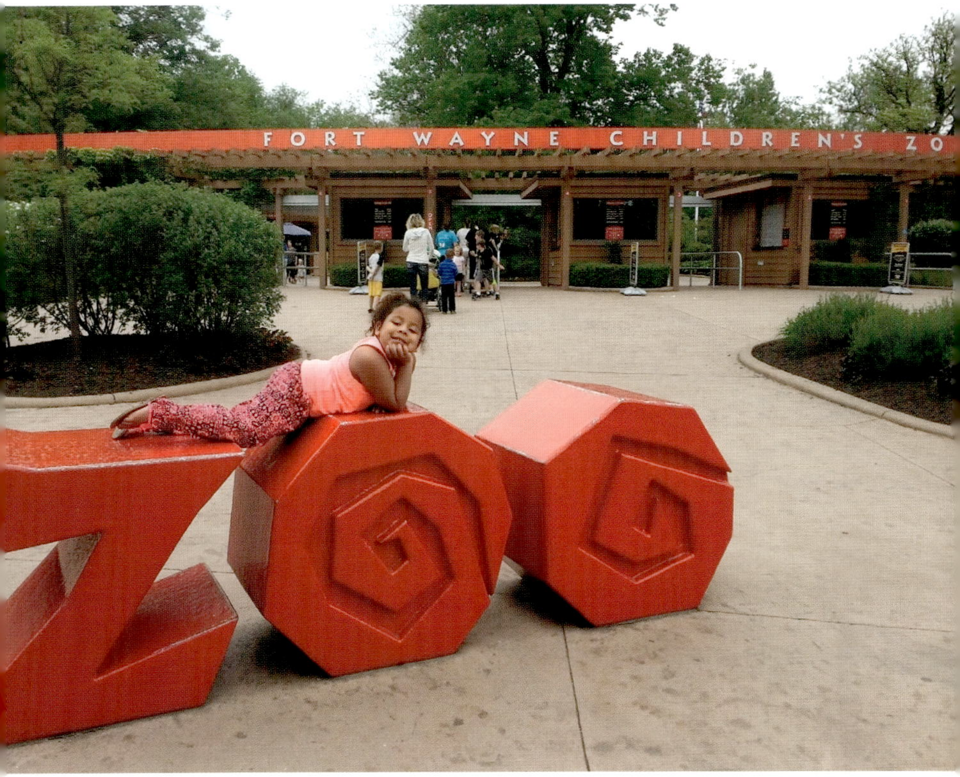

4:20 PM

Fort Wayne

My three-year-old granddaughter Anabelle
loves the zoo!

Photo by Laura Ochoa McCue

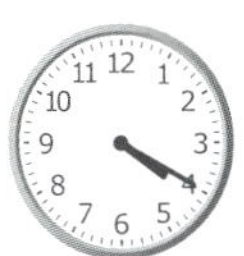

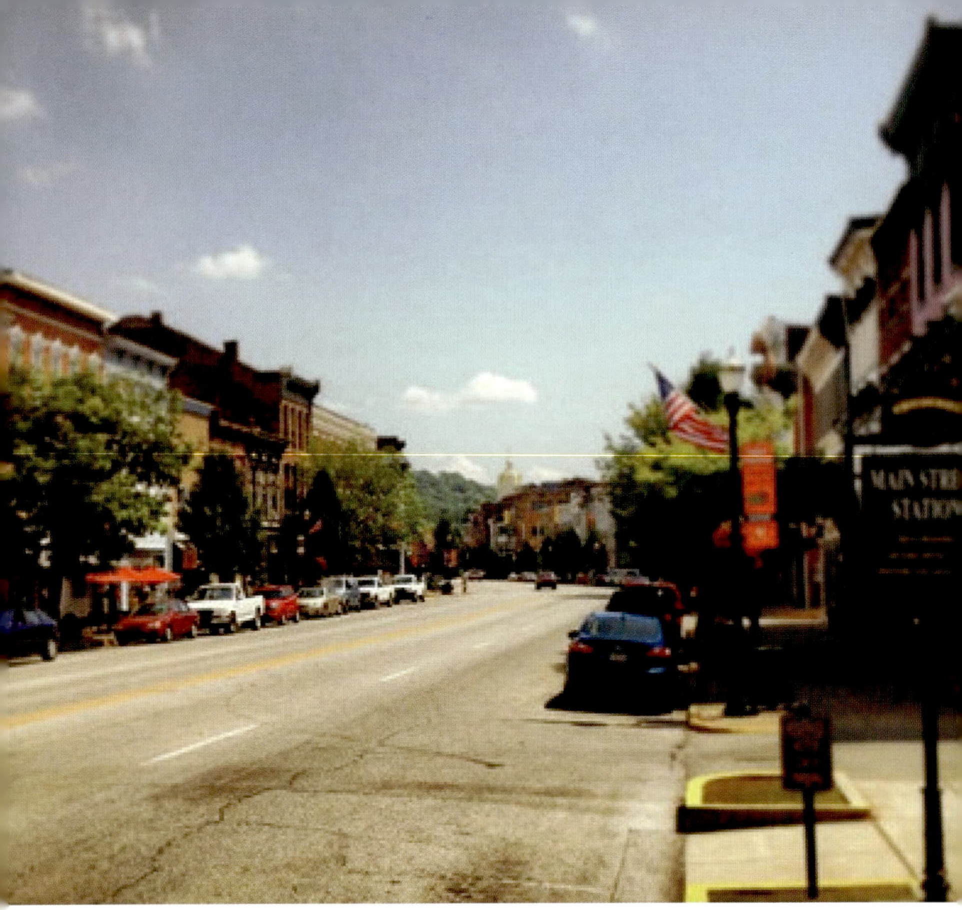

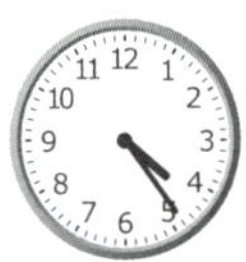

4:24 PM

Madison

The afternoon begins stretching long down beautiful Main Street.

Photo by Jennifer Watson

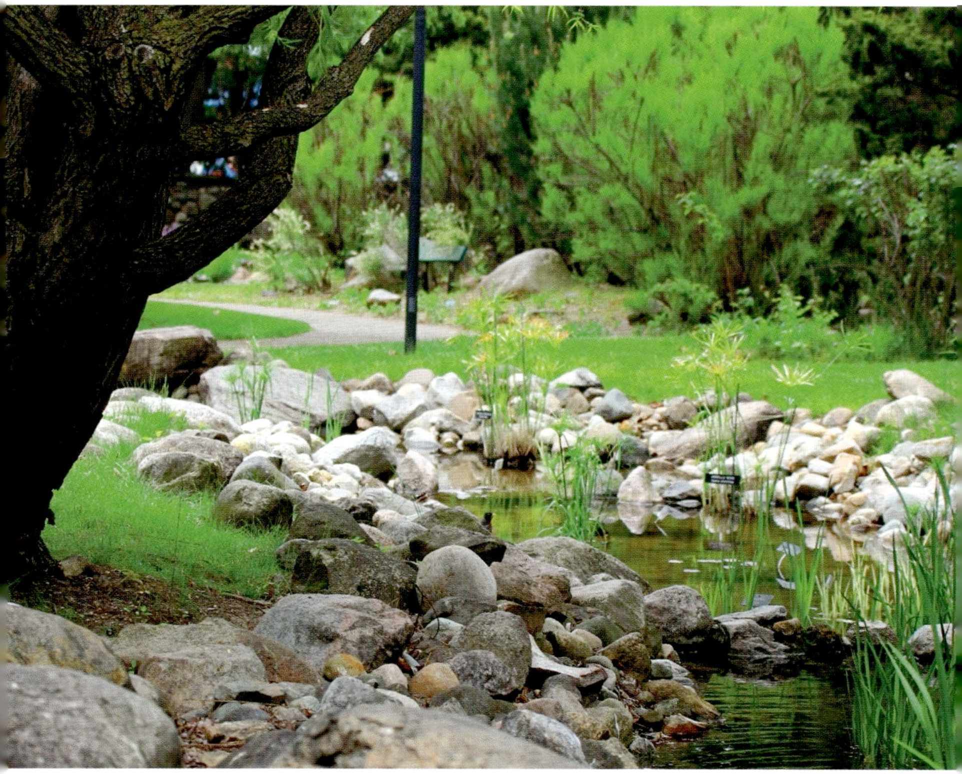

4:30 PM

Warsaw

Late afternoon in the Warsaw Biblical Gardens.

Photo by Angela Capps

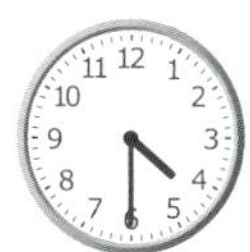

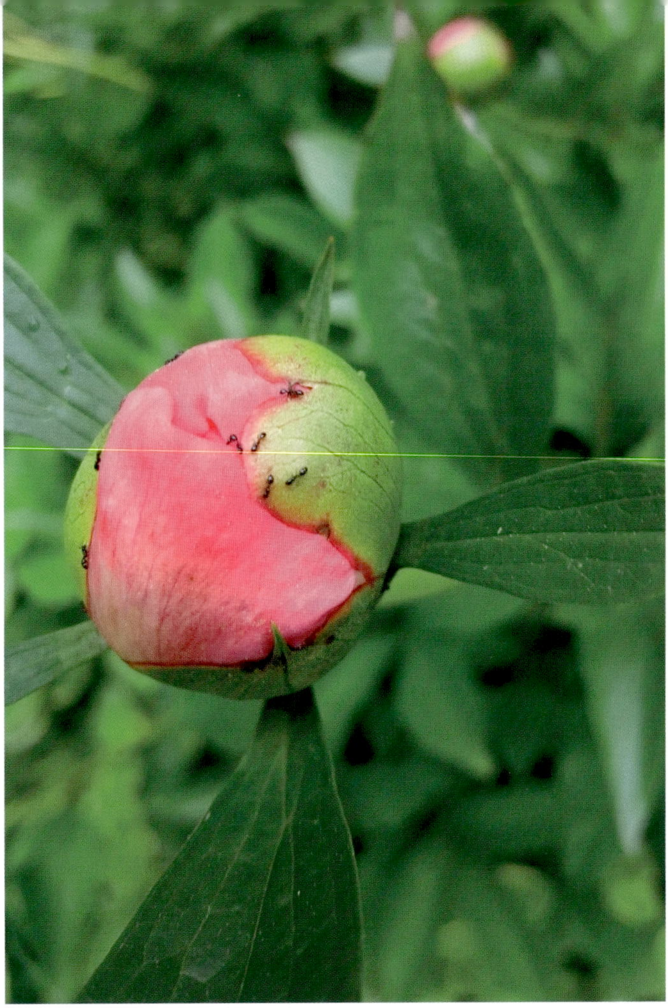

4:30 PM

Indianapolis

Even the ants are anxious for the peonies to pop!
Indiana's own state flower.

Photo by Kassie Ritman

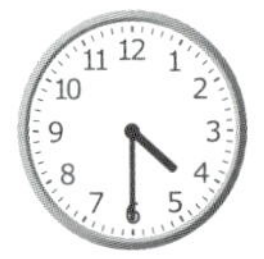

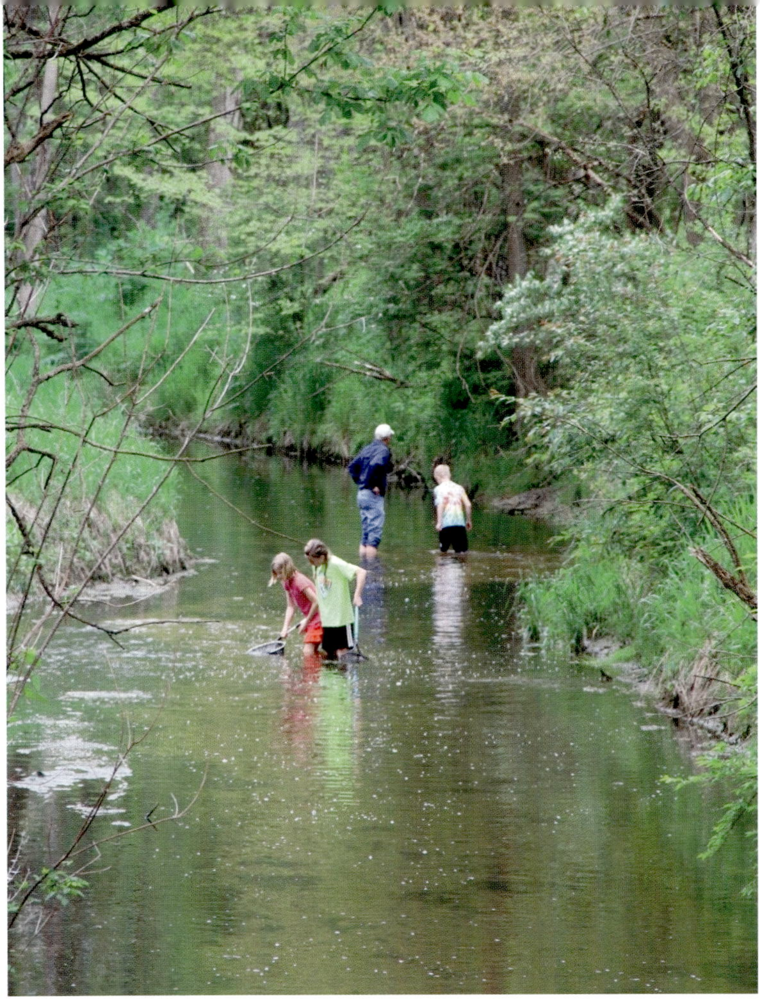

4:40 PM

Warsaw

Playing in the stream—again.

Photo by Jorie Bail

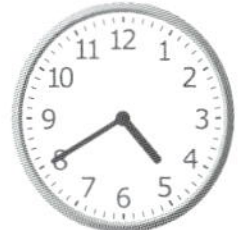

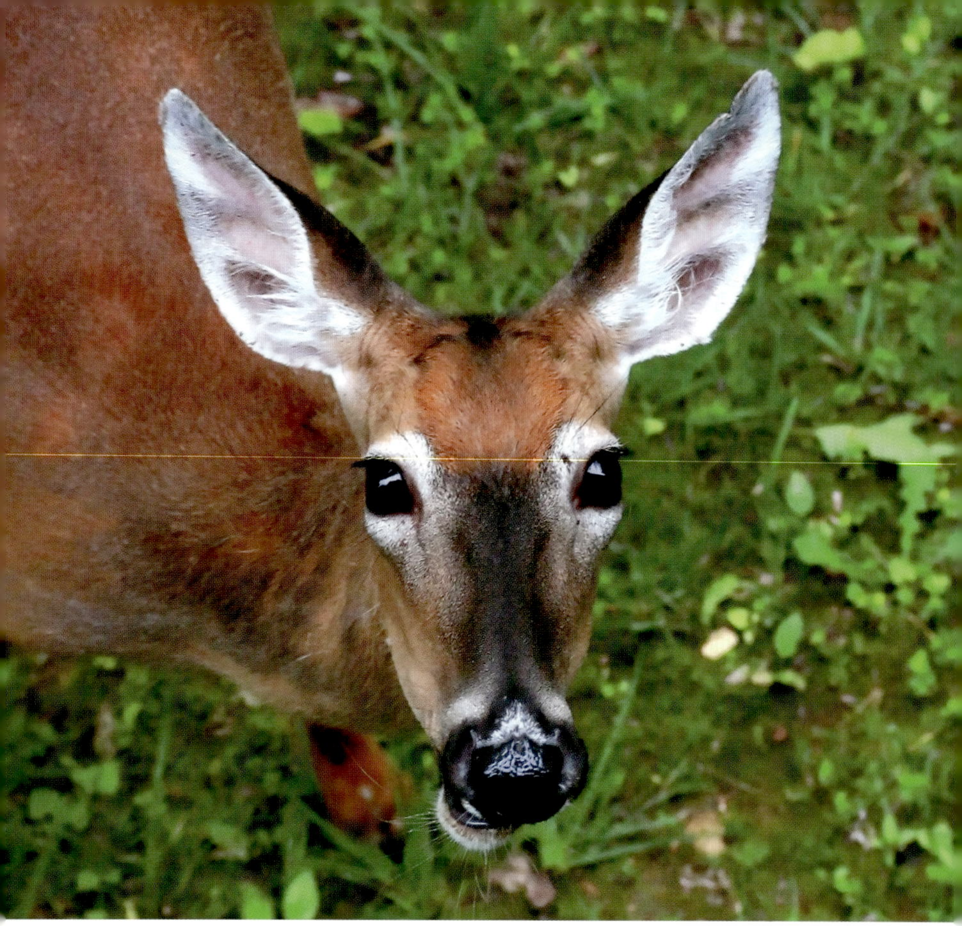

4:40 PM

Monroe County

Where's my apple? Making a new friend at Lake
Monroe.

Photo by Rick Holen

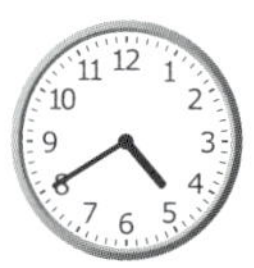

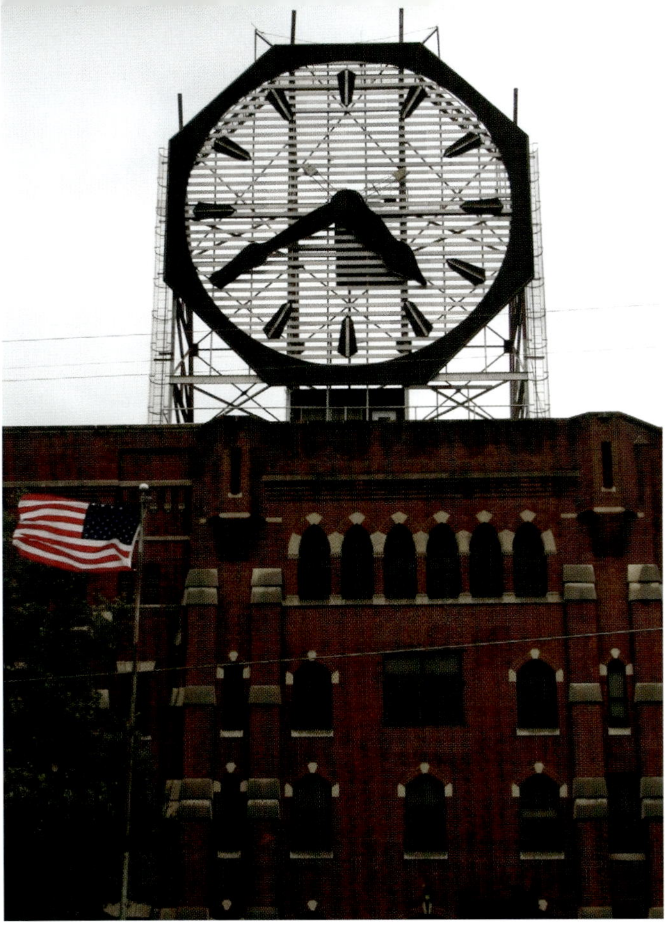

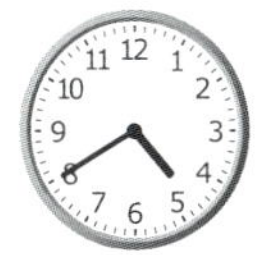

4:40 PM

Clarksville

Looking up at the ancient Colgate Clock, still on time on a rainy day. Built in 1906, the 40-foot icon of southern Indiana sits atop the old Colgate Palmolive factory, which closed in 2008.

Photo by Kelly Short

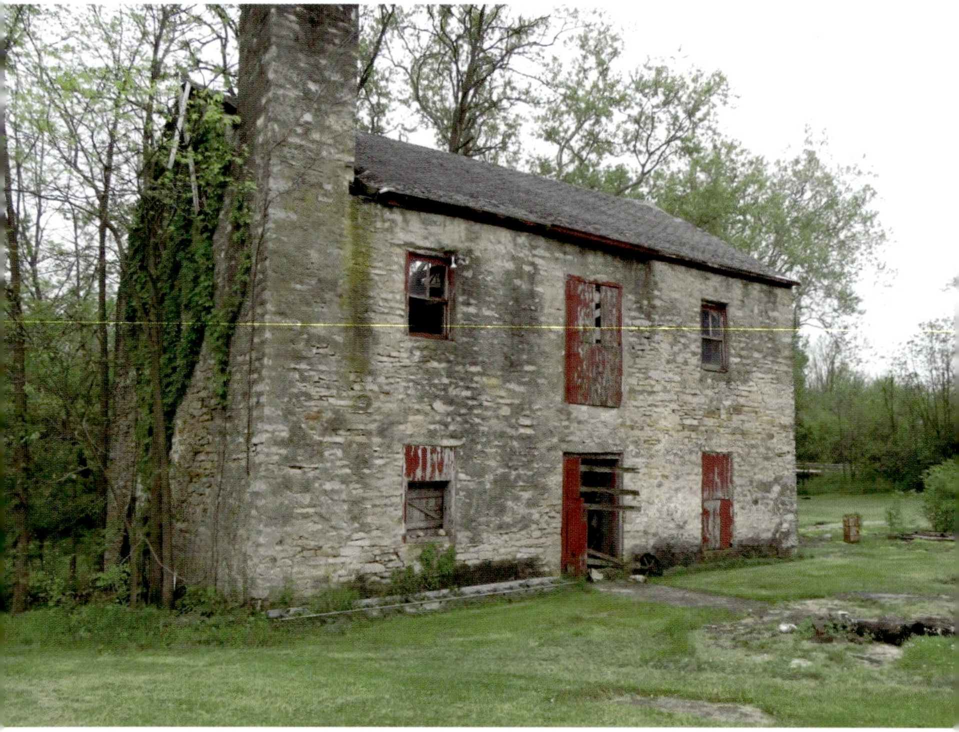

4:47 PM

Middleboro

Stopping by the Jeremiah Cox Mill, built in 1826.

Photo by Robert Williams

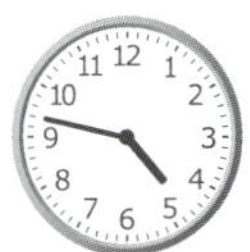

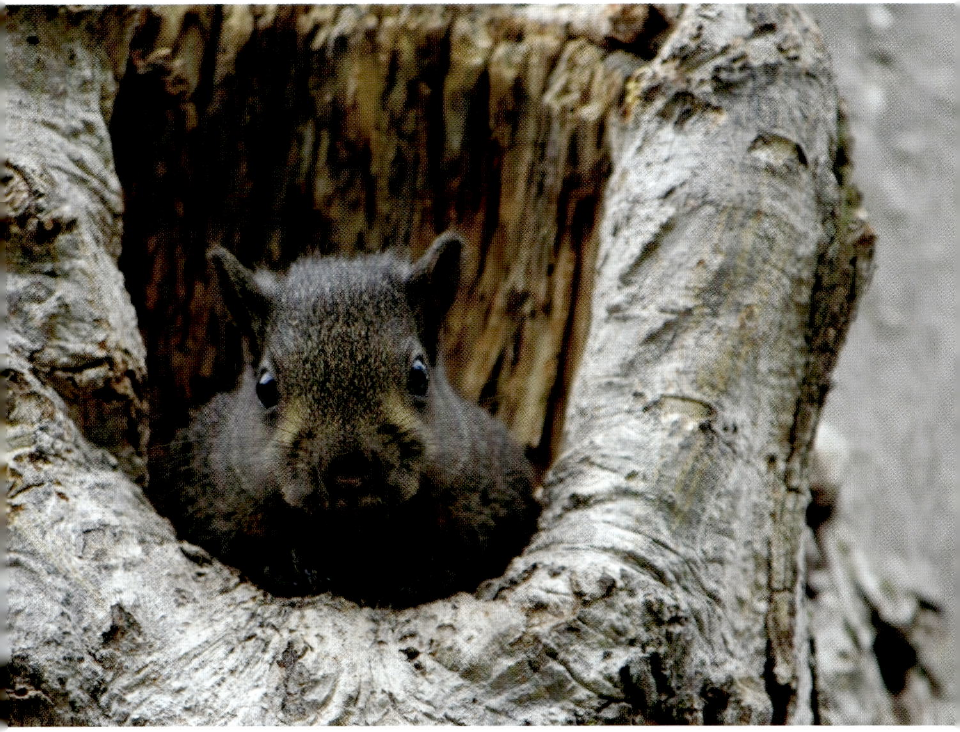

4:58 PM

Warsaw

It's a joy to see a young squirrel poke its head out
of the backyard hollow tree before it becomes brave
enough to venture beyond.

Photo by Donna Propp

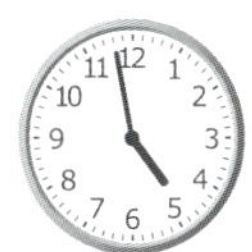

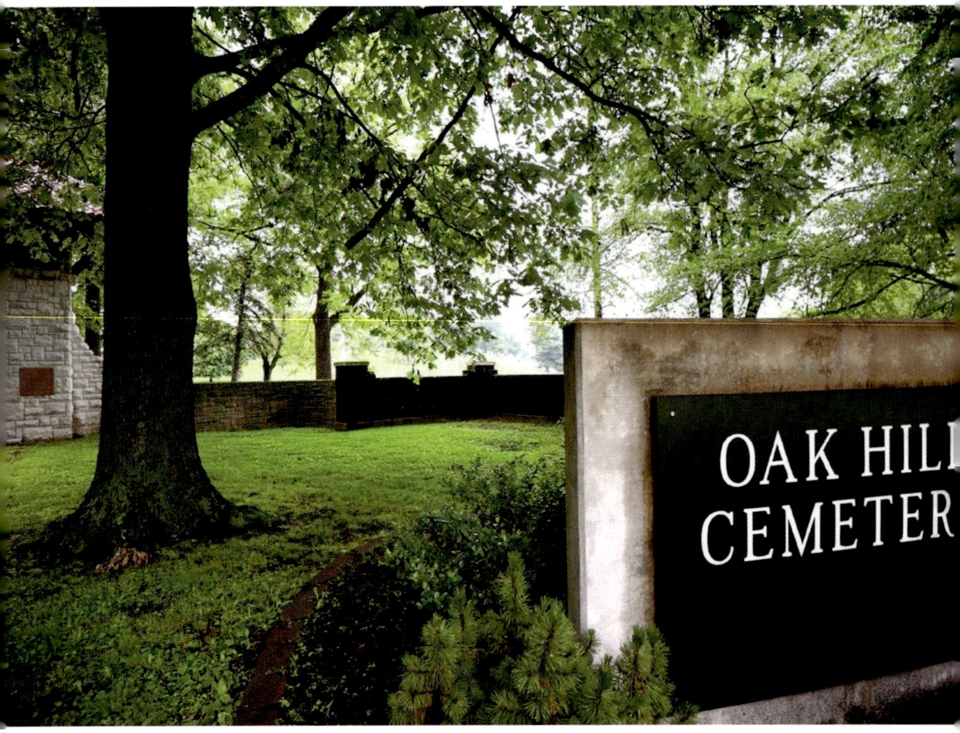

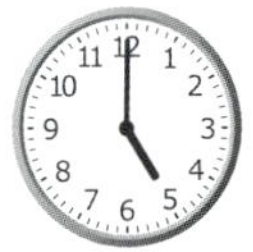

5:00 PM

Evansville

My dad died on May 20th several years ago and
I use this day to make the rounds, remembering
friends and relatives who have passed away.

Photo by Chuck Stinson

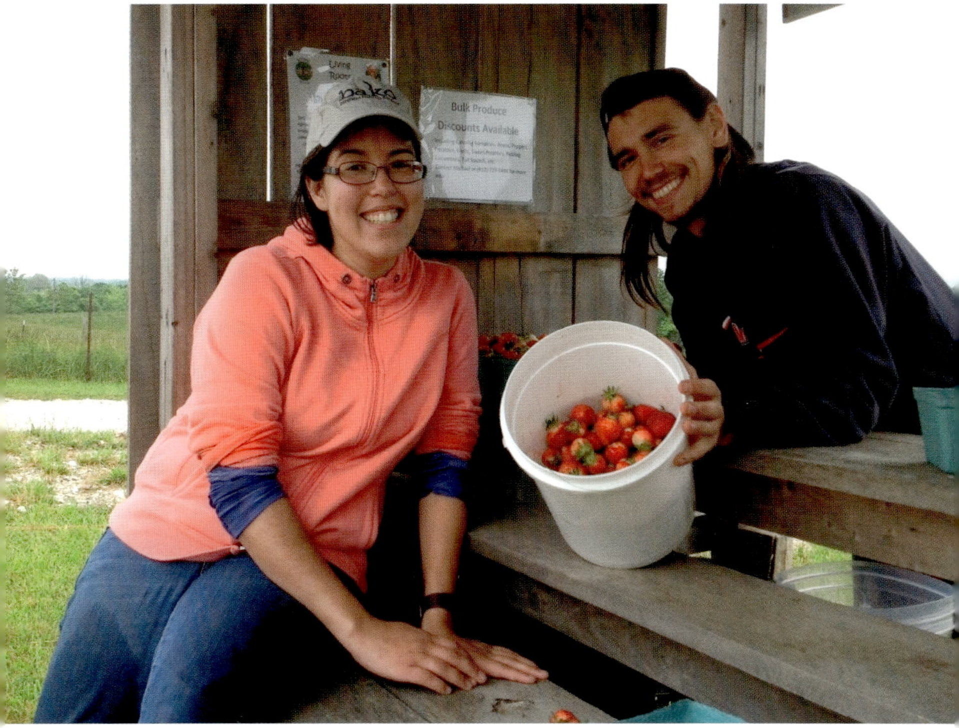

5:05 PM

French Lick

Picking organic strawberries at
Living Roots Ecovillage.

Photo by Beth Gazley

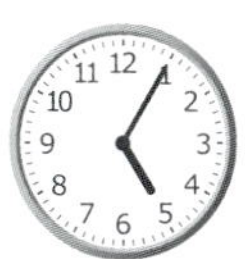

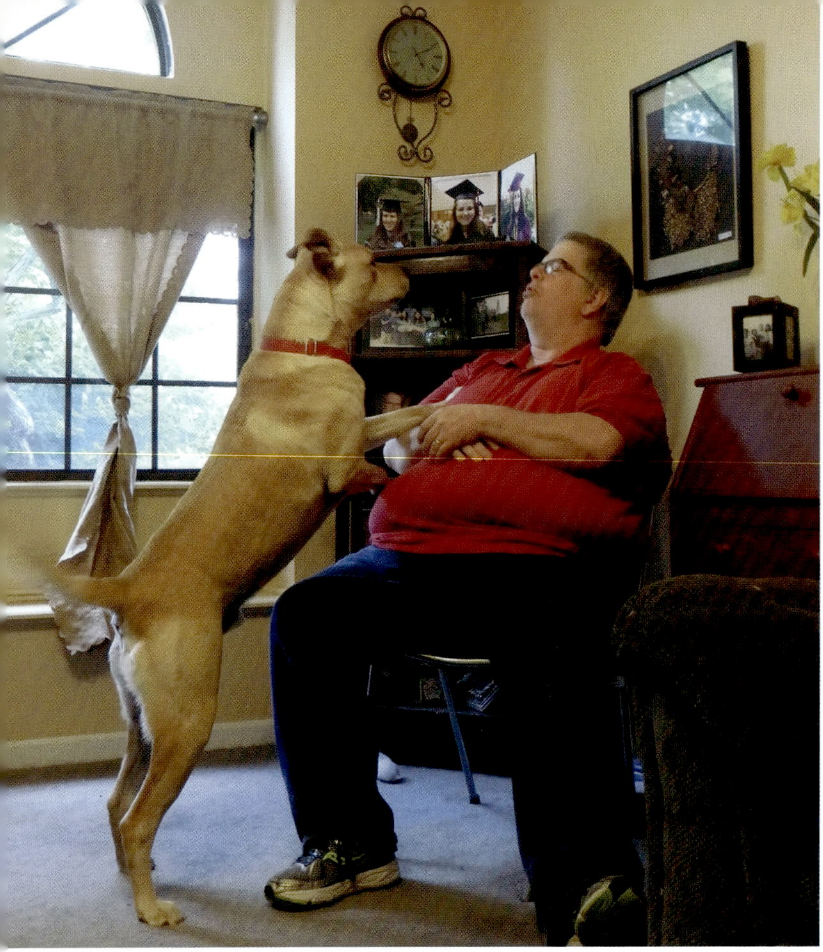

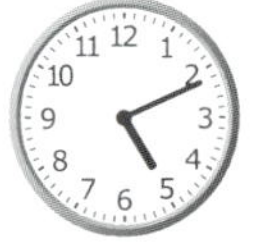

5:11 PM

Bloomington

It's the weekend, time to howl! Happy to be home to celebrate being together with our family, those we love . . . pets included.

Photo by Betty Watson

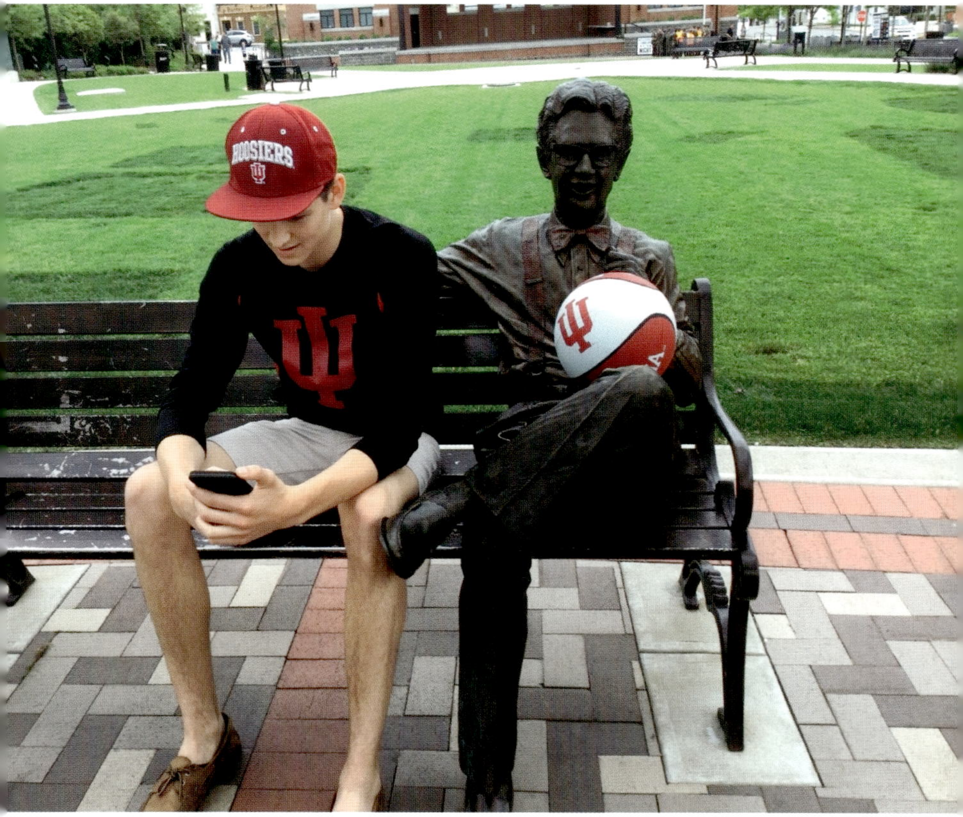

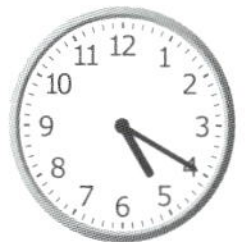

5:20 PM

Valparaiso

Two Hoosiers--a current IU student and Orville Redenbacher—sharing a bench in Central Park.

Photo by Frieda Davison

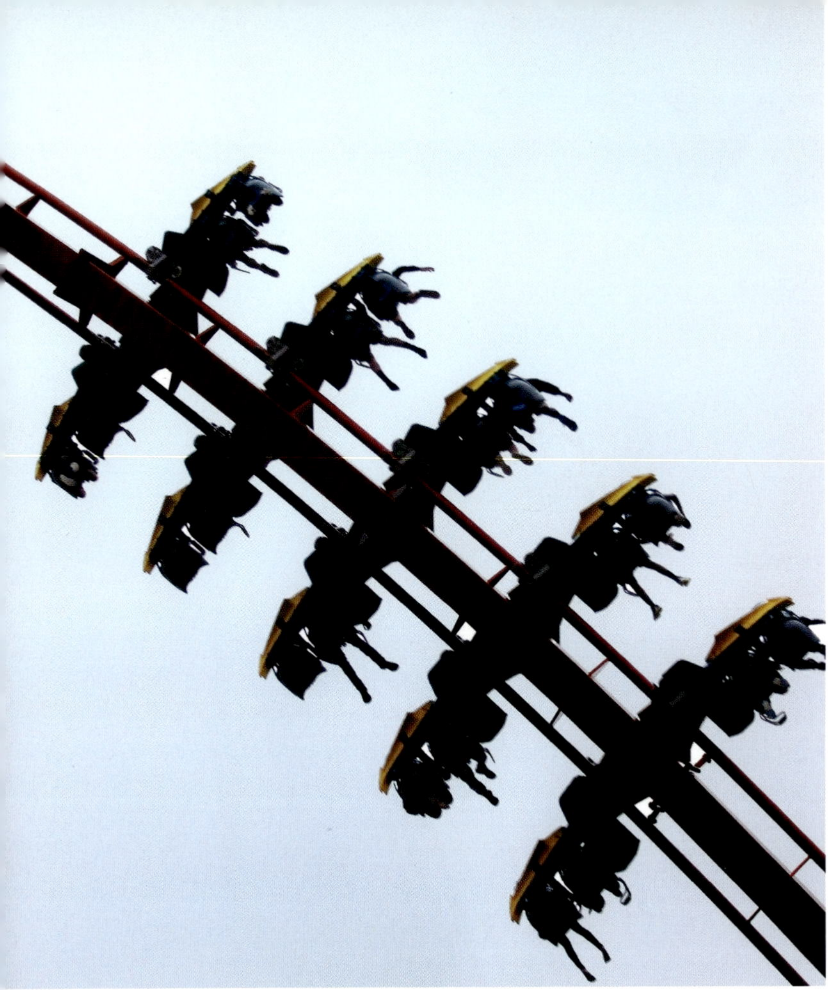

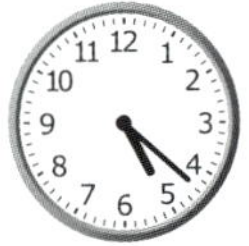

5:22 PM

Santa Claus

Hoosiers love riding rollercoasters—even in the rain!

Photo by Holiday World & Splashin' Safari

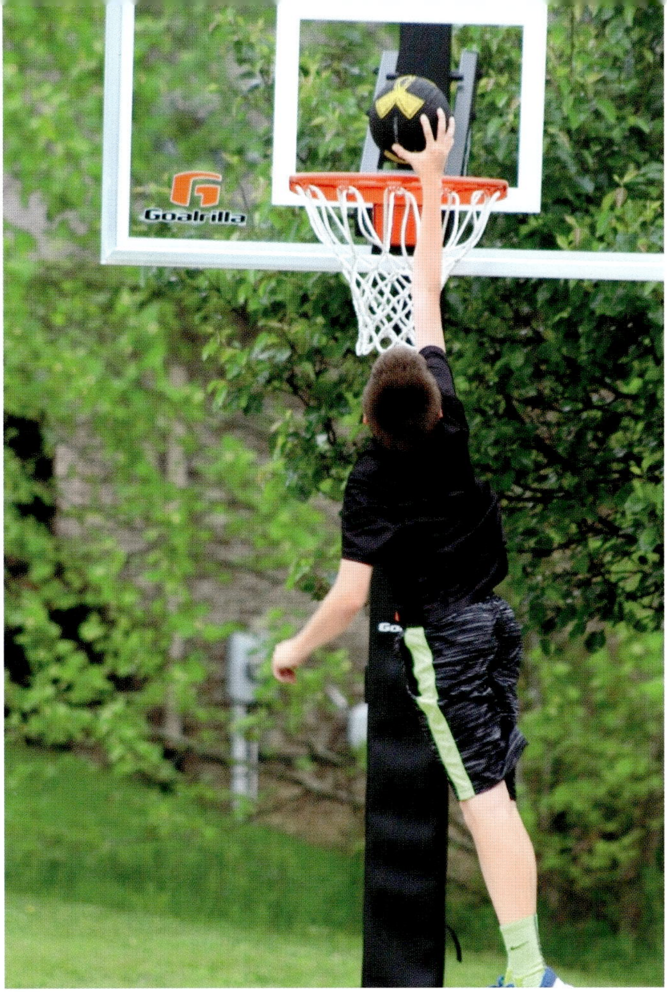

5:30 PM

Indianapolis

Elevating above the rim at his home basketball court.

Photo by Clarissa West

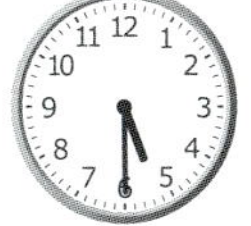

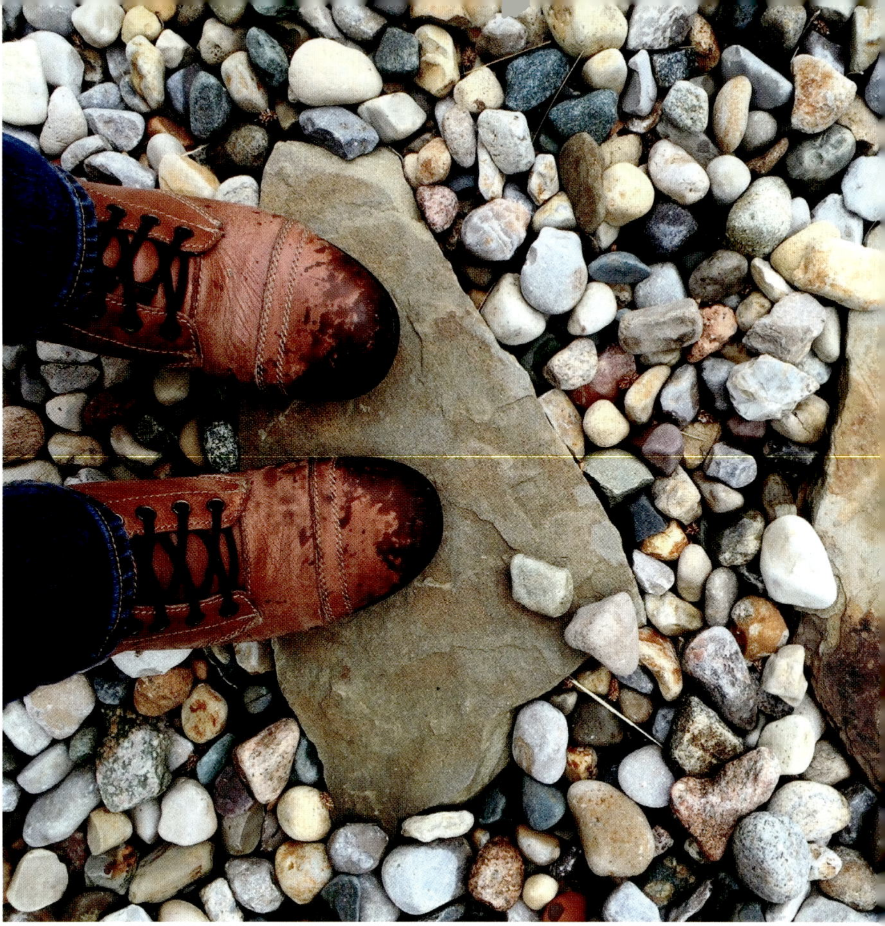

5:45 PM

Ellettsville

My favorite thing to do after a long day of work
is to play in the backyard with my dogs, Luna
and Molly. Wet boots on our colorful rock patio
represent serenity on this showery day.

Photo by Sarah Payne-Mills

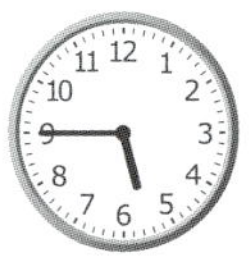

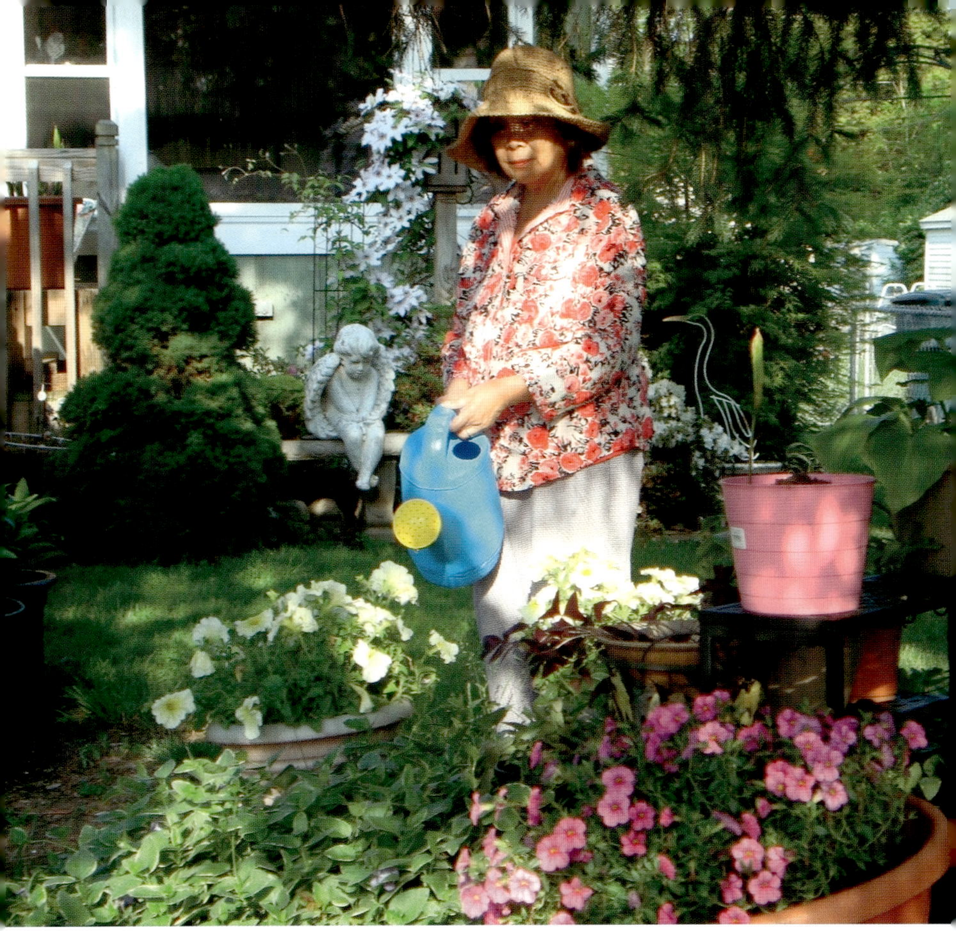

5:45 PM

Muncie

Enjoying the nature surrounding us with endless spring days.

Photo by John Ramsey

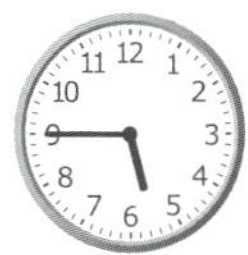

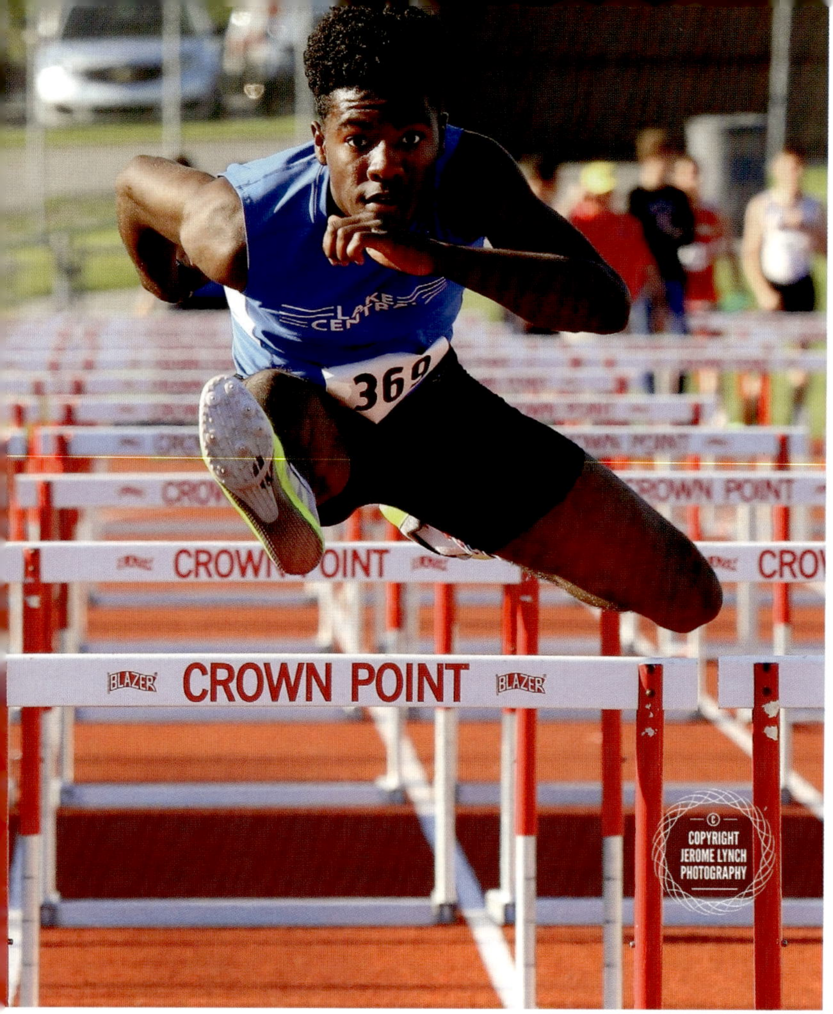

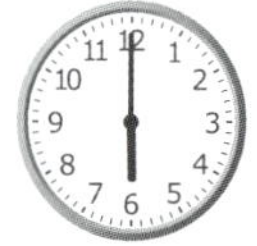

6:00 PM

Crown Point

Lake Central High School freshman Cameron Williams winning the 110-meter hurdles.

Photo by Jerome Lynch

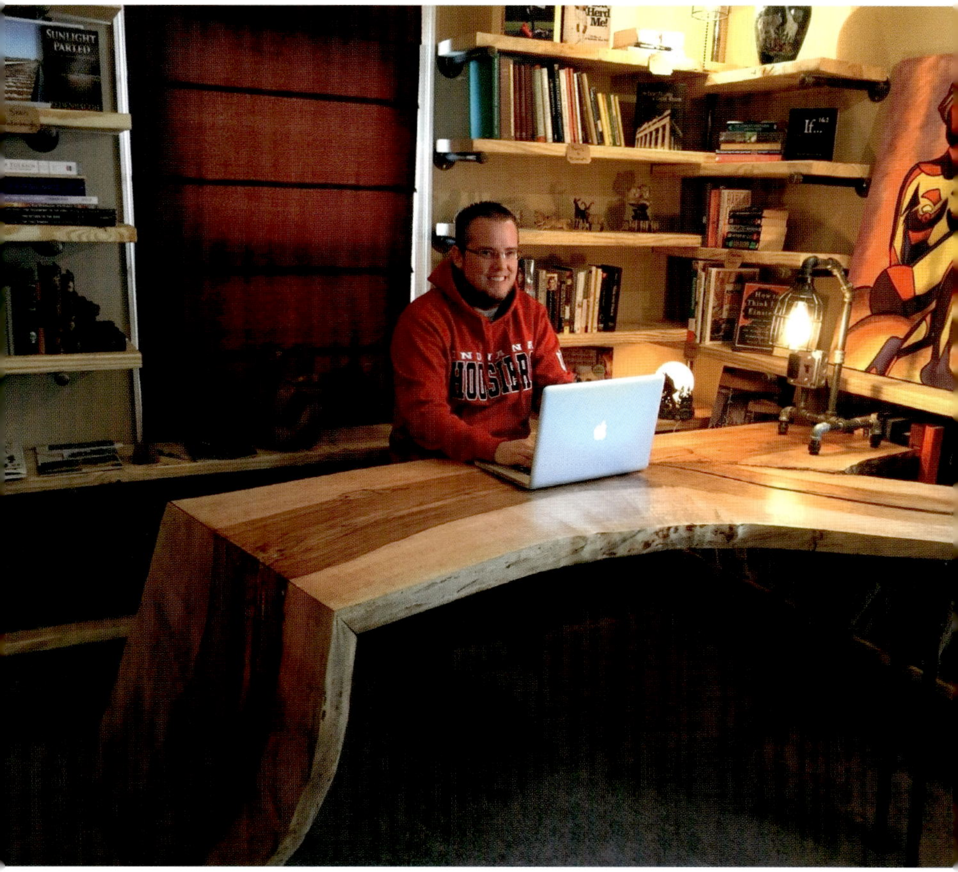

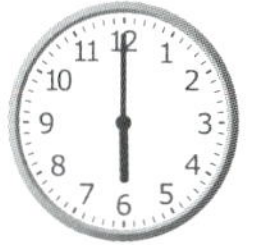

6:00 PM

Evansville

Working on a follow-up novel in my
handmade library.

Photo by Sean Redenbaugh

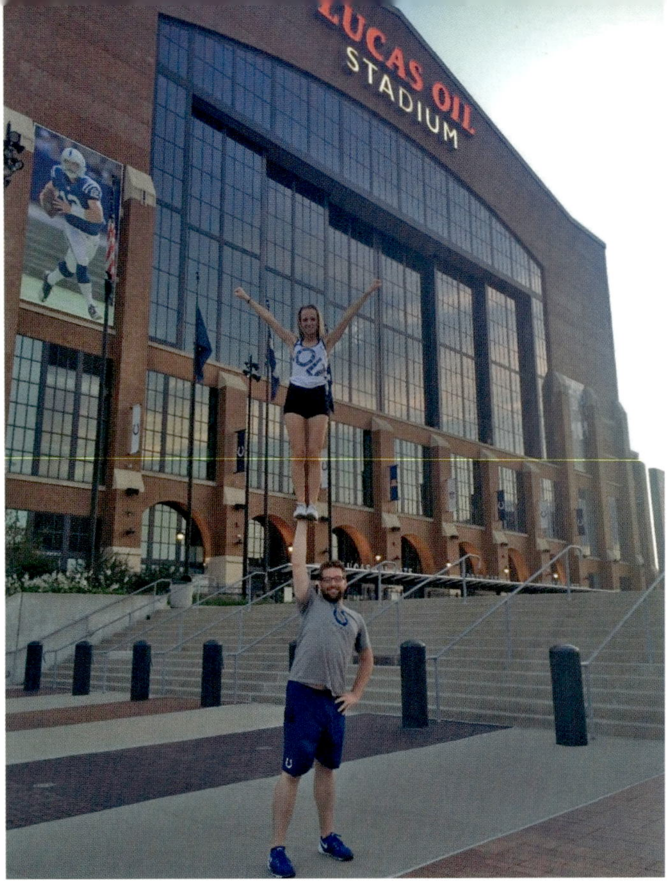

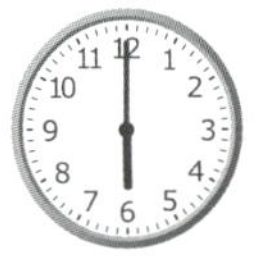

6:00 PM

Indianapolis

Indiana University cheer alumni and Indianapolis Colts Blue Stampede members stunting in front of the Lucas Oil Stadium after dinner.

Photo by Connor Norwood

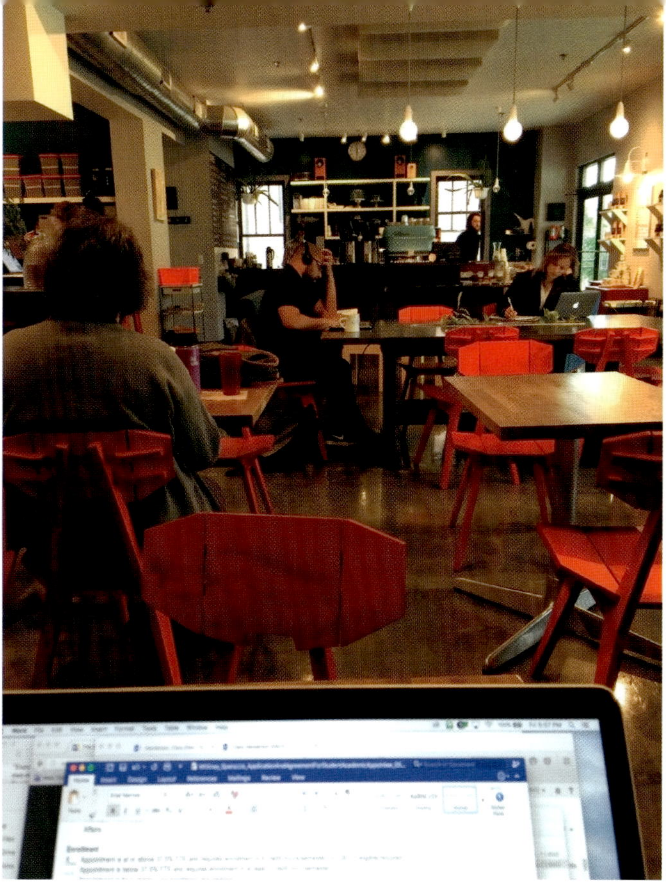

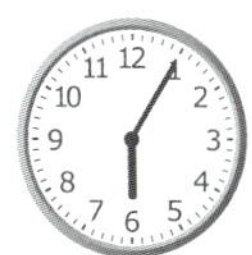

6:05 PM

Bloomington

Hopscotch Coffee along the B-Line in Bloomington
is my favorite Friday haunt for working on my book.
We die-hards remain at our computers until closing,
drinking our working day down to the dregs
before a Friday night in Btown.

Photo by Clara Henderson

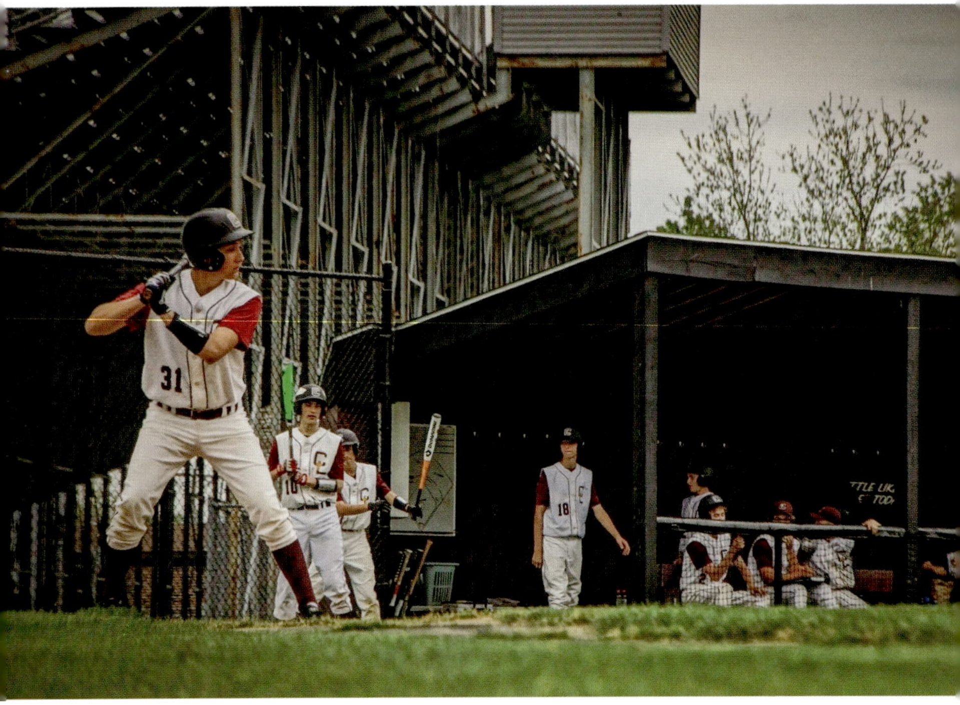

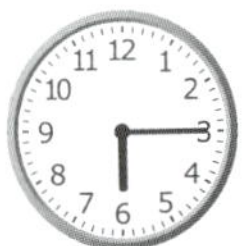

6:15 PM

Fort Wayne

Batter up! Concordia Lutheran High School Junior Varsity team playing for the win at Zollner Stadium.

Photo by Abby Miller

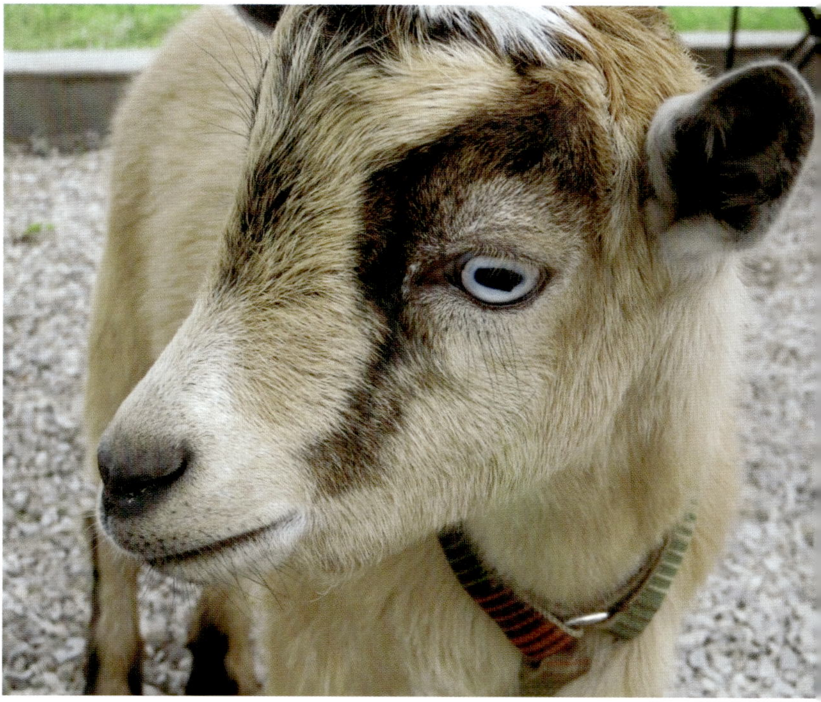

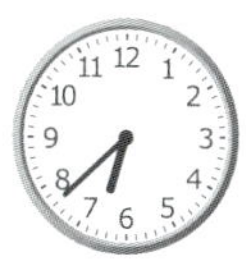

6:38 PM

Brown County

A goat greets visitors at the second Bean Blossom
Farmers' Market of the season.

Photo by Michelle Watson

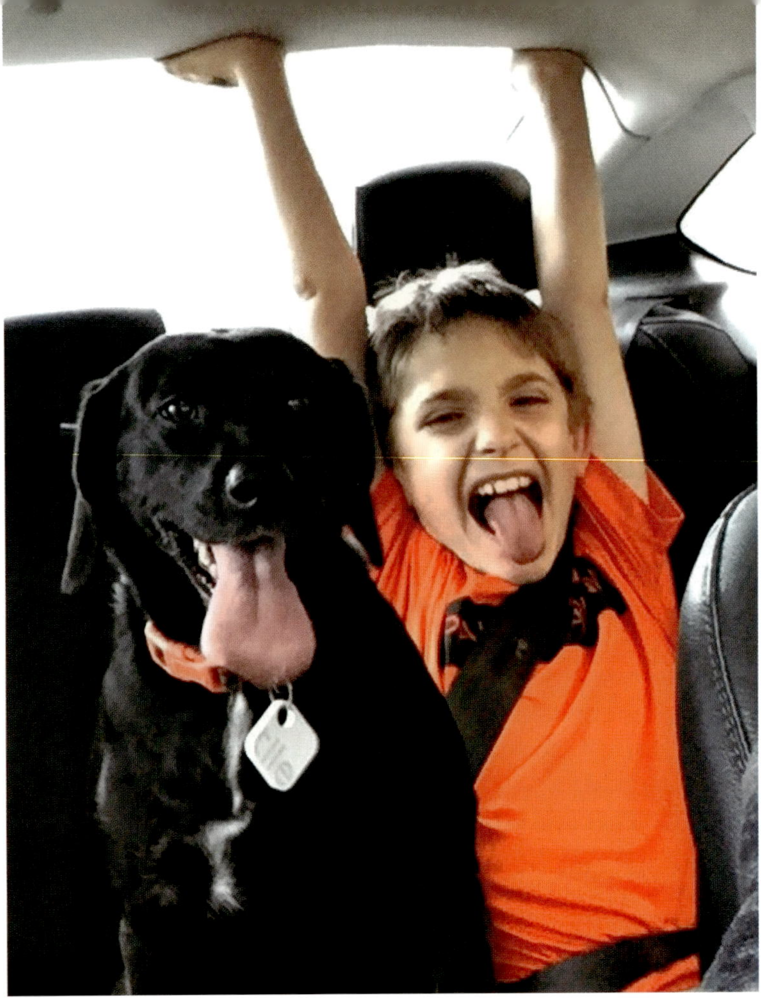

6:42 PM

Bloomington

On the way with dog Sammie to play
Little League baseball!

Photo by Daphne Siefert-Herron

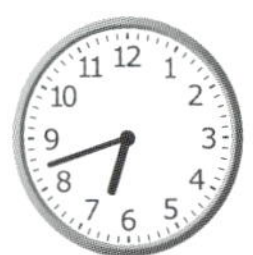

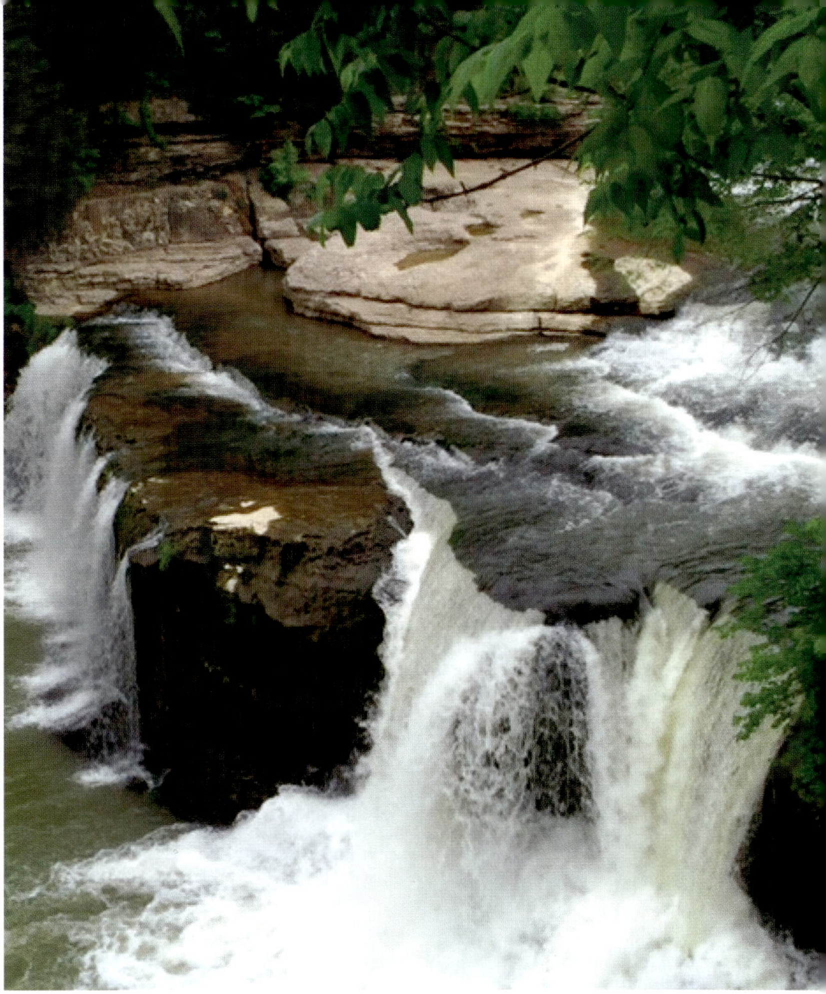

6:44 PM

Jennings Township

Taking in Cataract Falls before dusk.

Photo by Mary Fitzgerald Ball

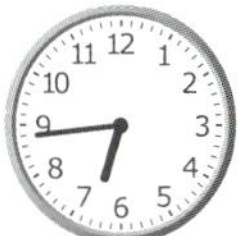

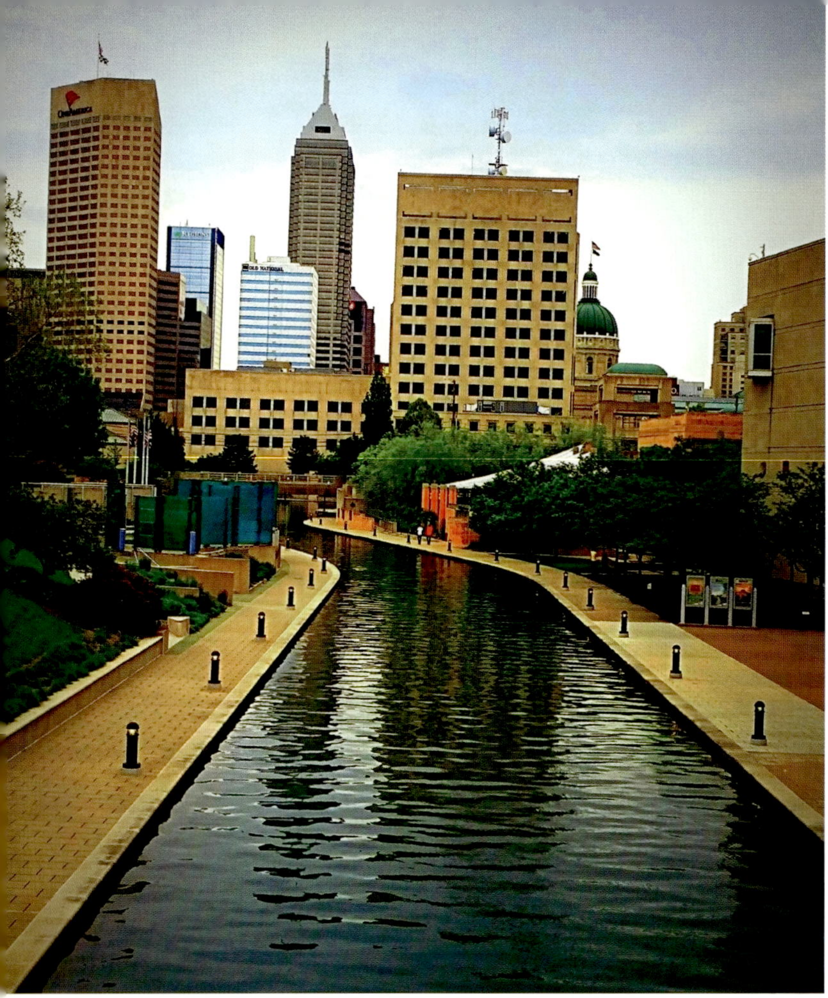

7:00 PM

Indianapolis

Stopping by the Indy Central Canal—
the Hoosier lifeline.

Photo by Ruchi Bansal

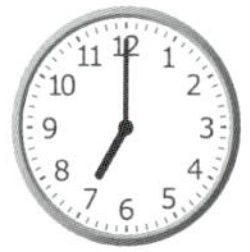

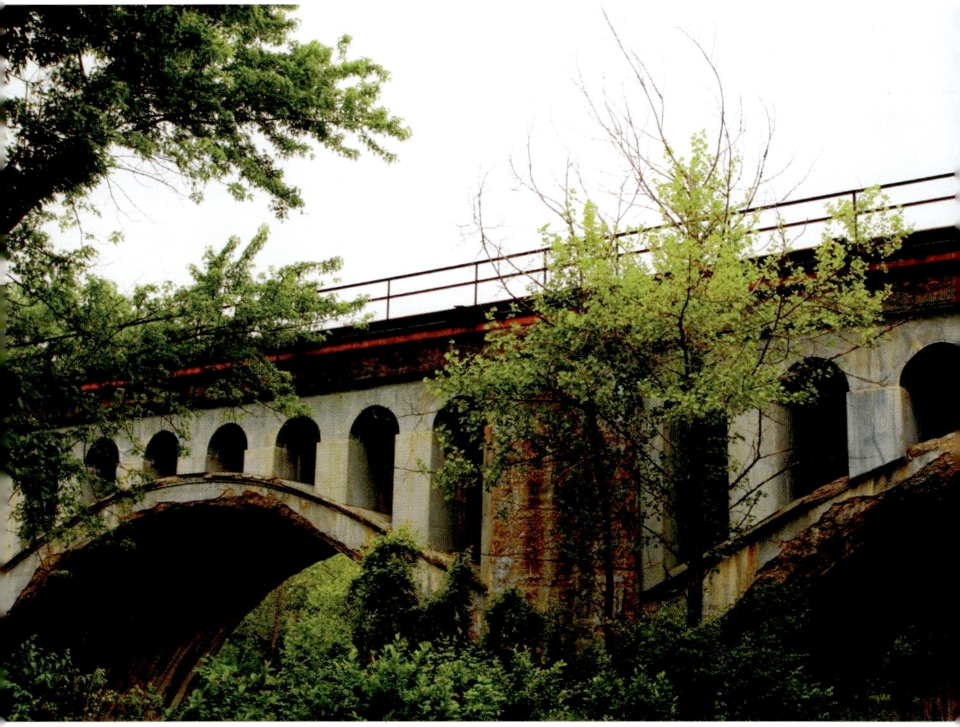

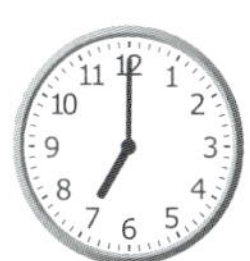

7:00 PM

Avon

The shadows gather at the Haunted Bridge.
Built in the 1850s, there are several legends
surrounding the haunting of the bridge.

Photo by Gary Dove

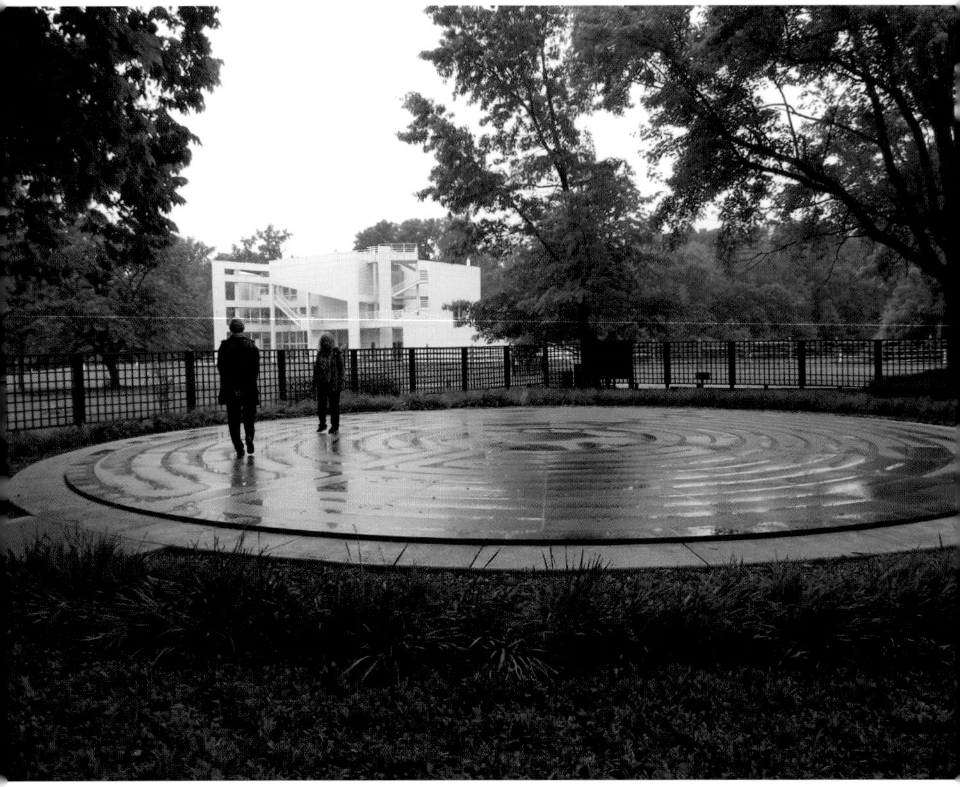

7:00 PM

New Harmony

Walking the Cathedral Labyrinth in the rain.

Photo by Liz Robb

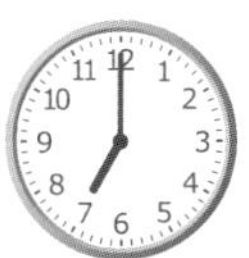

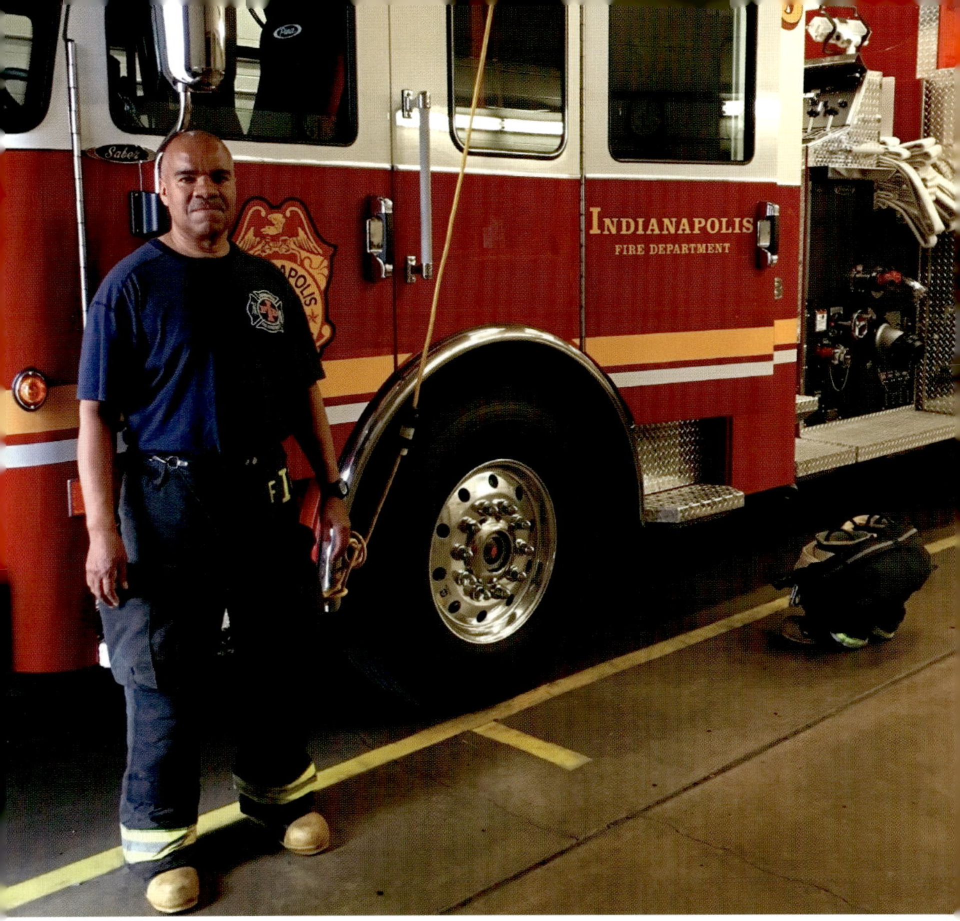

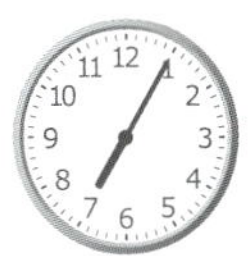

7:05 PM

Indianapolis

My firefighter husband on the job. I drove to the firehouse to spend time with my best friend on his duty day. I am so proud of what my husband does for the people of our city that we both love!

Photo by Susan Thompson

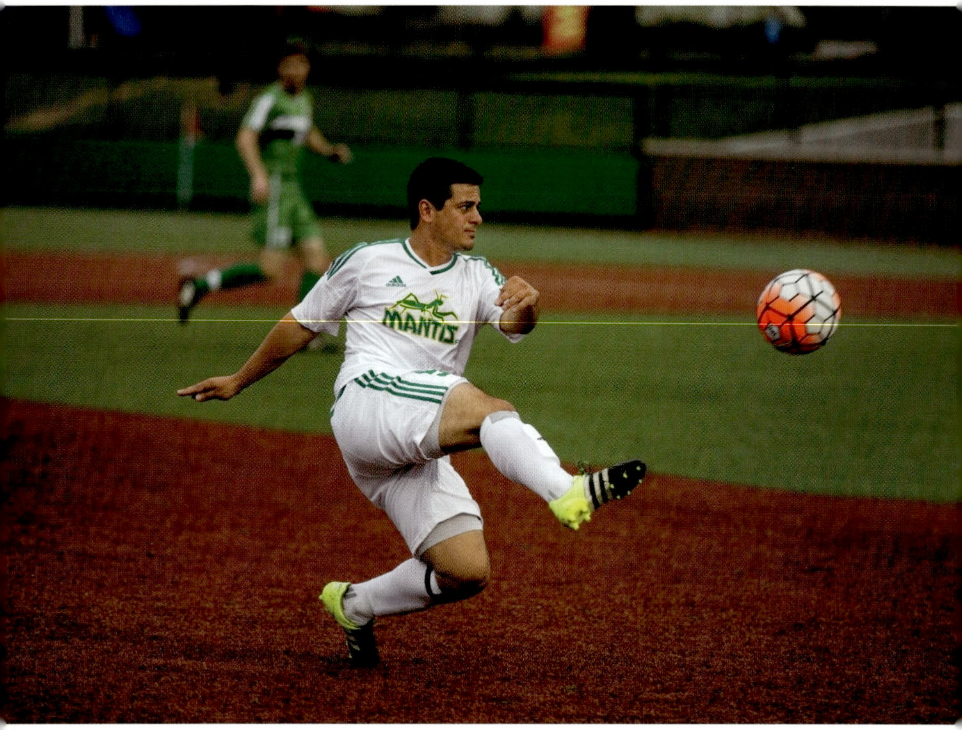

7:16 PM

Kokomo

First game (and win) for the Kokomo Mantis
soccer team!

Photo by Mike Dukes

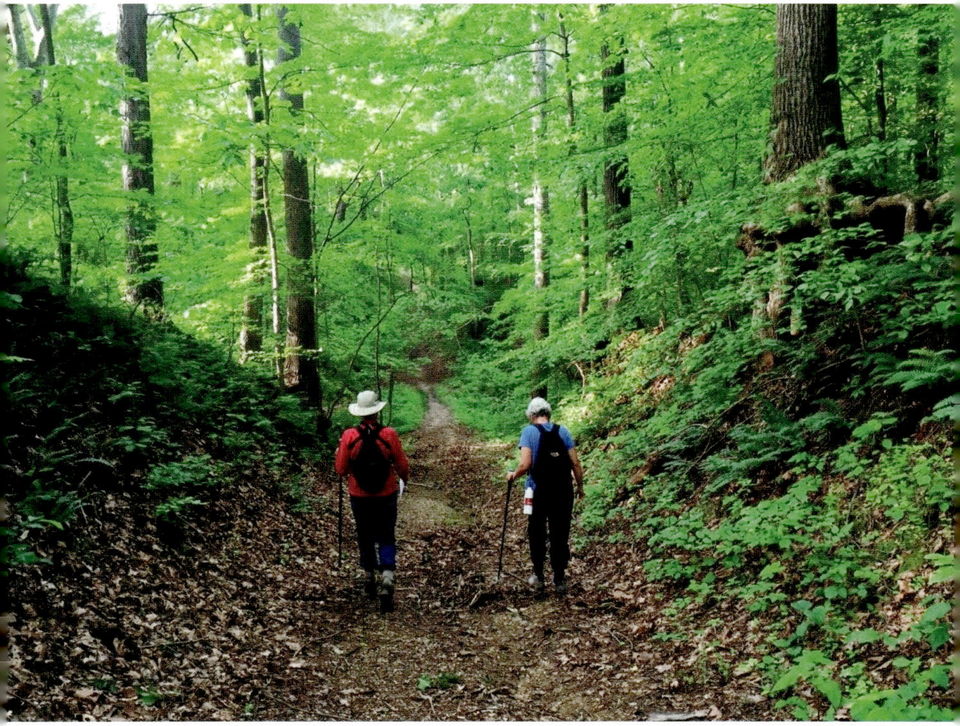

7:30 PM

New Harmony

End-of-the-day hike at Harmonie State Park.

Photo by Dottie Warmbier

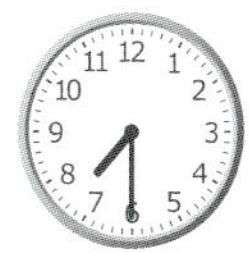

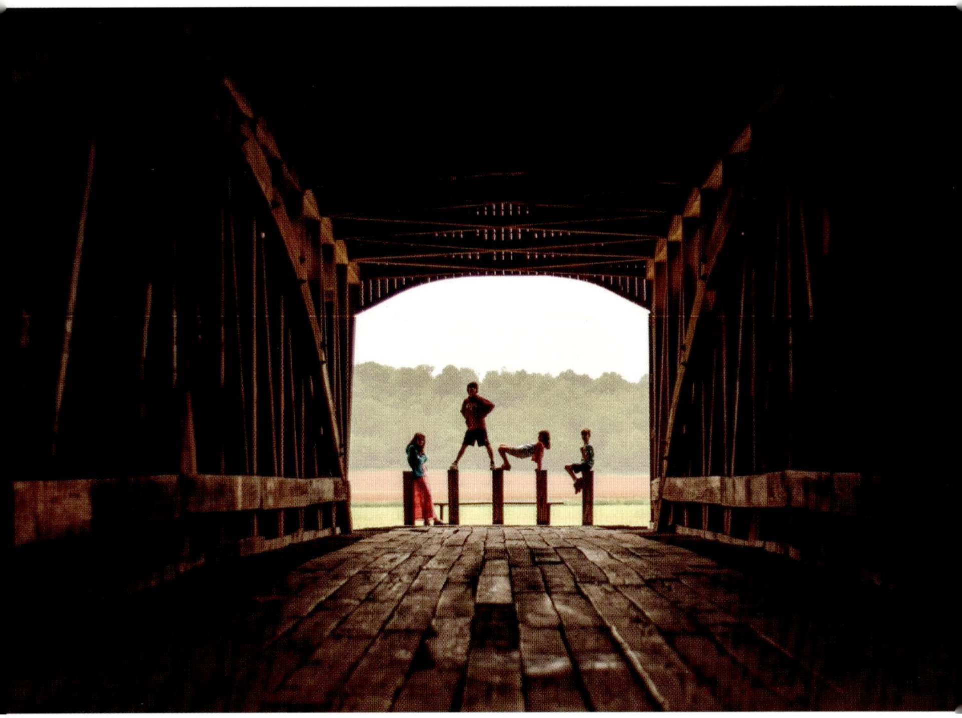

7:30 PM

Parke County

Rainy day play in Parke County's beautiful covered bridges.

Photo by Fatima Scott

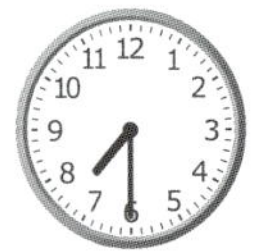

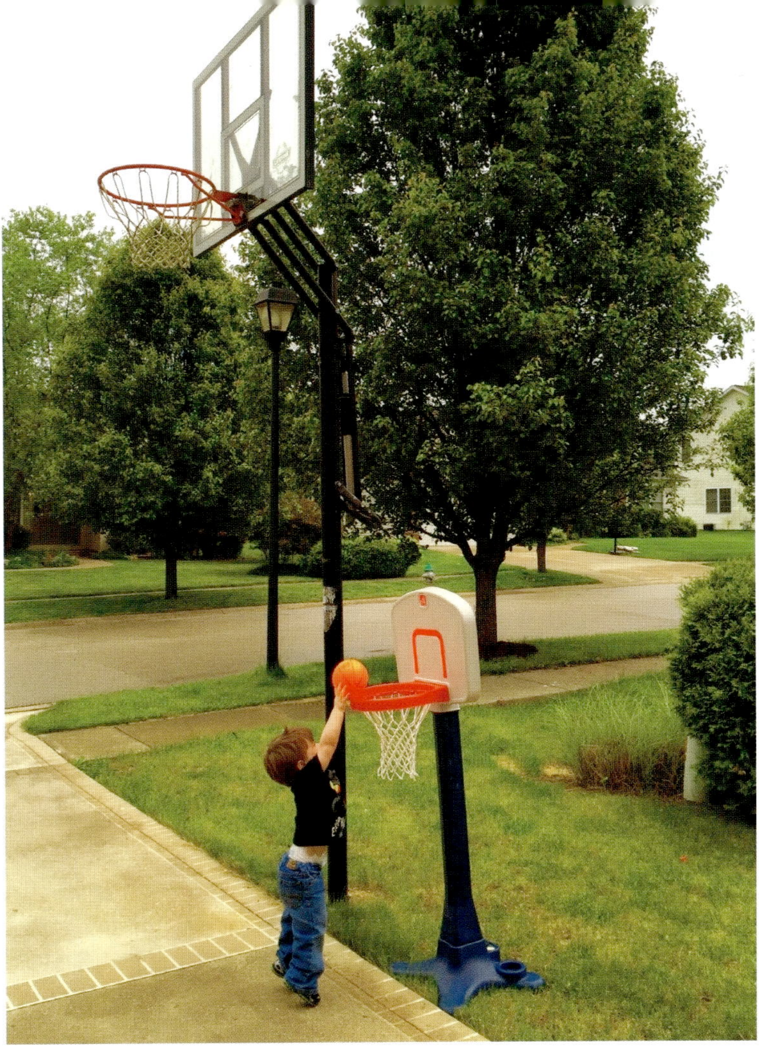

7:43 PM

Bloomington

Mr. Basketball!

Photo by Mandy Hussey

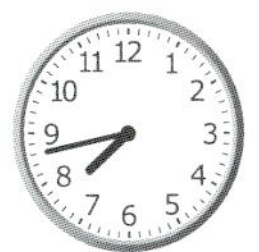

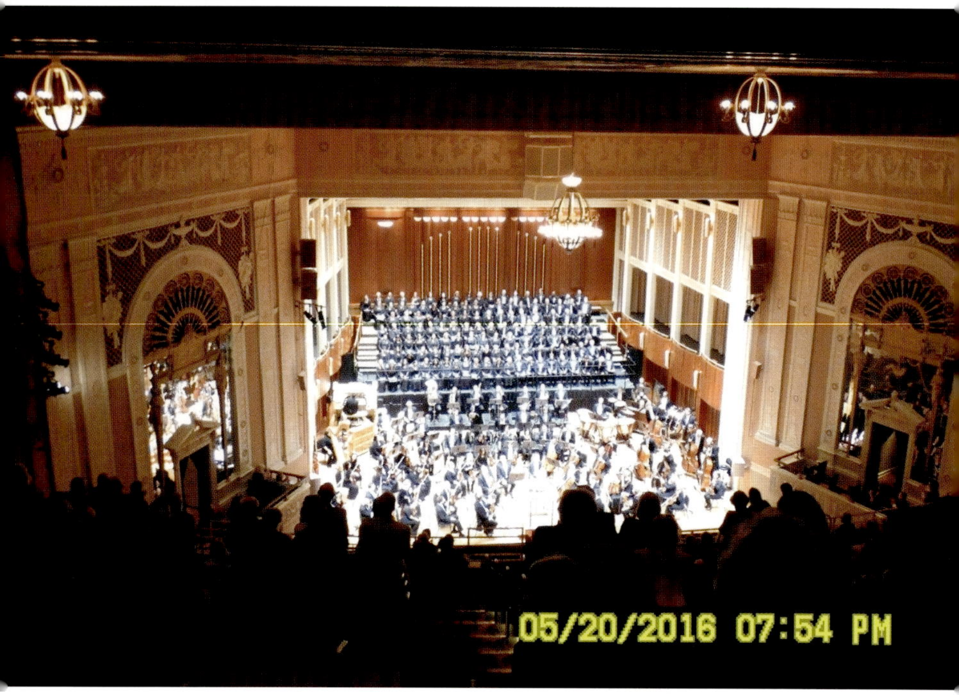

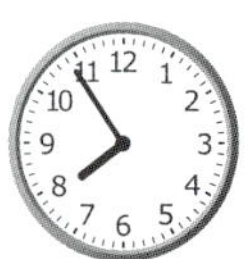

7:54 PM

Indianapolis

Beethoven's Pastoral Symphony performed at the
Hilbert Circle Theatre on Monument Circle.

Photo by Daniela Raicu

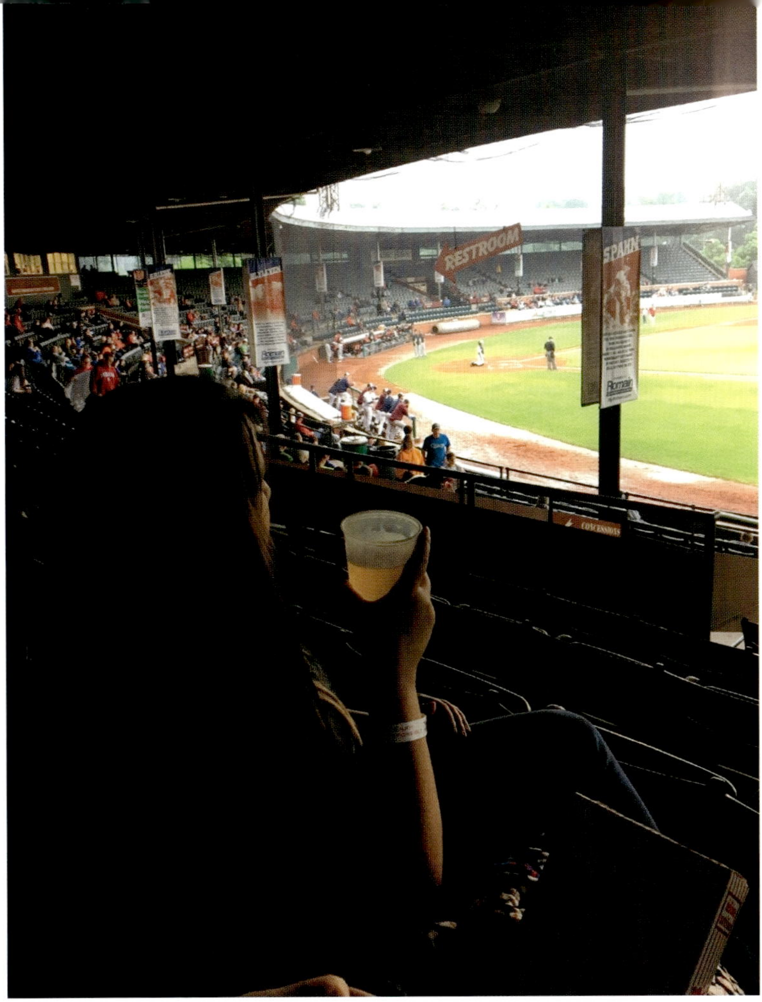

7:58 PM

Evansville

Friday night at Bosse Field!

Photo by Sally Gries

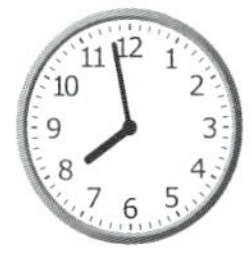

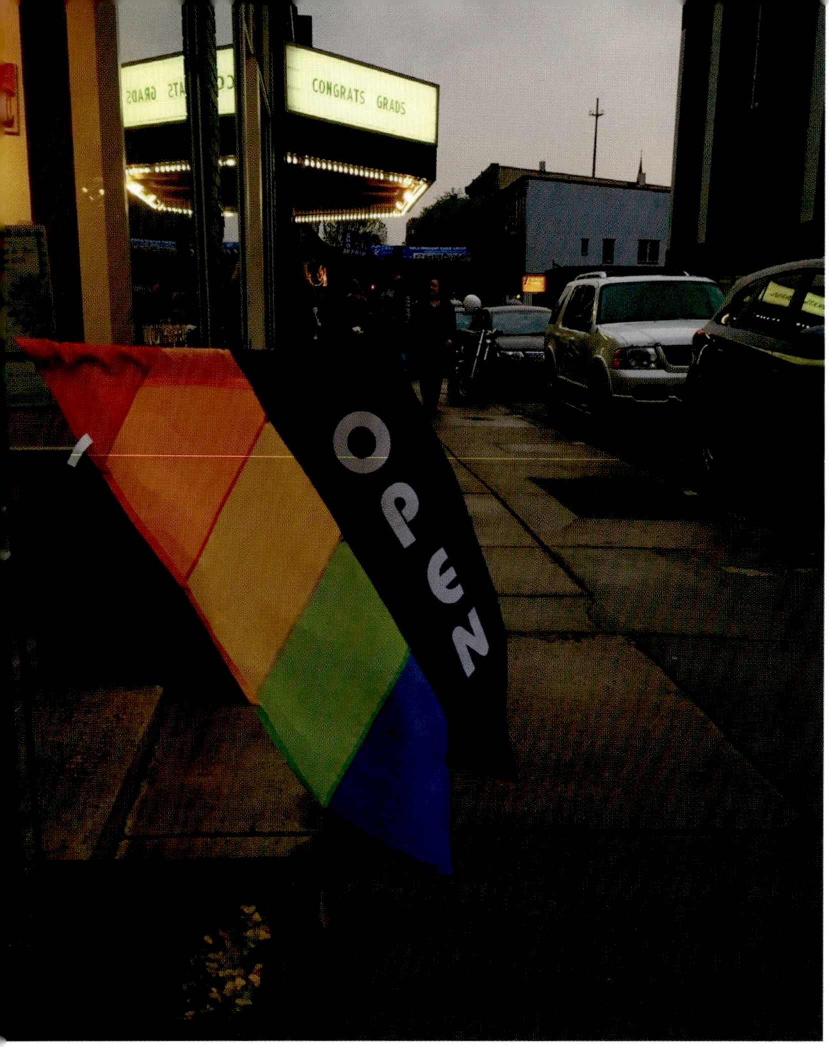

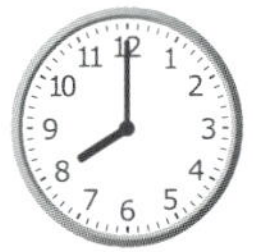

8:00 PM

Lafayette

Lessons learned. We serve everyone.

Photo by Angie Klink

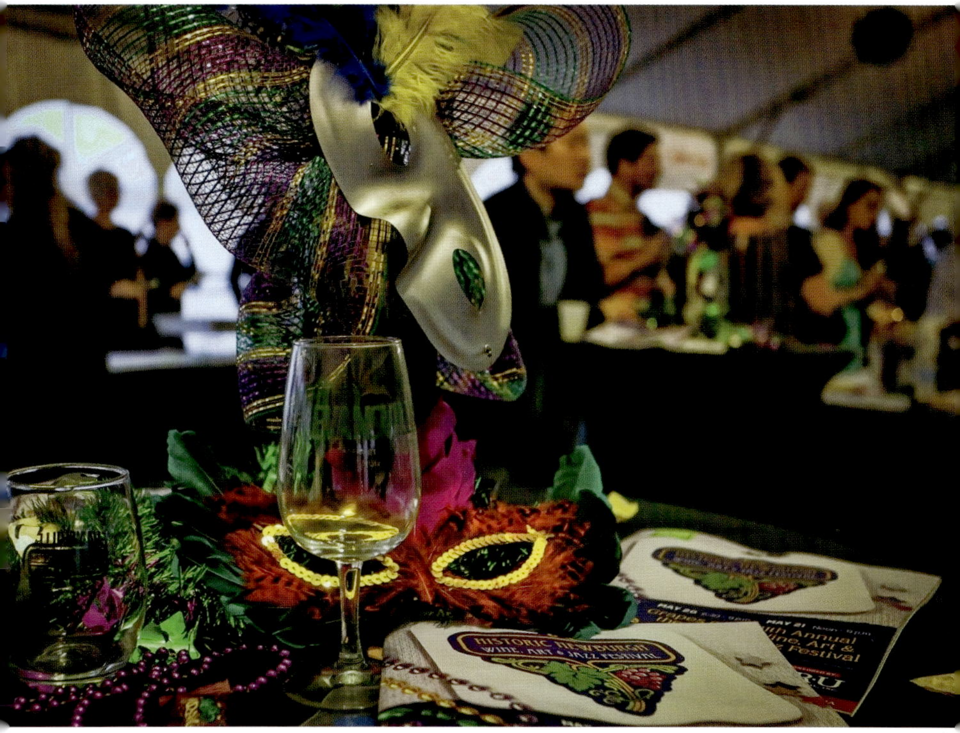

8:00 PM

Newburgh

Historic Newburgh's Grapes on the Grass Soiree kicks off the eleventh annual Wine, Art and Jazz Festival.

Photo by Ken May

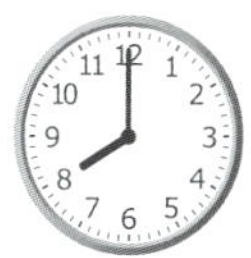

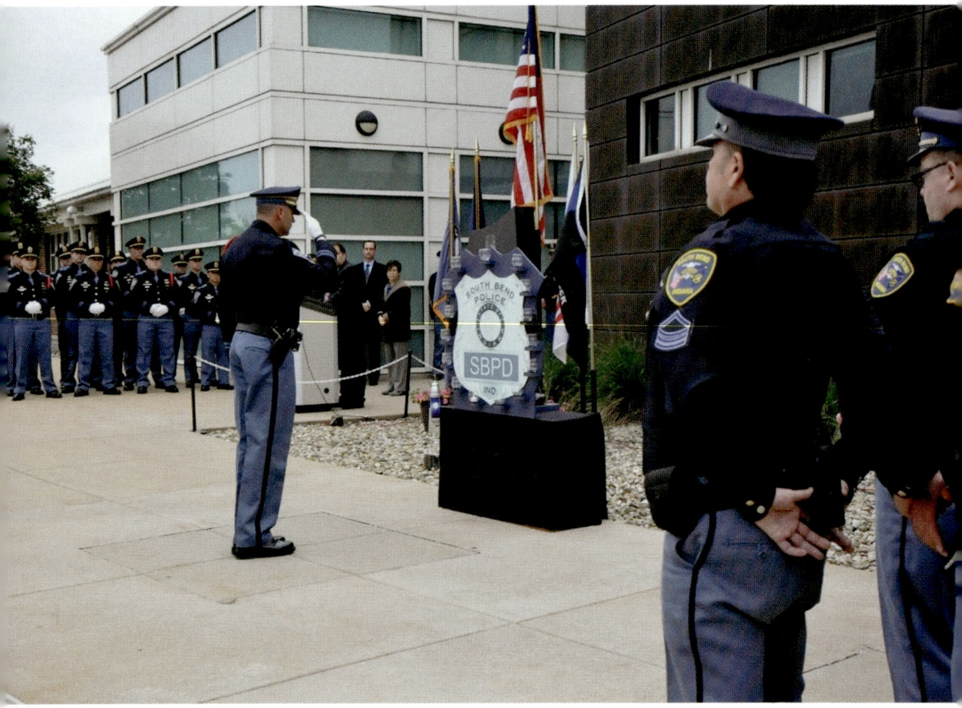

8:00 PM

South Bend

Police Chief Scott Ruszkowski salutes during the
National Law Enforcement Memorial Day ceremony.

Photo by Philip Mark

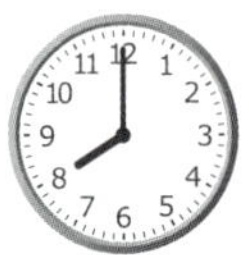

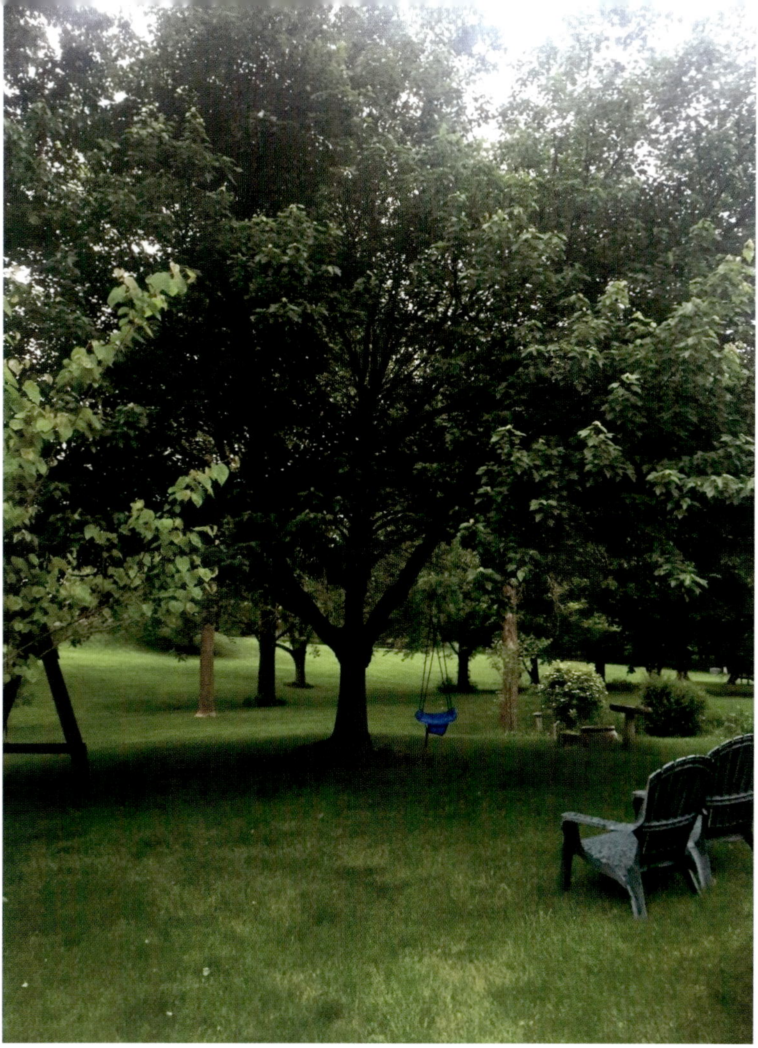

8:00 PM

Zionsville

Kids are in bed. Tranquility.

Photo by Kim Lewis

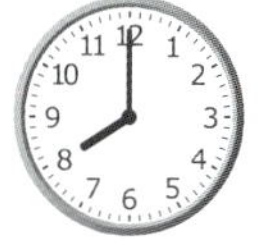

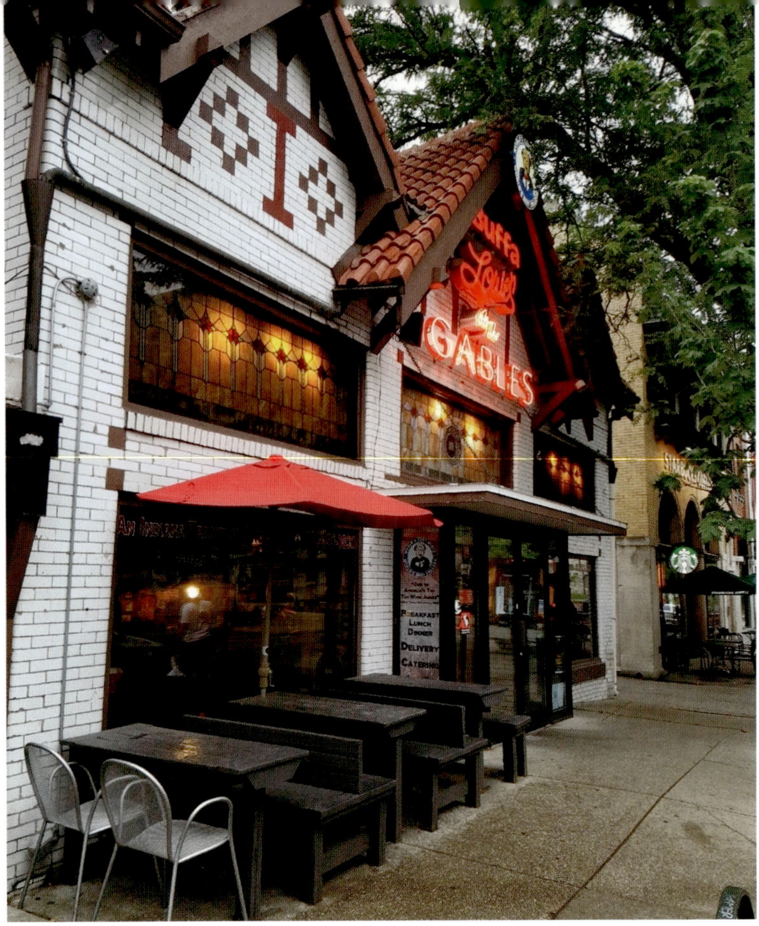

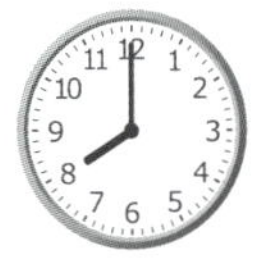

8:00 PM

Bloomington

It's time for Buffa Louie's at The Gables—
an IU tradition.

Photo by Anna Summitt

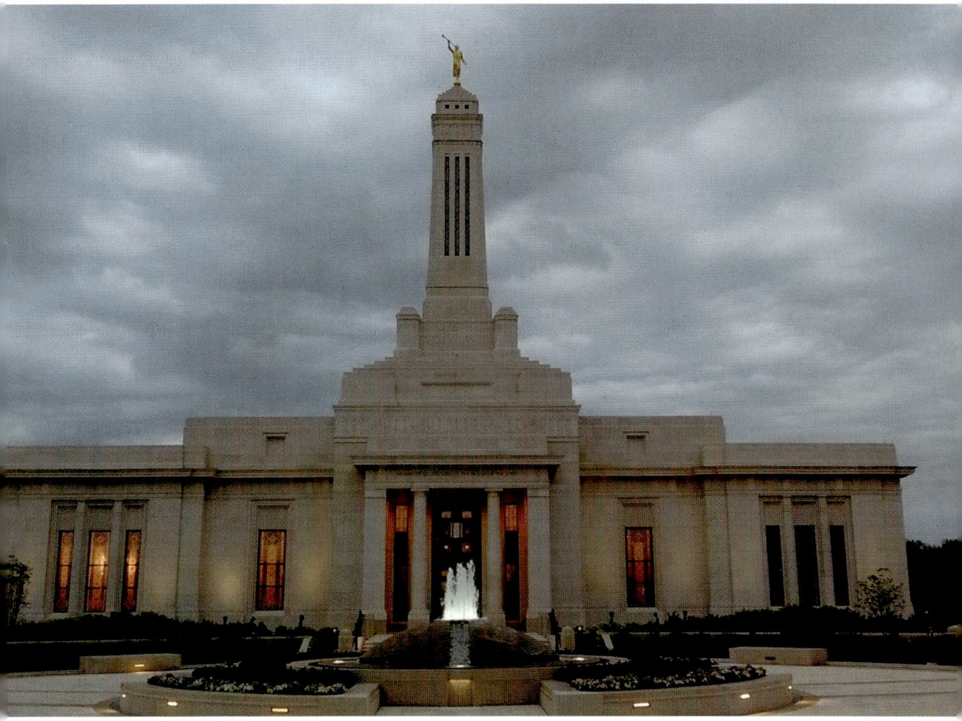

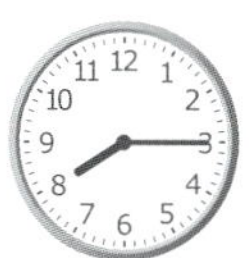

8:15 PM

Carmel

A spring night approaches at the Mormon Temple.

Photo by Gerald Smith

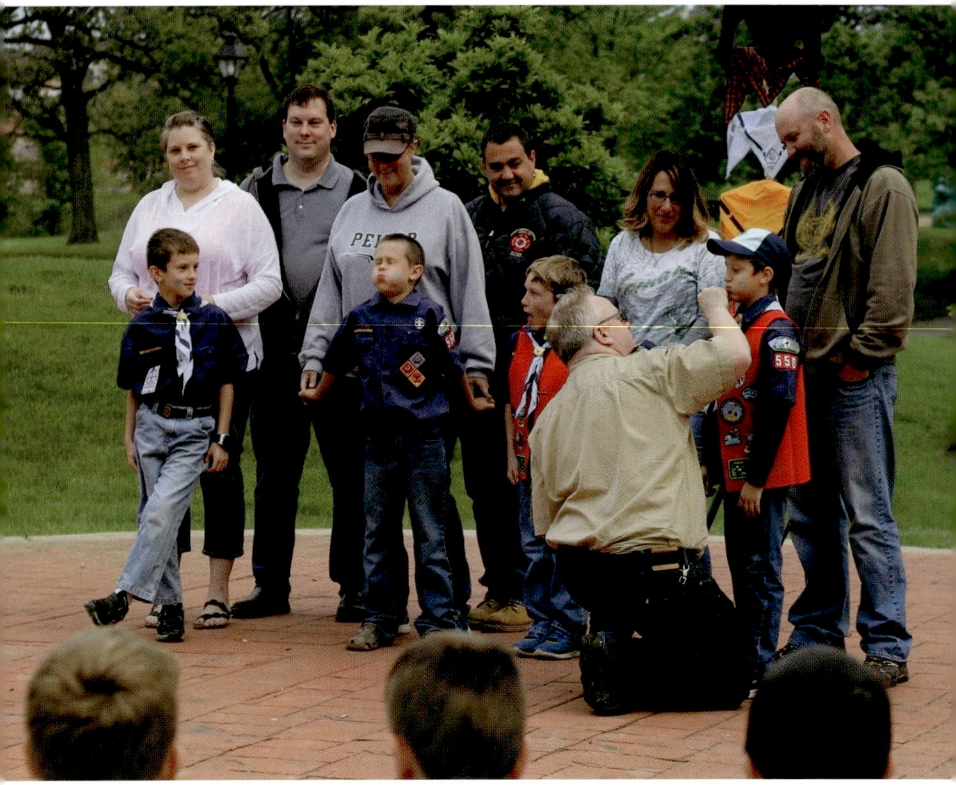

8:16 PM

St. John

Assistant Cubmaster Kiechle draws the Sign of the
Bear on the Cub Scouts of Pack 550 as they advance
to Webelos at the Rank Ceremony at Lake Hills
Park.

Photo by Marisa Snoreck

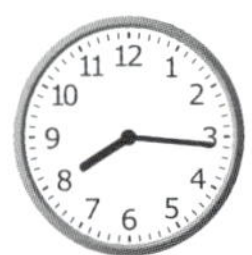

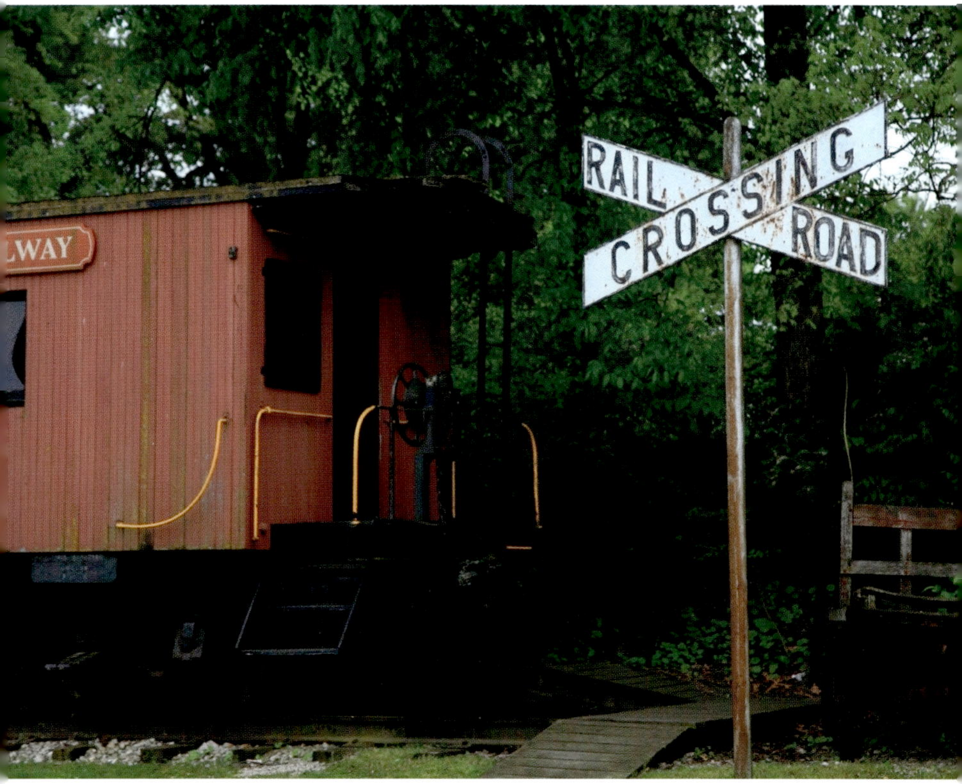

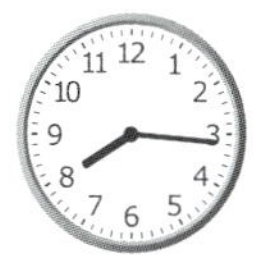

8:16 PM

Etna Green

Twilight gathering at the Crossroads of America. A display of a classic railway car and sign depicting what helped bring this country together, in the park next to the Etna Green Museum.

Photo by Katrina Fink

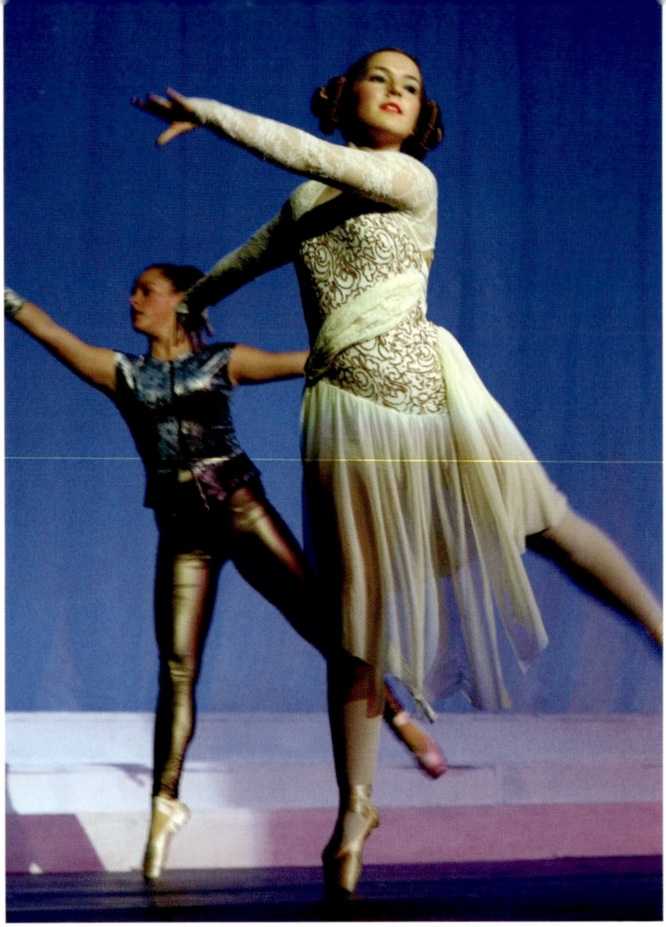

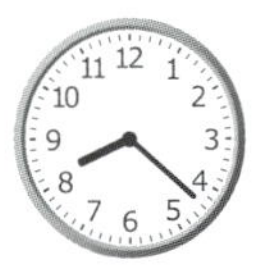

8:22 PM

Greenfield

Princess Leia (Cassondra Jones) and Han Solo (Dana Sutherlin) dance in the Wilkerson Dance Studio's performance of *Star Wars: The Ballet* at the Greenfield-Central High School auditorium.

Photo by Brigette Cook Jones

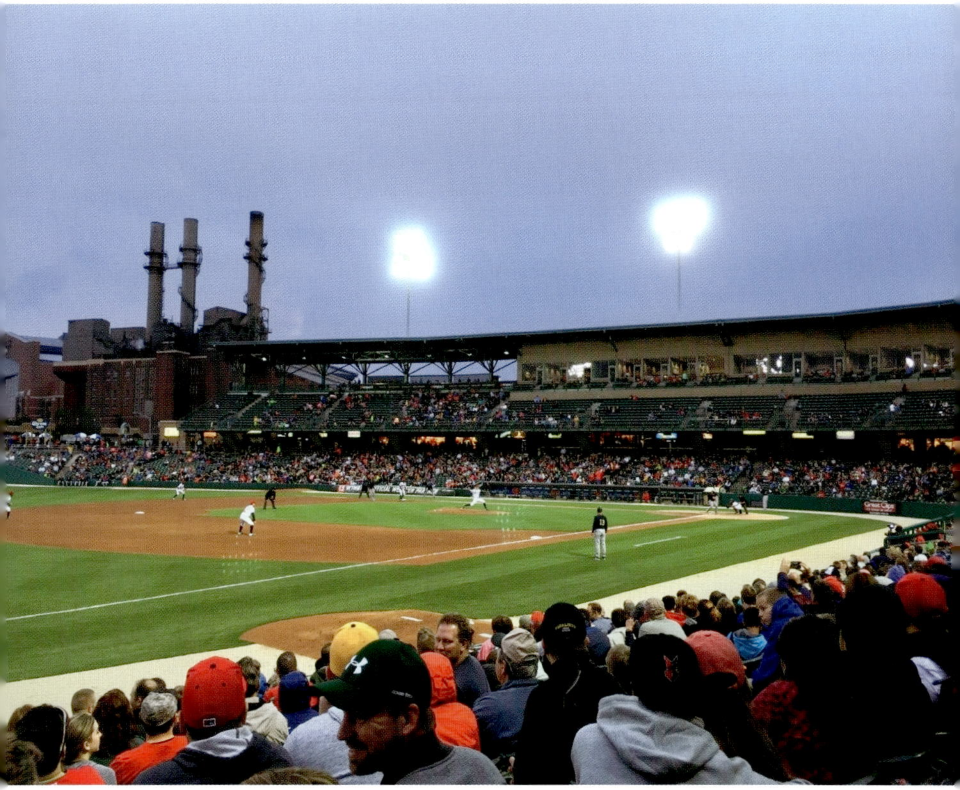

8:25 PM

Indianapolis

A great, albeit rainy, evening to watch the
Indianapolis Indians beat the RailRiders 5–1 at
Victory Field!

Photo by Kaitlyn Walker

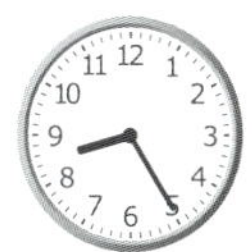

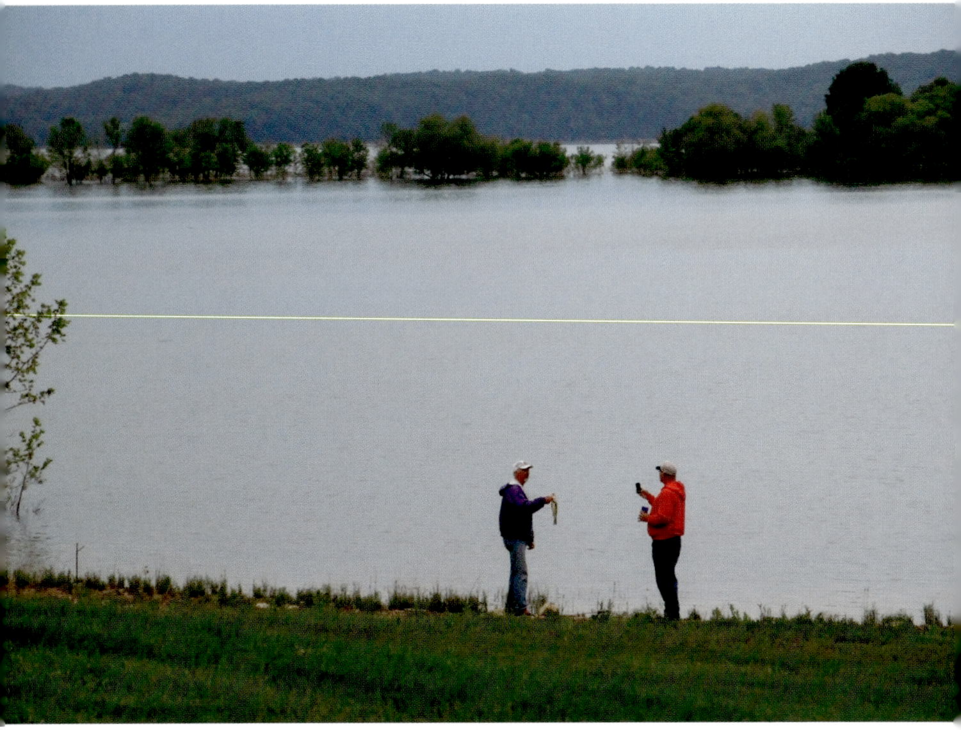

8:30 PM

Monroe County

Last catch of the day at Lake Monroe.

Photo by Ron Eid

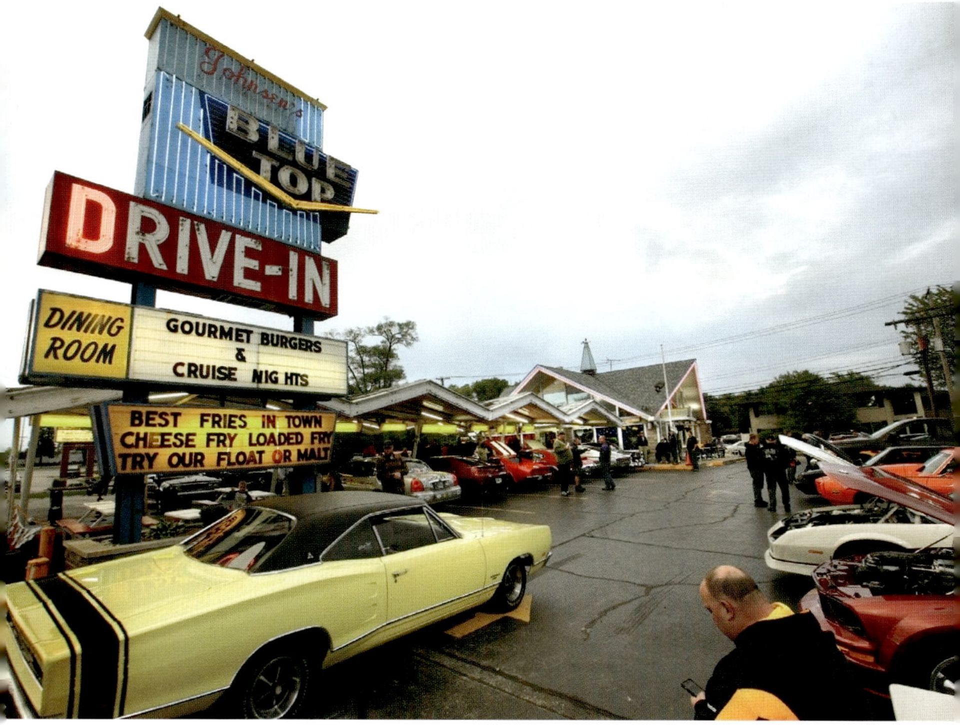

8:40 PM

Highland

On weekend evenings car enthusiasts gather at the Blue Top Drive-In to share their common love for custom and restored vehicles and proudly display them to the public.

Photo by Thomas Semesky

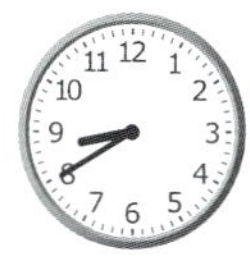

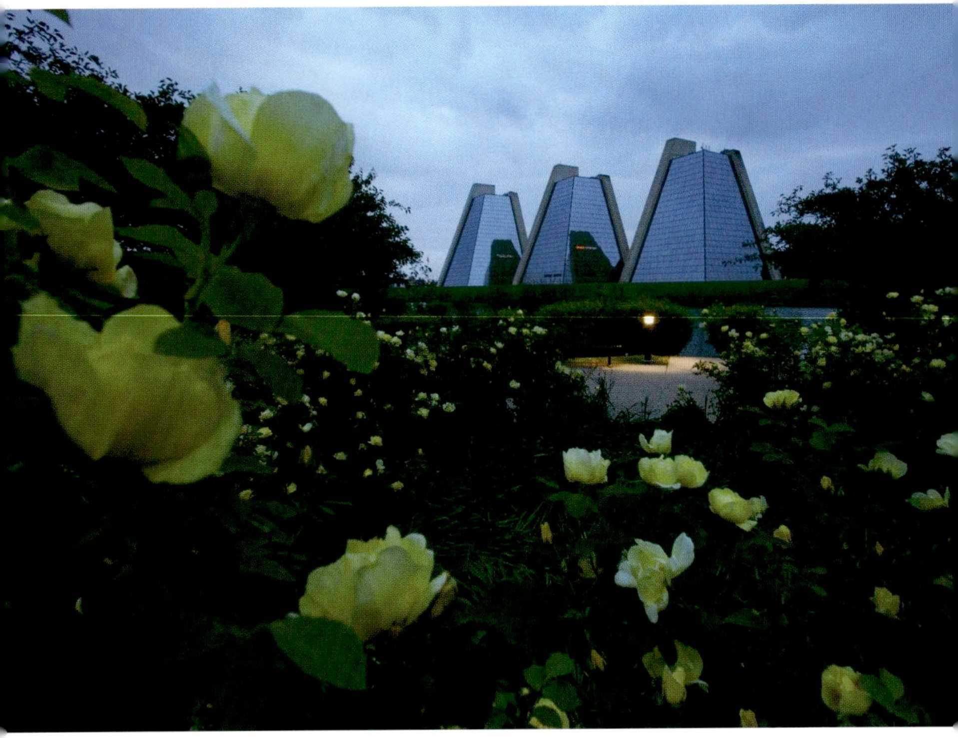

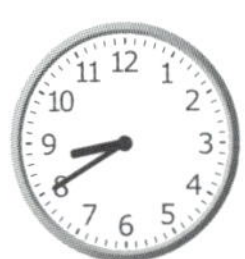

8:40 PM

Indianapolis

As the day slips away, May flowers frame the Pyramids on the northwest side of the city.

Photo by Daren Short

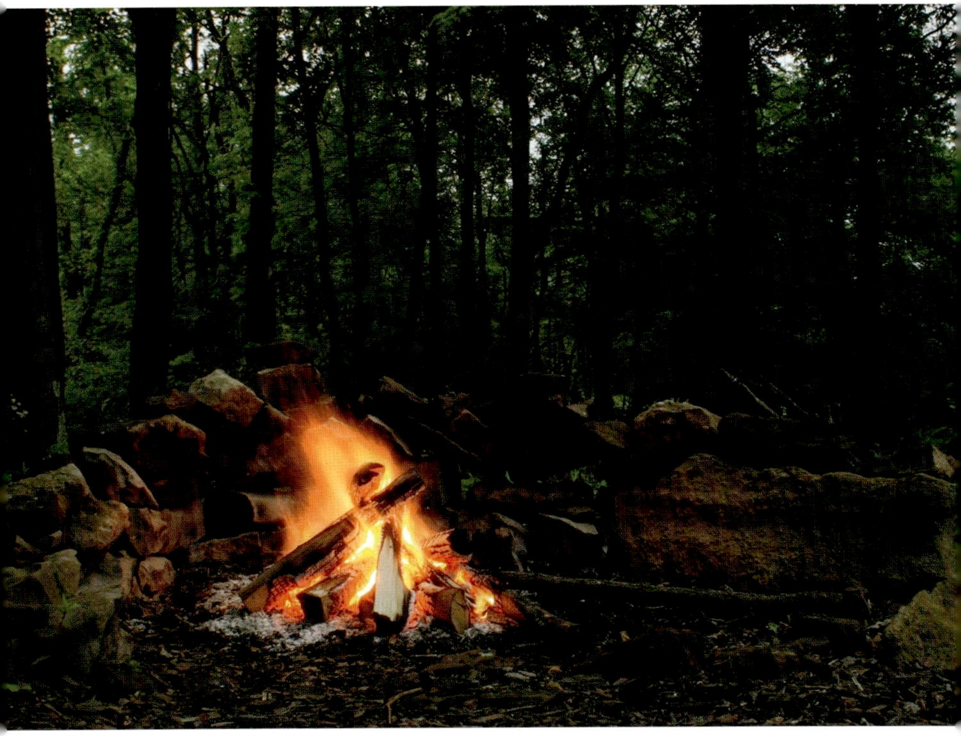

8:50 PM

Monroe County

Enjoying an evening fire through the
sprinkling rain.

Photo by Kelsey Daniel

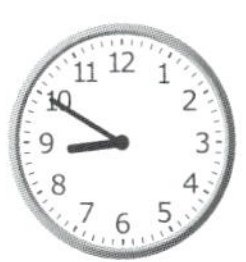

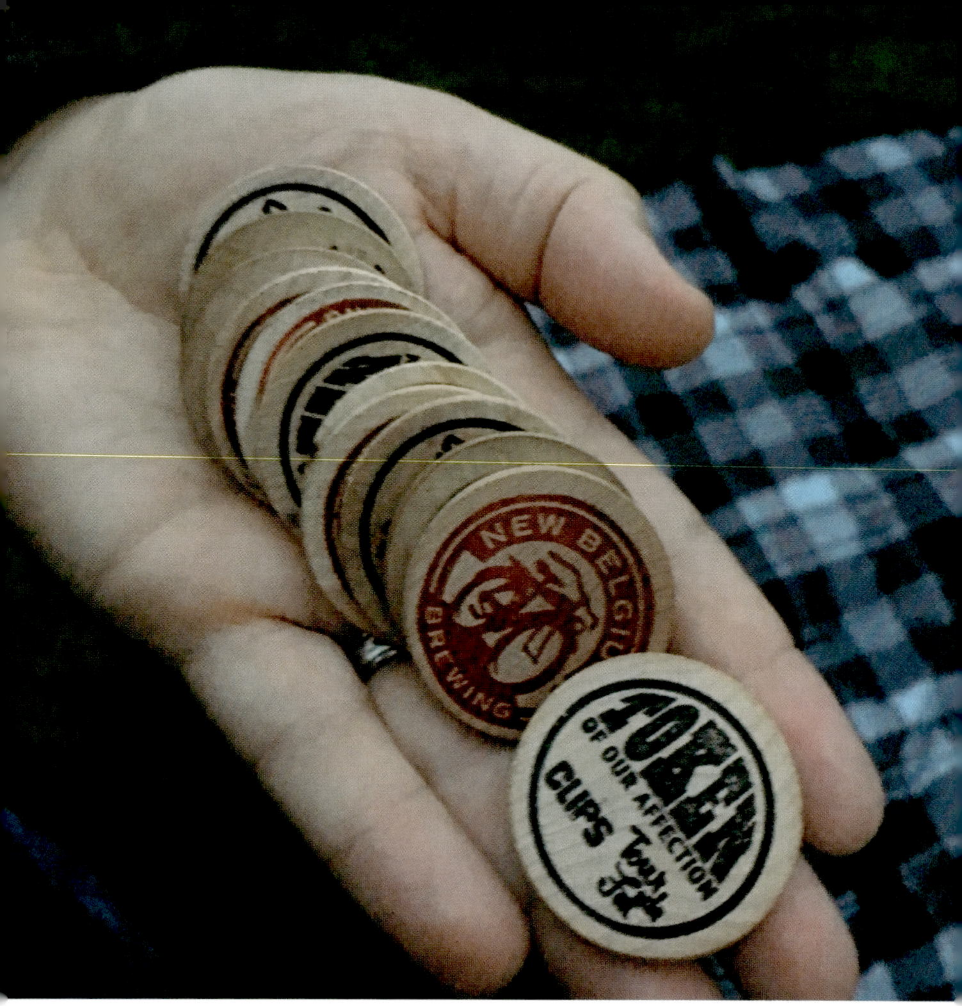

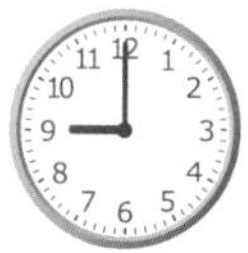

9:00 PM

Bloomington

Beer in the rain at the New Belgium
Clips festival at Bryan Park.

Photo by Melissa Myers

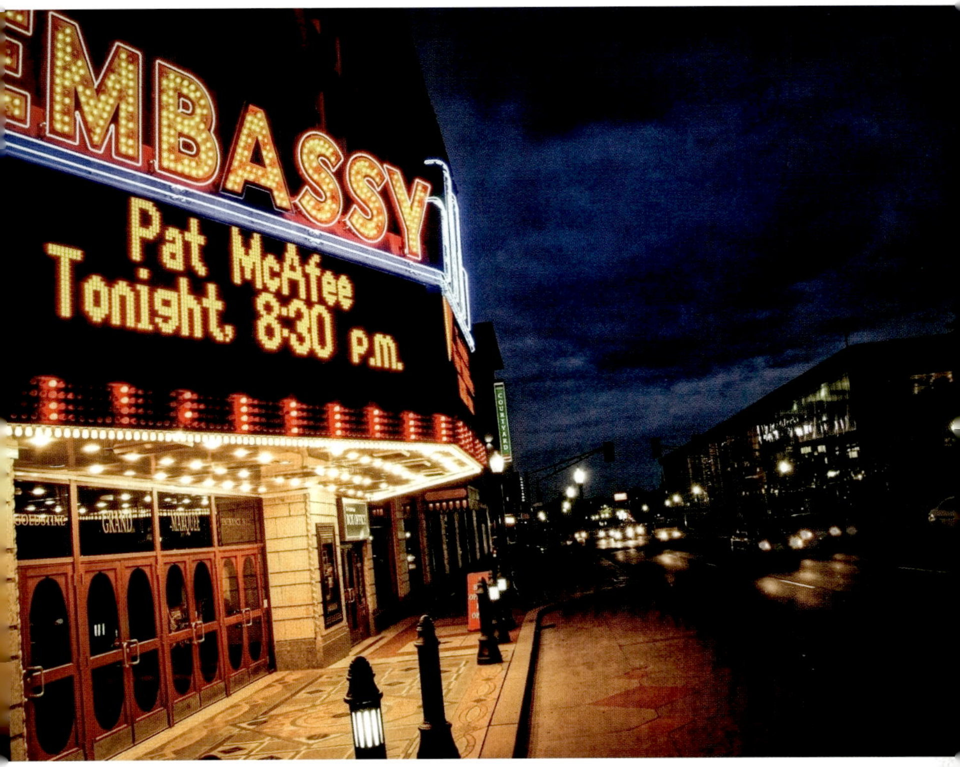

9:10 PM

Fort Wayne

Pat McAfee LIVE at the historic Embassy Theatre!

Photo by Michele Miller

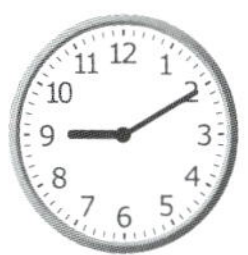

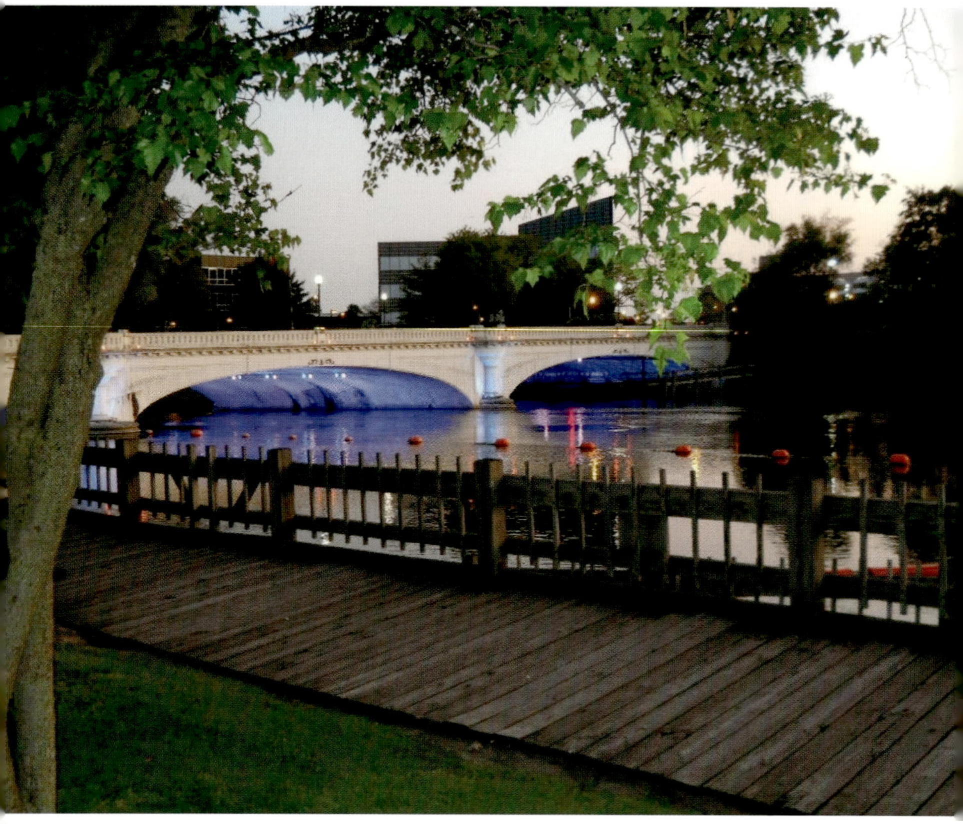

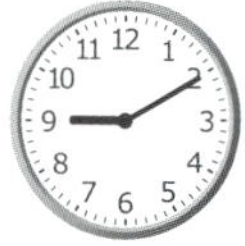

9:10 PM

South Bend

Strolling along the East Race, enjoying the River Lights. This interactive attraction is one of a kind for the community.

Photo by Renee Putman

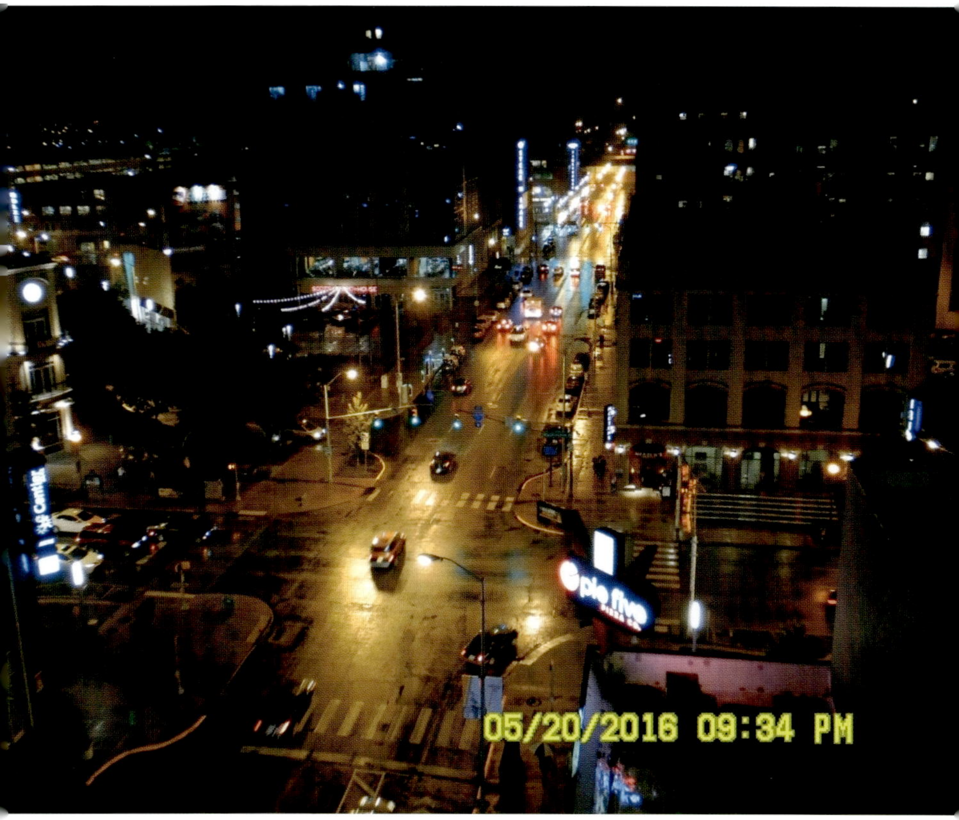

9:34 PM

Indianapolis

A drizzly downtown evening.

Photo by Tricia Clark

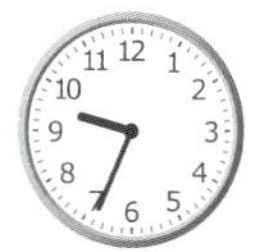

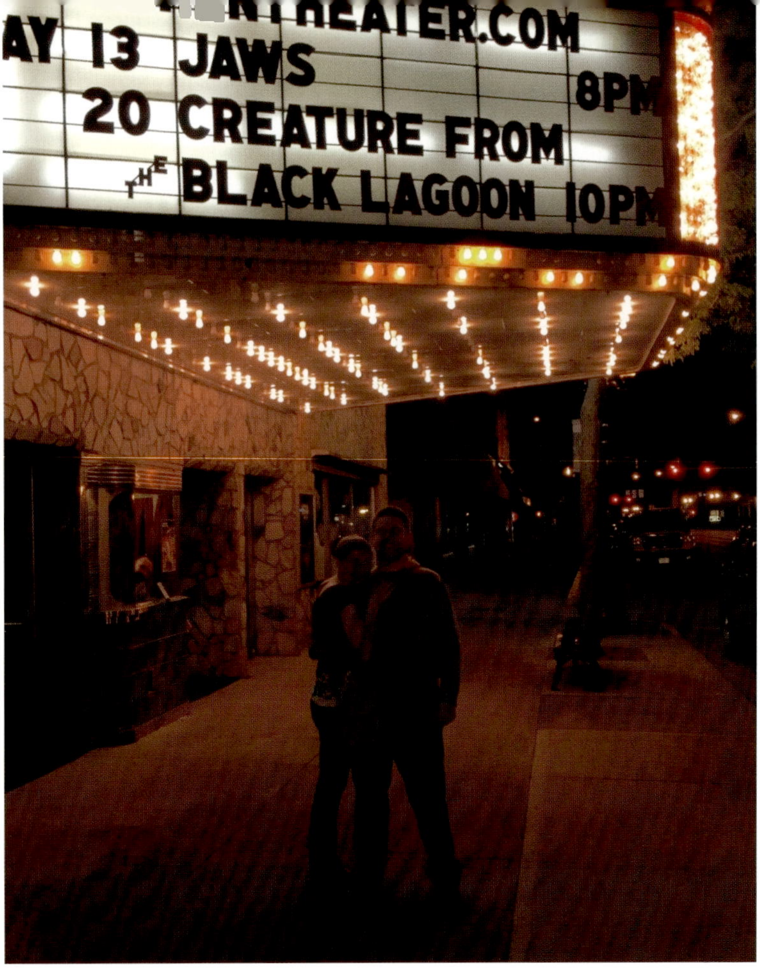

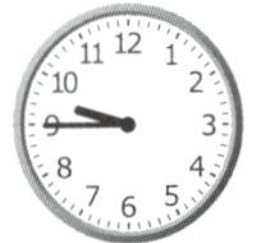

9:45 PM

Goshen

Can't wait to see *The Creature from the Black Lagoon* at the Goshen Theater! It's part of the theater and Art House's summer Creature Feature Film Series.

Photo by Ryan Pogotis

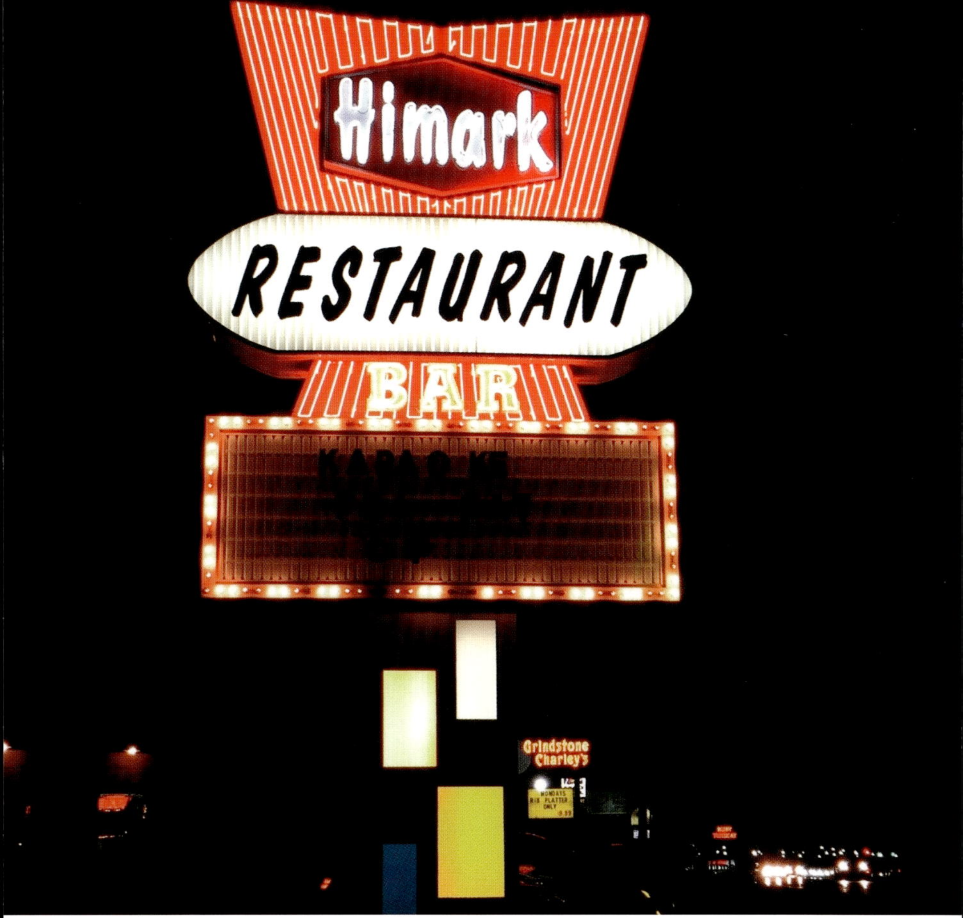

10:15 PM

Kokomo

Back home again to Kokomo and the Hi-Mark on a
rainy night.

Photo by Jennifer Akins

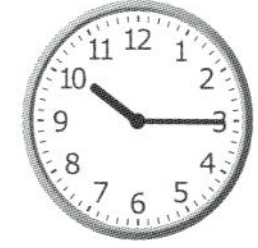

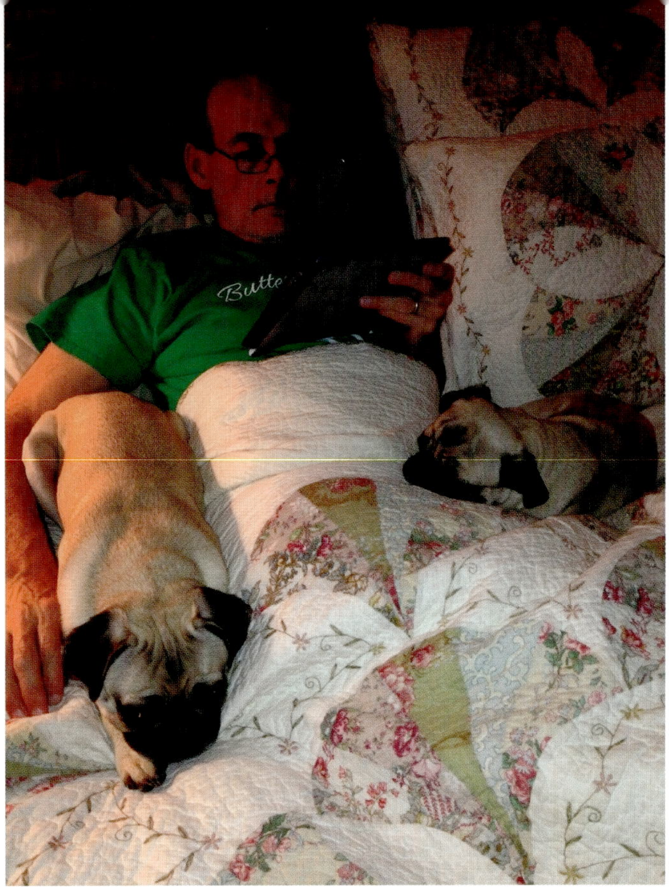

10:15 PM

Lakeville

Hoosiers not only read before sleeping, they take live warmers to bed with them if it's a chilly evening. Tonight was a two-dog night at our farm.

Photo by Joan Laudeman

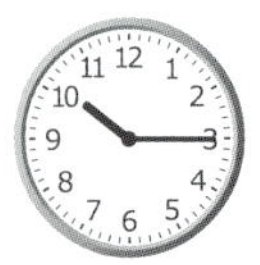

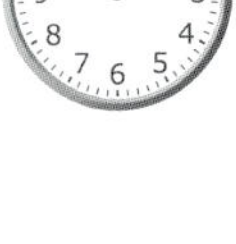

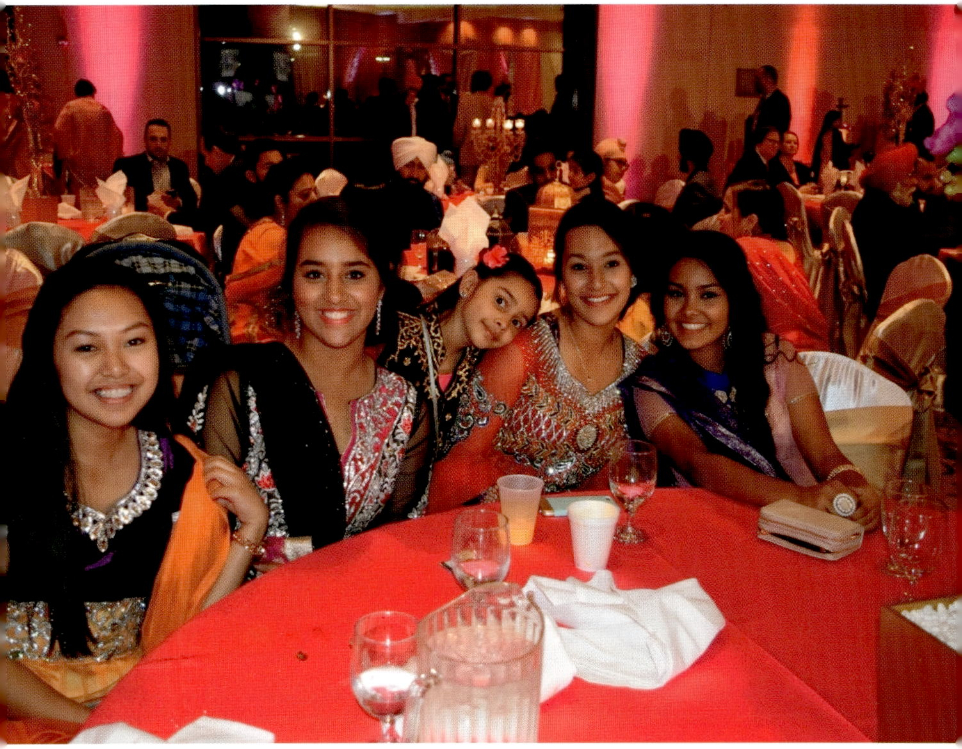

10:30 PM

Schererville

At a wedding reception for a family friend, all
wearing hand-made traditional Indian dresses and
ready to dance to traditional Indian music.
As a proud Hoosier family we love being able
to celebrate our culture!

Photo by Dilmeet Kaur

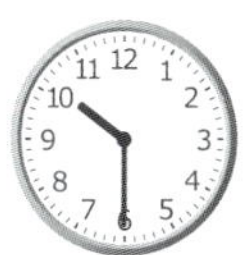

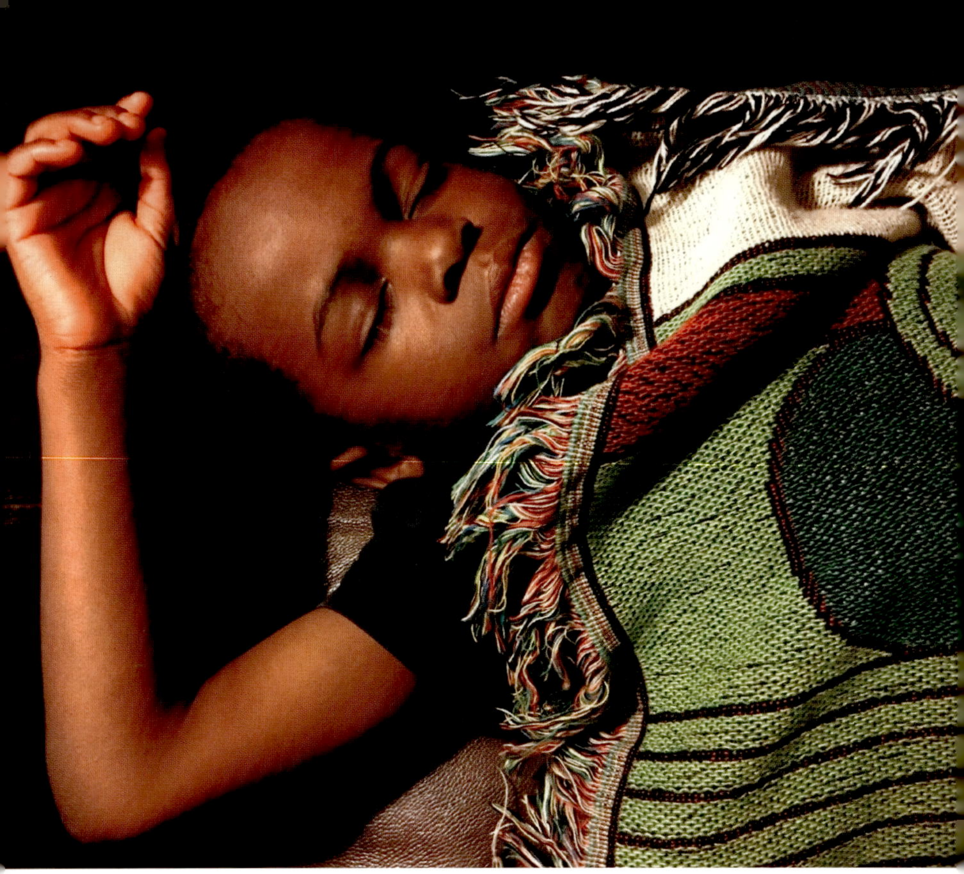

10:39 PM

Indianapolis

Finally asleep on the living room couch,
his favorite spot on a Friday night.

Photo by Georgia Wiltz

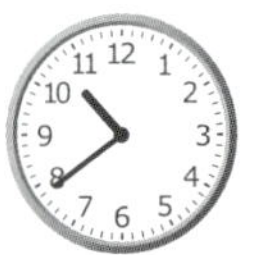

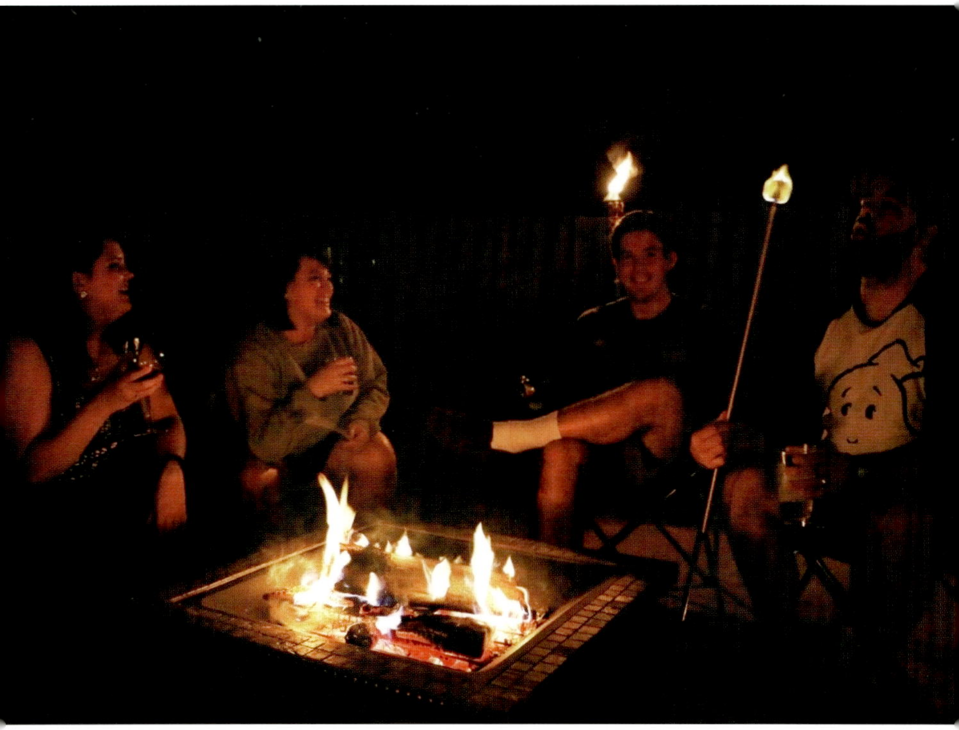

11:00 PM

Brownsburg

Fridays full of fire and friendship.

Photo by Jennifer Jones

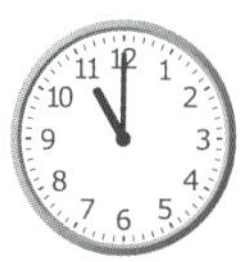

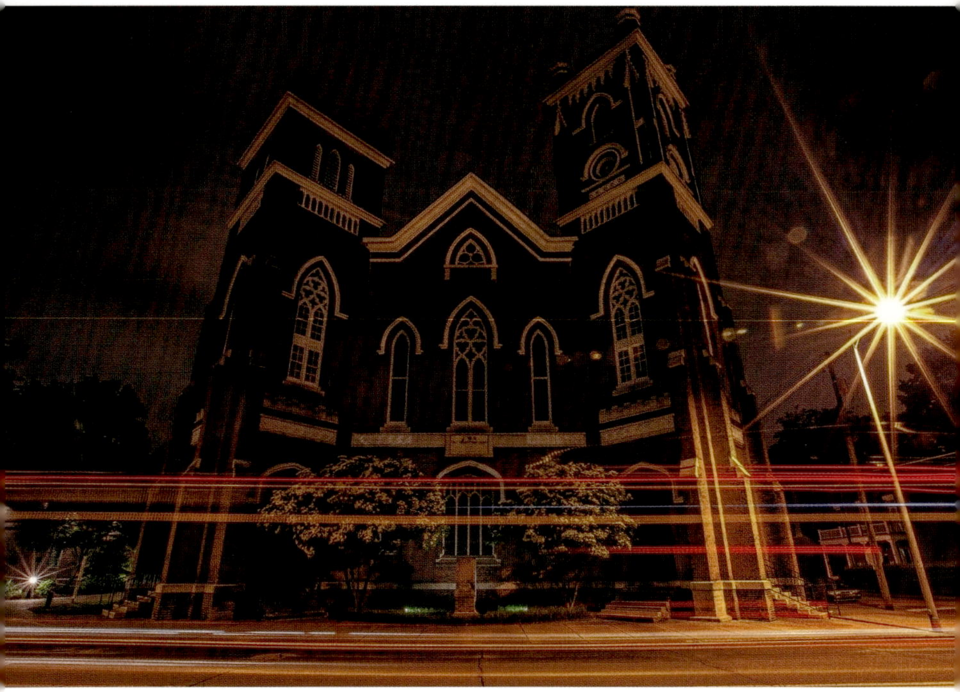

11:07 PM

Evansville

The First Presbyterian Church on Second Street.

Photo by Kiah Fuhrer

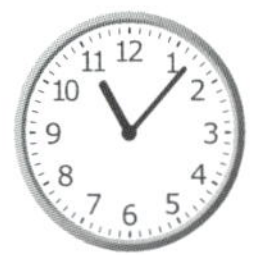

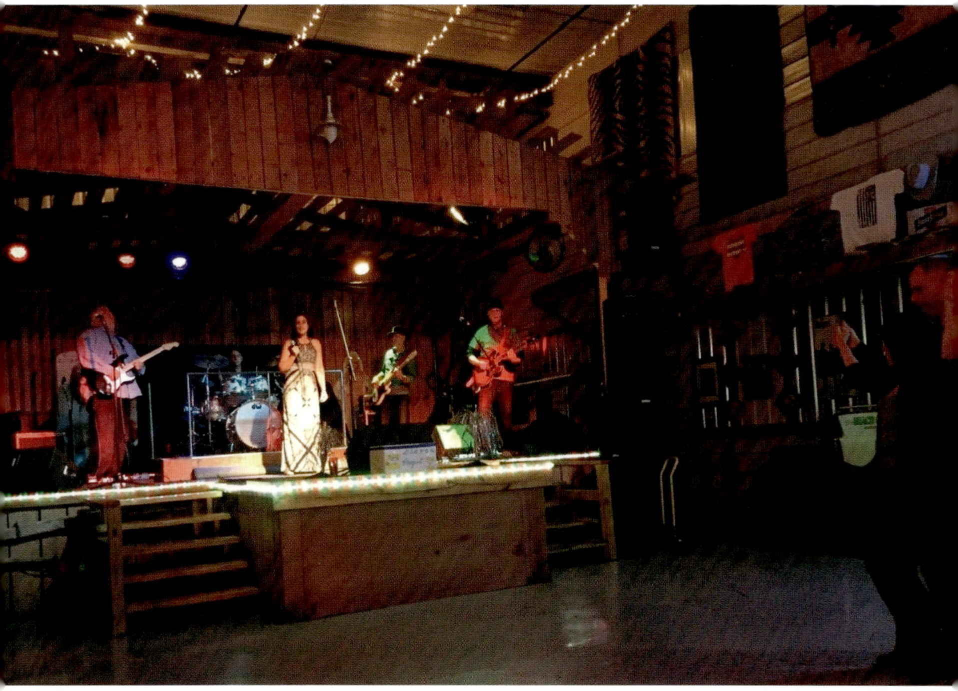

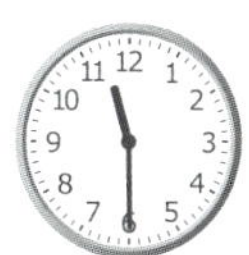

11:30 PM

Charlestown

Grooving to a band at the Rusty Bucket Saloon.

Photo by Amy Martin

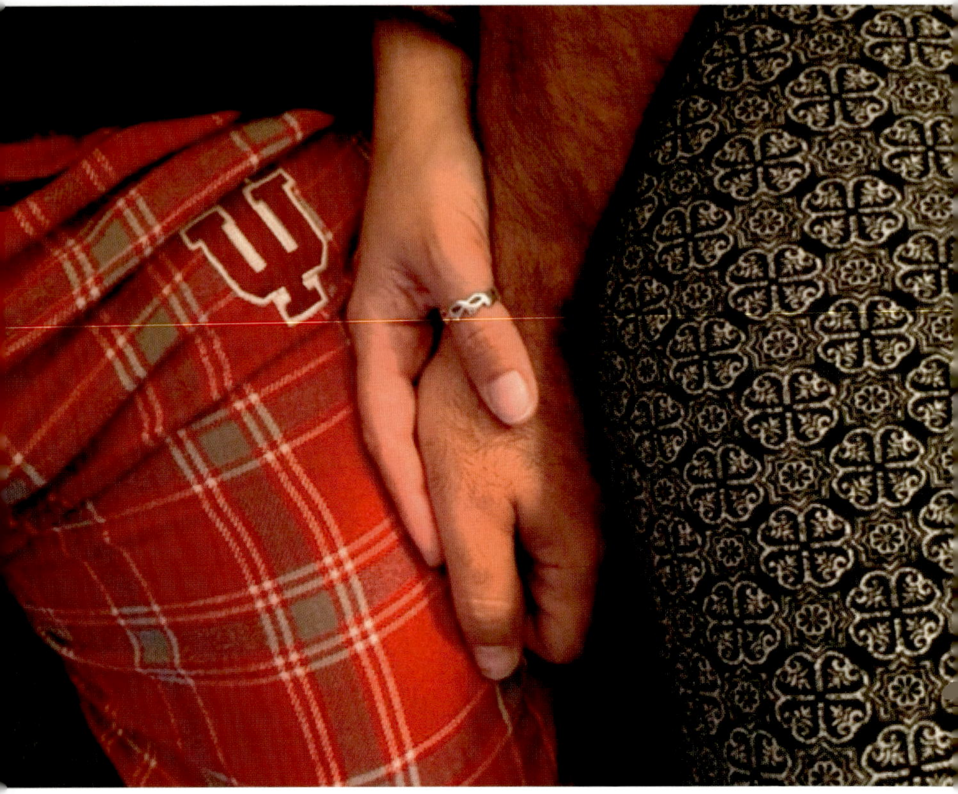

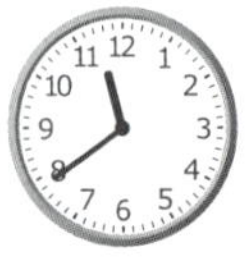

11:39 PM

Bloomington

Watching *The Late Show with Stephen Colbert* together, as we drift off to sleep.

Photo by Juliette Kniola

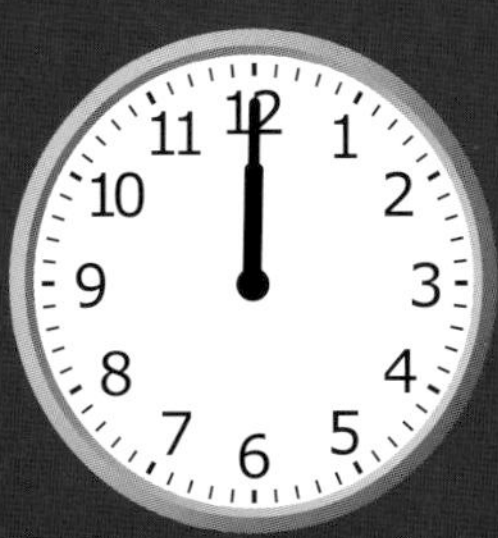

Good Night, Indiana

Editor: Gary Dunham

Book and Cover Designer: Jennifer L. Witzke

Project Manager/Editor: Nancy Lightfoot

Marketing and Sales Director: Dave Hulsey

Editorial and Production Director: Bernadette Zoss

Production Intern: Tiffany Joy Ignalaga

Printer: Four Colour Imports Ltd.